PRAISE FOR
KILL OR CAPTURE

"Klaidman . . . [was] clearly given extraordinary access to key players in the administration . . . Provide[s] scintillating details about internal deliberations that in some cases took place only months ago, giving [the] work an engaging sense of immediacy."

— **Dina Temple-Raston,** *Washington Post*

"A page-turner of drama and intrigue going on inside the White House."　　　　　— **Soledad O'Brien,** *Starting Point*

"Klaidman, a *Newsweek* reporter, sees a president wracked by indecision, torn between his commitment to legal ideals and his political pragmatism . . . A fascinating and detailed account of the administration's internal battles."　　— **David Cole,** *New York Review of Books*

"This is such an important book because of the news it breaks, but also it's so revealing about the kind of wartime president Barack Obama wanted to be and felt he had to be."

— **David Gregory,** *Press Pass*

"Daniel Klaidman's *Kill or Capture* divulge[s] the details of top-level deliberations — details that were almost certainly known only to the administration's inner circle."　　　　　— *Wall Street Journal*

KILL OR CAPTURE

THE WAR ON TERROR AND THE SOUL
OF THE OBAMA PRESIDENCY

Daniel Klaidman

Mariner Books
Houghton Mifflin Harcourt
BOSTON   NEW YORK

For my parents,
Kitty and Steve Klaidman, with love.

And to the memory of my grandparents,
Ernest, Ilonka, Moe, and Sis.

═══════════════════

First Mariner Books edition 2013
Copyright © 2012 by Daniel Klaidman

www.hmhbooks.com

Library of Congress Cataloging-in-Publication Data
Klaidman, Daniel.
Kill or capture: the war on terror and the soul of the Obama presidency /
Daniel Klaidman.
p. cm.
Includes index.
ISBN 978-0-547-54789-3   ISBN 978-0-544-00216-6 (pbk.)
1. War on Terrorism, 2001–2009. 2. Terrorism — Prevention — United States.
3. United States — Foreign relations — 21st century. 4. Obama, Barack.
I. Title.
HV6432.K56 2012
363.325'1560973 — dc23
2012008228

Book design by Brian Moore

Printed in the United States of America
DOC 10 9 8 7 6 5 4 3 2 1

CONTENTS

Cast of Characters vi

A Note on Sources x

Prologue 1

1. The Promise 13

2. Where the Fuck Is bin Laden? 37

3. Torture Debates and Murder Boards 65

4. Escape from Gitmo 93

5. Kill or Capture 117

6. How Not to Try a Terrorist 145

7. The Christmas Gift 173

8. From Warfare to Lawfare 199

9. "The President Is Anguished" 225

10. Textbook 241

Epilogue 266

Postscript 272

Acknowledgments 277

Index 281

CAST OF CHARACTERS

THE WHITE HOUSE

Barack Obama, President of the United States

Joe Biden, Vice President of the United States

Rahm Emanuel, Chief of Staff

William M. Daley, Chief of Staff (succeeding Emanuel)

Jim Messina, Deputy Chief of Staff for Operations

David Axelrod, Senior Adviser to the President

David Plouffe, Senior Adviser to the President (succeeding Axelrod)

John Brennan, Assistant to the President for Homeland Security and Counterterrorism

Greg Craig, White House Counsel

Robert Bauer, White House Counsel (succeeding Craig)

Daniel Meltzer, Deputy White House Counsel

Tom Donilon, Deputy National Security Adviser, National Security Adviser

Valerie Jarrett, Senior Adviser to the President

Robert Gibbs, Press Secretary and Senior Adviser to the President

Jim Jones, National Security Adviser

Denis McDonough, Chief of Staff to the National Security Council, Deputy National Security Adviser

Ben Rhodes, Speechwriter, Deputy National Security Adviser for Strategic Communications

Dan Pfeiffer, Deputy Communications Director, Communications Director

STATE DEPARTMENT

Hillary Rodham Clinton, Secretary of State

Harold Koh, Legal Adviser

Ambassador Daniel Fried, Special Envoy for the closure of the Guantánamo Bay detention facility

DEPARTMENT OF DEFENSE

Robert Gates, Secretary of Defense

Jeh C. Johnson, General Counsel

DEPARTMENT OF JUSTICE

Eric Holder, Attorney General

David Ogden, Deputy Attorney General

Robert Mueller, FBI Director

Kevin Ohlson, Chief of Staff for the Attorney General

Amy Jeffress, National Security Adviser for the Attorney General

Matthew Miller, Director of Public Affairs

Matthew Olsen, Executive Director, Guantánamo Review Task Force

Andrew Tannenbaum, Deputy Director, Olsen task force

David Barron, Office of Legal Counsel

Preet Bharara, US Attorney, Southern District of New York

David Raskin, chief prosecutor of the New York Southern District Court's terrorism unit

DEPARTMENT OF HOMELAND SECURITY

Janet Napolitano, Secretary of Homeland Security

David Martin, Principal Deputy General Counsel, Department of
Homeland Security

MILITARY & INTELLIGENCE

Admiral Michael "Mike" Mullen, Chairman of the Joint Chiefs of Staff

General James "Hoss" Cartwright, Vice Chairman of the Joint Chiefs of
Staff

William H. McRaven, Commander, Joint Special Operations
Command; Commander, US Special Operations Command

General James Mattis, Commander, US Central Command

Michael Hayden, Director of Central Intelligence

Leon Panetta, Director of Central Intelligence (succeeding Hayden)

Stephen "Steve" Kappes, Deputy Director of Central Intelligence

Michael "Mike" McConnell, Director of National Intelligence

Dennis Blair, Director of National Intelligence (succeeding McConnell)

AL-QAEDA AND ITS AFFILIATES

Osama bin Laden, al-Qaeda leader

Ayman al-Zawahiri, bin Laden's deputy

Khalid Sheikh Mohammed, high-level al-Qaeda operative and
principal architect of 9/11 attacks

Saleh Ali Saleh Nabhan, leading al-Qaeda operative in East Africa

Anwar al-Awlaki, chief of external operations for al-Qaeda in the
Arabian Peninsula

Abu Zubaydah, alleged al-Qaeda member

Umar Farouk Abdulmutallab, the "Christmas Day bomber"

Baitullah Mehsud, leader of Pakistani Taliban

Richard Reid, the "Shoe Bomber"

Najibullah Zazi, would-be terrorist, planned attack on New York
subway system

Faisal Shahzad, the would-be "Times Square bomber"

Mohammed Saleh Mohammed Ali al-Kazemi, code name "Akron," deputy, al-Qaeda in the Arabian Peninsula

Ahmed Abdulkadir Warsame, Shabab member, liaison to al-Qaeda

OTHER PLAYERS

Sabin Willett and Susan Baker Manning, defense attorneys representing Uighur detainees at Guantánamo

Thomas Wilner, lawyer for Guantánamo detainees

Richard Clarke, counterterrorism adviser to candidate Obama

Sen. Lindsey Graham, R-SC, powerful player on counterterrorism issues

Sen. Sheldon Whitehouse, D-RI, supported Justice Department effort to investigate Bush-era torture

Bruce Riedel, former CIA official who led a White House review of US policy in Afghanistan and Pakistan

Laurence Tribe, Harvard law professor and Obama adviser

Sharon Malone, wife of Eric Holder

Michelle Obama, First Lady

Anthony Romero, Executive Director, American Civil Liberties Union

Tom Malinowski, Washington Director, Human Rights Watch

A NOTE ON SOURCES

For this book I drew on interviews with more than two hundred sources, most of whom are current or former Obama administration officials. I also benefited from the valuable perspective of many who served in previous administrations, both Democratic and Republican. I talked to numerous academics and legal experts for their insights on the range of issues covered herein. As often as possible, I consulted internal government documents, including contemporaneous notes of key meetings taken by participants and private emails. I also relied on the transcripts of speeches, press conferences, and background briefings provided by the White House and other government agencies. In those instances where I rely on exclusive reporting in newspaper or magazine stories, I cite them in the body of the text.

Ultimately, narrative accounts of events unfolding essentially in real time depend on the willingness of participants to speak candidly to reporters about what they've observed firsthand. Most of the interviews for this book were conducted on background, which means I agreed not to attribute direct quotes by name. For a variety of reasons, individuals working in presidential administrations are simply unwilling to discuss the inner workings of government — how important decisions are made, how ethical dilemmas are resolved, or the human dimensions of their jobs — without a grant of anonymity. That is especially the case when the subject is national security. The late *Washington Post* editorial-page editor and columnist Meg Greenfield once observed that "the off the record part is where the reality and authenticity are to be found."

But implicit in allowing sources to speak anonymously is a reporter's obligation to carefully verify the accuracy of their accounts, and to give readers a glimpse into the reporting process so that they can assess the credibility of the information themselves. There are many techniques reporters use to authenticate the accounts of their sources. Most important is cross-referencing what they say with other sources, something I have endeavored to do throughout this book. When I quote President Obama or other key characters, I do so only if that quote was relayed to me by a source who personally heard it. Where possible, I have checked those quotes against contemporaneous notes taken by participants in meetings. Ultimately, I am dependent on the memory of my sources.

Occasionally I write about the emotional state and interior thoughts of President Obama and his top aides. In doing so, I am not taking literary license. Those accounts are based on reporting — either from specific comments the president has made that directly express his state of mind, or from reasonable inferences from sources I have interviewed who have observed and spoken to him.

One final point in the interest of transparency: in some instances, to add an extra layer of insurance, I strayed from a journalistic convention and read certain sections of my book to sources. Journalists have been known to frown on this practice, fearing it could lead sources to try to edit the manuscript or to take back things they said. Those are valid concerns. But reporting a fact-intensive book is a large undertaking. Many sources gave up a lot of their valuable time to help me tell this story. Some did so at considerable personal risk. I believe I owed it to them to take extra steps to faithfully reflect their accounts. I only did this with the understanding that it was for the purpose of ensuring accuracy, capturing the correct nuances, and providing proper context. When I did it, I believe that all of my sources acted in good faith.

PROLOGUE

ON THE AFTERNOON of January 29, 2010, a bleak, cold day in Washington, Barack Obama's top counterterrorism and political advisers gathered in the White House Situation Room. Obama arrived a few minutes late, wearing his customary game face. There was no small talk, just a crisp beckoning from the president for the group to take their seats. Some noticed a slight spring in his step — perhaps because he'd just returned from a feisty sparring session with House Republicans at their annual retreat in Baltimore. Otherwise the mood in the White House was grim. Two days before, New York mayor Michael Bloomberg had abruptly withdrawn his support for the administration's plan to try 9/11 mastermind Khalid Sheikh Mohammed and four coconspirators in a federal court in downtown Manhattan. Obama knew Attorney General Eric Holder's initiative was politically fraught. Now, its thin layer of cover had been stripped away. Bloomberg's about-face sparked a full-blown congressional revolt. Obama was being lacerated on the cable news shows and the op-ed pages for "criminalizing" the war on terror, and for the decision to bring one of the world's most infamous terrorists into the heart of New York City. Yet the president knew that if he retreated from the plan to try Mohammed in federal court, he would be excoriated by liberals for abandoning the rule of law and perpetuating the policies of George W. Bush.

Obama had been elected as a change maker — "change we can believe in." He promised, among many other things, to move America "beyond the politics of fear."

He had campaigned as the anti–George W. Bush: he would close the Guantánamo Bay detention facility, end preventive detention, and bring terrorists to justice in civilian courts, among other sweeping changes. The United States would show the world that America was a nation of laws, not unchecked powers. Yet the challenges Obama faced upon taking office one year earlier were dominated by a financial crisis greater than any since the Great Depression, and he was determined to put health care reform at the top of his agenda. Health care costs represented an economic threat, and at the same time, the crisis seemed to present a unique opportunity to pull together a massive overhaul of a complex industry. The rule-of-law agenda would have to wait, as the health bill soon overwhelmed many other initiatives, subordinating almost all other questions. White House staffers called it "triage," the inescapable reality, as they saw it, of a president's having to choose among policy priorities. They used the abbreviation AHC, or "after health care," to refer to everything else they hoped to accomplish.

Obama was caught between his own pragmatic impulses and his commitment to "first principles." The question of where and how to put Khalid Sheikh Mohammed — or KSM, as the spies and soldiers called him — on trial was symbolically important: Obama was determined to show that the American criminal justice system was a strength, not a weakness. Politically, this was a tough sell, since most Americans wanted the senior al-Qaeda operative kept far away and interrogated to the last drop of his useful intelligence. Obama's advisers were sharply split. The January meeting had come against the backdrop of months of brutal infighting over counterterrorism policy. Obama had run a disciplined and drama-free campaign, and yet he had come to preside over a White House that seemed striking for its acrimony and dysfunction. No issue laid bare the divisions more than KSM. Sometimes the tensions played out openly, with profanity-laced outbursts in the halls of the West Wing. Other times they took the form of subterfuge, end runs, or a quiet knife in the back. The policy rivalries masked deeper, more personal animosities.

The two main protagonists in this drama were Rahm Emanuel, Obama's intense and volatile chief of staff, and Holder, Obama's friend. From the beginning Holder had struggled politically. He had been muzzled by Emanuel and the White House message police after some early gaffes, and he had fought increasingly lonely — and often unsuccessful — policy battles. Yet the president had his back. So did Valerie Jarrett, Obama's senior adviser and a longtime friend of the president's.

Obama's affection for Holder bred resentment within the White House, especially with the chief of staff. "Of all of the twelve cabinet members, why does the boss like Eric the most? We should all throw him in a pit and kick him," commented one of the president's top advisers, sarcastically alluding to the biblical story told in *Joseph and the Amazing Technicolor Dreamcoat,* the 1970s Broadway musical about a father's preference for one of his sons, and his brothers' jealous plot to undermine him.

The disagreement on KSM played out against a larger internal war over domestic policy that Emanuel would memorably characterize as "Tammany Hall" versus "the Aspen Institute." The Tammany faction, named for the infamous Democratic Party machine, was made up of the political operatives, the hardheaded realists. Opposing Tammany were the idealists and policy wonks who found a philosophical home at think tanks like the Aspen Institute, known for its lofty seminars dedicated to creating a more just society. In Emanuel's conception, the Aspenites sailed naively against the political tide, fighting for unpopular causes long beyond their ability to prevail, often at the expense of the president's standing. Tammany came to believe that many of the president's promises to reform the war on terror were simply out of step with the American people. Its outlook was epitomized by one charter member's cutting remark about the attorney general: "Your job is to take the shit off of the president, not to put the shit on him. KSM put the shit on the president." The idealists, for their part, believed that Tammany's eagerness to appease Republicans in Congress at the expense of core principles was self-fulfilling: the less the White House was willing to take on the right, the more it was rolled. The $64,000 question throughout these battles was always, "Where does Obama stand?" The president stayed so far above the fray, sometimes for excruciatingly long periods, that it was difficult to know which way he was leaning, much less where he would eventually settle.

National security policy has always been a presidential proving ground. American leaders, from Woodrow Wilson to Jimmy Carter to George W. Bush, have been defined by their crusades: to make the world safe for democracy, to put human rights at the center of foreign policy, to spread democracy around the world. They all faced pragmatic critics, and sometimes those critics were right. They also faced idealistic critics. For all of George W. Bush's talk about spreading democracy, it was his assertion of executive power, from indefinite detentions to warrantless wiretapping, that drove liberals crazy. Now, with one of the world's most famous terrorists coming to New York to stand trial — unless Obama reversed Holder's decision — the Obama administration faced a focused, defining decision.

For Emanuel the decision to try KSM in civilian court in New York City was a self-inflicted wound, pure and simple. Sticking with it would be suicidal. It had only been a month since the "Christmas Day bomber," Umar Farouk Abdulmutallab, a twenty-three-year old Nigerian al-Qaeda operative, had mocked American defenses and nearly brought down a packed airliner with explosives secreted in his underwear. Republicans were torching Obama as soft and ineffectual on terrorism. With an eye already on the midterm elections, the White House's pollsters had begun noticing a worrying trend: independents were abandoning Obama in large numbers, and national security issues were part of the reason. When Scott Brown, an obscure Republican politician from deep-blue Massachusetts, captured Ted Kennedy's Senate seat in a special election on January 19, it heralded the arrival of the Tea Party as an electoral force and struck fear deep into the White House political operation. In his acceptance speech, Brown returned to a theme that had resonated with voters throughout his insurgent campaign. "Our Constitution and laws exist to protect this nation," he bellowed. "They do not grant rights and privileges to enemies in wartime."

What Emanuel wanted to know now was whether Obama was really going to risk a second term to protect the constitutional rights of a bunch of terrorists held in Guantánamo. Was this the issue he wanted to stake his presidency on?

Obama could certainly be ruthlessly pragmatic, subordinating even cherished ideals to his political needs. But he struggled with national security dilemmas, sometimes to the point of Hamlet-like indecision, trying to balance security and liberty. Throughout the campaign he'd rejected the "false choice" between protecting the country and upholding its values. It wasn't just a poll-tested talking point. He believed America's strength was rooted in its ideals. After a year in office, Obama also knew that presidential decisions could create powerful precedents. His preoccupation with his legacy included an element of vanity — he'd sometimes tell advisers, "I don't want my name" on a policy that might be judged harshly in the future. For all these reasons, he agreed with Holder that Khalid Sheikh Mohammed should be tried in civilian court, public opinion notwithstanding. So he had summoned his advisers to assess the damage of Mayor Bloomberg's reversal, and to help him identify a politically feasible path forward.

Robert Bauer, the White House counsel, "set the table," stating the agenda for the meeting. Obama nodded to Holder to lead off. Rather than a full-throated defense of his decision, however, the attorney general laid out the president's meager options. Holder did not fill the room with a booming voice or sway it with the force of his legal reasoning. He didn't have Bob Gates's "command presence" or Hillary Clinton's lawyerly precision. He was more phlegmatic and didn't seem to crave the room's approval. What he had was the president. Six months before, on the Fourth of July, they had stood together on the White House roof terrace, watching fireworks explode over the National Mall. "I'm leaning toward prosecuting KSM in federal court," he had told Obama, careful not to cede his independence by seeking approval. "It's your call, you're the attorney general," Obama had responded flatly.

Now, after Holder finished, Rahm let loose with a brutally concise message for the president: If you go ahead with this, you'll lose and they'll make you pay.

Seated to the left of Obama was Harold Hongju Koh, the former dean of Yale Law School, now serving as the State Department's top lawyer. Round, perpetually rumpled, and possessing an enormous intellect, Koh was a combative infighter on behalf of his liberal convictions. His writings in favor of "transnational jurisprudence" and a strong deference to international law made him a darling of the human rights community. The right had vilified him as an elitist whose theories would undermine American sovereignty. Even some of his colleagues in the Obama administration saw him as a moralizing academic. He was outranked by virtually everyone at the table — but Obama liked having him around in these settings. A former constitutional law professor himself, the president respected Koh's academic pedigree and knew that he would push the intellectual boundaries of the debate. Koh understood and seemed to relish his role. For this meeting he had carefully prepared his remarks and rehearsed them before his staff.

Looking directly at the president, Koh pointed out that terrorists had been tried successfully in traditional American courts hundreds of times, and that there had never been any security problems. (Indeed, for all its tough talk, the Bush administration had routinely used the criminal courts to try terrorists.) Moreover, Koh argued, when our closest allies had suffered major al-Qaeda attacks, they tried the perpetrators in the cities where the strikes had occurred, whether it was London, Madrid, or Mumbai. To try KSM in Manhattan would "show confidence in our system," it would be a "redemptive act," precisely because it is what the terrorists don't want us to do. Finally, Koh skillfully framed the debate as a showdown between Obama and the terror mastermind himself. "If KSM is tried in a military commission," he told the president, "you will be playing completely into how KSM wants to be viewed — as a fearsome person and a great military leader, when in fact he is just a common criminal."

Holder pulled out some highlighted, slightly worn papers from his leather binder and prepared to pass them down to Obama, but Koh beat him to the punch. Some of the president's aides eyed each other nervously as they watched the unvetted papers reach the president, a breach of ministerial protocol. Back and forth the argument bounced, between liberal ideals and populist realpolitik. Obama did not say much; he mostly sat back and listened. When he did intervene, he seemed to vacillate between his own high principles and cold pragmatism. At one point he told the group that he wasn't willing to lose his administration over the issue. But later in the conversation, Obama lifted the discussion out of the purely tactical. "We all know where terrorism is going," he said. "Ten years from now an American teenager is going to be accused of trying to blow up the mall in Minneapolis." He paused for effect. "I'm not going to be responsible for a separate system of justice for that kid." Holder could not figure out where the president would finally come down on the matter. But he did notice that Obama kept glancing at the papers that had been passed to him.

Emanuel asked Phil Schiliro, the White House legislative liaison, how many votes the White House could expect to get if the KSM issue was brought before the House. Schiliro, an expert vote counter, didn't even have to think about it: "Less than 200," he replied — far fewer than the 217 votes the president would need to prevail. The ship had sailed, he seemed to be saying. But Holder pointed out that the administration had not properly prepared the ground with Congress or the public for the decision. Obama cut in, gently chiding his attorney general. "Now, Eric, to be fair, you didn't do this right."

The comment stung. "I wasn't allowed to," he said acidly. The two friends were now touching on something that had been a source of tension throughout the first year of the administration. There was an impression among many White House staff that Holder was politically inept and had botched the public presentation of difficult policy decisions. For their part, Holder and his aides believed that the White House was so spooked by its critics, it wasn't willing to truly engage Congress and fight for what it believed in. Emanuel had made Holder announce the KSM decision late on a Friday, and then, rather than allowing the attorney general to defend it boldly on the Sunday-morning news programs and on the op-ed pages, he was told to appear only on the PBS *NewsHour*—an outlet with modest ratings.

Typically, when White House meetings descended into squabbling, the president would try to lead his team to higher ground. Now, Obama picked up the papers lying in front of him. They contained a sentencing statement delivered in 2003 by US District Judge William Young in a federal courtroom in Massachusetts, directed at Richard Reid, the so-called shoe bomber, who had attempted to blow up a civilian airliner in December 2001. Young gave Reid multiple life sentences without parole—along with a stirring speech, which Obama now began to recite.

This is the sentence that is provided for by our statutes. It is a fair and a just sentence. It is a righteous sentence. Let me explain this to you. We are not afraid of any of your terrorist co-conspirators, Mr. Reid. We are Americans. We have been through the fire before. There is all too much war talk here. And I say that to everyone with the utmost respect. Here in this court, where we deal with individuals as individuals, and care for individuals as individuals, as human beings we reach out for justice. You are not an enemy combatant. You are a terrorist. You are not a soldier in any war. You are a terrorist. To give you that reference, to call you a soldier gives you far too much stature. Whether it is the officers of government who do it or your attorney who does it, or that happens to be your view, you are a terrorist. And we do not negotiate with terrorists. We do not treat with terrorists. We do not sign documents with terrorists. We hunt then down one by one and bring them to justice.

So war talk is way out of line in this court. You're a big fellow. But you're not that big. You're no warrior. I know warriors. You are a terrorist. A species of criminal guilty of multiple attempted murders. In a very real sense Trooper Santiago had it right when first you were taken off that plane and into custody and you wondered where the press and where the TV crews were and you said you're no big deal. You're no big deal. What your counsel, what your able counsel and what the equally able United States attorneys have grappled with and what I have as honestly as I know how tried to grappled with, is why you did something so horrific. What was it that led you here to this courtroom today? I have listened respectfully to what you have to say. And I ask you to search your heart and ask yourself what sort of unfathomable hate led you to do what you are guilty and admit you are guilty of doing. And I have an answer for you. It may not satisfy you. But as I search this entire record it comes as close to understanding as I know.

It seems to me you hate the one thing that to us is most precious. You hate our freedom. Our individual freedom. Our individual freedom to live as we choose, to come and go as we choose, to believe or not believe as we individually choose. Here, in this society, the very winds carry freedom. They carry it everywhere from sea to shining sea. It is because we prize individual freedom so much that you are held here in this beautiful courtroom. So that everyone can see, can truly see that justice is administered fairly, individually, and discretely.

It is for freedom's sake that your lawyers are striving so vigorously on your behalf and have filed appeals, will go on in . . . their representation of you before other judges. We care about it. Because we all know that the way we treat you, Mr. Reid, is the measure of our own liberties. Make no mistake, though. It is yet true that we will bear any burden, pay any price, to preserve our freedoms. Look around this courtroom. Mark it well. The world is not going to long remember what you or I say here. Day after tomorrow it will be forgotten. But this, however, will long endure. Here, in this courtroom, and courtrooms all across America, the American people will gather to see that justice, individual justice, justice, not war, individual justice is in fact being done. The very President of the United States through his officers will have to come into courtrooms and lay out evidence on which specific matters can be judged, and juries of citizens will gather to sit and judge that evidence democratically, to mold and shape and refine our sense of justice.

See that flag, Mr. Reid? That's the flag of the United States of America. That flag will fly there long after this is all forgotten. That flag still stands for freedom. You know it always will. Custody, Mr. Officer. Stand him down.

Obama put down the speech and looked around the room. He didn't fix his gaze on anyone in particular; he just stared for several moments. Then he spoke. "Why can't I give that speech?" Without another word, he rose and walked out of the room.

1

THE PROMISE

O
N MAY 16, 2007, Richard Clarke's driver pulled up to a shabby block of Massachusetts Avenue, in Northeast DC. Clarke got out of the car, looked around, and wondered if he was in the right place. Two days earlier he'd spoken to Susan Rice, a democratic foreign policy mandarin and a top adviser in Barack Obama's nascent presidential campaign. The two had worked together in the Clinton White House, and Rice was now looking to put together a team to advise Obama on counterterrorism. Clarke seemed perfect. He was a veteran of the terror wars, having worked for four presidents stretching back to Ronald Reagan. Moreover, he had seen George W. Bush's war on terror go awry from the inside. When the country was attacked on September 11, 2001, Clarke was Bush's principal counterterrorism adviser, but he broke with Bush over the decision to invade Iraq, testifying in dramatic public fashion at televised hearings of the 9/11 Commission and publishing a scathingly critical book about the administration's conduct of the war on terror, in 2004.

Rice had arranged for Clarke to meet Obama at the rundown apartment the Illinois senator had rented for discreet policy sessions and to plan his presidential campaign. The scruffy building, which housed a Subway sandwich shop, reminded Clarke of the tenement where he'd grown up in Boston. It hardly looked like a presidential launching ground for the young, charismatic politician who'd taken Washington by storm three years before.

There were a few ragtag NGOs listed on the building directory, but no mention of Obama. Clarke called the cell phone number he'd been given and an aide came down to collect him. After greeting Clarke, Obama led him down the dismal hallway to a small, sparsely furnished room badly in need of a paint job. The two men chatted amiably for a few minutes, but the pleasantries masked a mutual doubt. Obama had reason to be wary of his visitor. Clarke was both a supple thinker and a hard-charging man of action, a rare combination in a lifelong bureaucrat. But he could also be arrogant and headstrong. For his part, Clarke was intrigued by Obama and thought the younger man might be able to provide a fresh start in the fight against al-Qaeda. But was he too much the effete intellectual? Could he really feel the threat of Islamic terrorism in his gut?

As they talked, Obama cogently and efficiently analyzed the litany of failures that had plagued American foreign policy. Iraq topped the list: instead of harnessing the goodwill of the international community after 9/11, the United States had wandered into the valley of Mesopotamia to fight a disastrous war against the wrong enemy. It was time to pull out of Iraq and finish the job in Afghanistan, he insisted. At the same time, the United States needed to reclaim its moral authority in the world, which had been compromised in the CIA's secret torture chambers or "black sites," at Abu Ghraib, and in the detention cells of Guantánamo. Finally, America needed to urgently change its message to the Muslim world; the United States was not at war with Islam, and until that perception was fundamentally altered, the nation could not win the ideological struggle against al-Qaeda. Clarke agreed with every word. But there was still the question of inner toughness: did Obama understand that as president he would be up against irredeemable people, for whom the only options would be to kill or capture them?

Clarke had spent a lifetime immersed in the dark corners of the terror wars; he had no illusions about what it would take to prevail against a nihilistic enemy like al-Qaeda. A president had to have a warrior instinct — an ability to be brutal at times. He made the point as directly as he knew how. Looking the senator in the eye, Clarke stated a simple fact. "As president, you kill people." He wasn't just talking about sending troops into battle — in the shadow wars, presidents know the names and addresses of people they have killed. Obama stared back at Clarke for several seconds. "I know that," he said very quietly and calmly. "He didn't flinch," Clarke later recalled.

For all of Obama's soaring rhetoric and appeals to idealism, and despite many observers' assumptions about his time as a community activist, he was a foreign policy realist by the time he ran for president. Obama's instincts were generally center-left, but he was skeptical of rigid ideology and pat solutions to complicated problems. He sought compromise and consensus, working within the system as it was, not as he wanted it to be. He aspired to be an "idealist without illusions," in John F. Kennedy's phrase. But his challenge now, as a presidential candidate with no military experience, was to sell himself as a credible commander in chief.

Clarke knew that Obama began with considerable disadvantages. Among other things, he was saddled with forty years of Democratic heritage — the perception that ever since Eugene McCarthy broke with the party to oppose the Vietnam War, Democrats had been weak on national security. Then there was his own personal heritage:

part black, part white, with Muslim and African ancestry, his advisers knew he would be viewed suspiciously by a large swath of the voting public.

Obama's bet was that those political vulnerabilities could, over time, be turned into strengths. After eight years of George W. Bush's feel-it-in-the-gut, shoot-from-the-hip approach to counterterrorism, the country might be ready for a cooler, more deliberative strategy. But Obama's cosmopolitan background also gave him a more visceral feel for how much of the rest of the world lived — and how they viewed America. He'd visited his own poor relatives in African villages, and as a child he witnessed the squalid poverty of Jakarta. In 1981 Obama traveled through South Asia with a Pakistani college friend. They spent three weeks in Karachi, where Obama discovered a sprawling, congested city throbbing with sectarian strife and tense with the threat of communal violence. These experiences helped shape Obama's belief that what most people around the world desired was adequate food, shelter, and security — lives of dignity, free of the daily humiliations of poverty and ignorance. They were the basis for a coherent set of views about the roots of Islamic rage and the underlying conditions that breed Islamic extremism — the economic despair, the social and political dysfunction that lead young men to become terrorists.

For Clarke, Obama's intuitive understanding of the forces driving Islamic extremism was an enormous asset. And yet he also knew that the slash-and-burn politics of a presidential campaign would not be friendly to Obama's more nuanced approach. He would need a thick layer of political insulation to protect him against the inevitable attack ads questioning his positions on terrorism. The challenge was to weave together Obama's notions of soft power and hard power into a new paradigm for the war on terror, one that could be framed as tough but smart. It was time to begin laying out a blueprint for how Obama would redirect the fight against al-Qaeda.

Three months after his meeting with Clarke, Obama prepared a major national security address. The speech was set for August 1, 2007, at the Woodrow Wilson Center in DC. Clarke and Rand Beers, a longtime counterterrorism expert with three decades of experience in Democratic and Republican administrations, consulted with Obama on the speech a few days before. They advised the candidate that he had two primary political objectives. First, he had to get out in front of any terrorist attack that might occur during the campaign. Clarke, who ran a global-security consulting firm, was regularly tapping his network of spook and counterterrorism sources to measure the threat environment. He believed the odds of an attack were high and potentially catastrophic to Obama's campaign. "We told him quite explicitly to get on the record putting the blame on the [present] administration," Clarke recalled. "We wanted him to show causality between what the Bush administration did and the continuing terrorism threat." This was a hard sell: for many Americans, the Bush administration had projected strength in its war on terror, and the argument that America was now less safe hinged on the abstract threat of backlash as a result of the war in Iraq — not on a weak national security response. Second, Obama needed to show he was willing to use force, confidently but more prudently than the current administration.

In the speech that resulted, Obama argued that a strategy of hunting down terrorists by itself would lead to Pyrrhic victories. His goal, he told the Wilson Center audience, was to "dry up support for terror and extremism." As president he would pledge $1 billion in aid for poverty reduction and for secular education to counter the radical madrasas, the Islamic schools that inculcated Muslim youth with anti-Western sentiment. Obama invoked the "thousands of desperate faces" looking up at American military helicopters from conflict zones and refugee camps. "Do they feel hope, or do they feel hate?" America's security hung in the balance, he argued.

But the softer talk of American values, hope, and economic empowerment was shot through with steel: Obama called for the deployment of at least two more brigades to bolster US counterterrorism operations in Afghanistan. (Clarke had had to instruct him that three to five thousand soldiers constituted a brigade.) America was exhausted from years of war and imperial overstretch, and yet Obama proposed to send thousands more American troops into battle. But the risk was carefully calculated. For many Democrats, Afghanistan was still "the good war," at least as compared with Iraq. The United States needed to be focused on the enemy that attacked it, the real center of the war on terror: al-Qaeda and the Taliban.

In the end, it was another line in the speech that proved the more controversial. In retrospect, it may have done more than anything in the campaign to protect him against charges of being soft on terrorism. A little less than halfway through the address, Obama, his voice rising, accused the Bush administration of fecklessness in the fight against the terrorists. "It was a terrible mistake to fail to act when we had a chance to take out an al-Qaeda leadership meeting in 2005," he charged. Then, in a rare moment of chest thumping, he vowed, "If we have actionable intelligence about high-value terrorist targets and [then Pakistani president Pervez] Musharraf won't act, we will." In early 2005 the Bush administration had planned a secret operation to drop American commandos into North Waziristan, the mountainous region of Pakistan bordering Afghanistan. The daring "snatch and grab" operation was aimed at capturing al-Qaeda biggies, including bin Laden's number two, Ayman al-Zawahiri. But at the last minute

(Navy SEALs had already boarded the military planes), Defense Secretary Donald Rumsfeld aborted the raid, in part because the Bush administration didn't want to disturb relations with the Pakistanis.

Hillary Clinton, Obama's main challenger for the Democratic nomination, pounced on the line at a February 2008 campaign debate in Cleveland. "He basically threatened to bomb Pakistan, which I don't think was a particularly wise position to take." Republican Party candidate John McCain would later echo Clinton's line of attack, accusing Obama of wanting to "invade" Pakistan. At the time it seemed like clever political jujitsu: take Obama's muscular rhetoric and try to paint him as naive. But the controversy would also presage a dilemma of the Obama presidency: can you kill or capture bad guys wherever you find them while staying true to American values and the rule of law?

While the campaign would later be dominated by the flailing economy, there were still flare-ups on terrorism. In June 2008 the Supreme Court issued a decision in *Boumediene v. Bush,* restoring the rights of prisoners held at Guantánamo Bay to challenge their detention in federal court. By then, Obama had the Democratic nomination sewn up. He and John McCain had both pledged to close down the Guantánamo detention camp. Yet they disagreed sharply over this announcement. Obama praised the decision and lauded the effectiveness of the American justice system as a weapon against terrorists. The McCain campaign immediately unleashed its surrogates, asserting the need to continue the Bush administration's policy of trying terrorists as "enemy combatants" in military tribunals, and attacking Obama as "naive" and "delusional." Former New York City mayor Rudy Giuliani, who had endorsed McCain after ending his own presidential run, laid out the central criticism: "Barack Obama appears to believe that terrorists should be treated like criminals — a belief that underscores his fundamental lack of judgment regarding our national security." Obama punched back hard. The Republicans lacked the credibility to criticize him on the issue. They were in charge, after all, when Osama bin Laden slipped away after the military had him pinned down in Tora Bora. And it was their disastrous war in Iraq, Obama stated, that diverted critical resources away from Afghanistan, the central battlefield in the war against al-Qaeda.

In the end, Obama won the election not on the basis of his foreign policy views but because the US economy was in free fall. The Iraq war was no longer uppermost in voters' minds, and Obama's national security positions were in fact not significantly different from his opponent's. In addition to promising to close Guantánamo, McCain had vowed to shut down the CIA's secret prisons and end torture. By the end of 2008, Obama's priorities, and the country's as well, clearly lay elsewhere: with economic recovery.

The approach Obama would take to national security as president, therefore, would be less a matter of political necessity, more one of character and symbolism. Although Americans were tired of the Iraq war, and many liberals loudly denounced the executive-power claims of the Bush administration (from warrantless wiretapping to "extraordinary rendition" to military tribunals to detentions without trials), the public as a whole wasn't clamoring for a change of course — Americans just wanted to regain lost jobs and see that the country was moving again. Obama would not be compelled to walk back the Bush agenda on the war on terror.

But symbolically, and as a test of personal conviction and resolve, Obama's decisions about whether and how to change that agenda would indicate much not only about his deepest beliefs and principles, but also his style of presidency. Where did he fall on the pragmatist-idealist spectrum? Did he care more about the long-term legacy he left for his successors, and the powers they could assert, or about short-term political wins and losses? How strong were his convictions? How hard was he willing to fight for them? Who, in the end, was Barack Obama? His conduct of the war on terror, as much as anything else, would reveal answers to these questions and define him in the minds of many Americans.

Two days after the presidential election, on November 6, Vice Admiral Mike McConnell was on a plane bound for Chicago to deliver Obama's first intelligence briefing as president-elect. McConnell was the director of national intelligence, the government's top intel officer, who oversaw the country's vast spy bureaucracy. The two men had met once before, shortly after Obama had captured the Democratic nomination. Much of that briefing had focused on the covert war in Afghanistan, where momentum was swinging dangerously toward the Taliban. A key reason, McConnell told Obama, was Pakistani duplicity. Pakistan's spy service, the ISI, was colluding with the Afghan Taliban, which it saw as a strategic counterweight to India on its western flank. The ISI, with the tacit support of Musharraf, was playing a cynical double game, one that was costing American lives.

Now that Obama had won the presidency, McConnell was prepared to divulge the intelligence community's deepest secrets. They met in a tiny room — a sensitive compartmented information facility, or SCIF — in the Kluczynski Federal Building. Despite the gloomy outlook in Afghanistan, there was one positive story to be told, one that reflected the very best abilities of America's frontline spies. McConnell, according to the account in Bob Woodward's 2010 book *Obama's Wars,* revealed to the president the inner workings of the CIA's covert drone program. Agency operators, manipulating joysticks at CIA headquarters in Langley, Virginia, had destroyed much of al-Qaeda's senior leadership. Astonishing precision technology had enabled mechanized death from thousands of miles away. But the pilotless drones were useless without targeting intelligence. That required humint, or human intelligence — spies on the ground in the vast, lawless border areas between Pakistan and Afghanistan. After years of stagnation, the agency had finally begun to make important gains recruiting and training local tribesmen to be their spotters. These were the crown jewels of American spying in the region, and they were now Obama's.

A few days after the McConnell briefing, Obama asked John Brennan to come to his Chicago transition office. The two had never met. Brennan was a twenty-five-year veteran of the CIA who'd served both overseas and at Langley. He spoke fluent Arabic and had been the agency's station chief in Saudi Arabia, where he maintained valuable relationships with members of the desert kingdom's security services. Obama was looking for a CIA director, and Brennan had come highly recommended by Anthony Lake, a wise man of democratic foreign policy circles and a trusted Obama adviser. Brennan was also a survivor of the Bush administration's intel wars, having served at one point as a top aide to former CIA director George Tenet.

Brennan liked what he'd heard from Obama during the campaign, but he wanted to take the president-elect's measure before making a decision to return to the maelstrom of national security politics. The two spent an hour together in the Kluczynski building and quickly established a bond. They talked about how their travels as young men in the Muslim world had helped shape their worldviews. Obama recalled his time in the teeming metropolis of Karachi. Brennan had studied at the American University in Cairo in the mid-1970s during a period of turmoil and simmering anti-Americanism.

Terrorism dominated their conversation. Brennan was an unsentimental intel warrior, and he told Obama he had no reluctance to use hard power against the terrorists when appropriate. But he also emphasized that America could not prevail in the war on terror without tackling the "upstream factors" that push young Muslim men toward violent radicalism in the first place. Their views were so complementary that Obama found himself finishing Brennan's sentences. When it came to the use of force, Obama and Brennan agreed on the need for a more surgical strategy, one that focused on demonstrable threats to the United States, rather than a "mow them all down" approach. It was like attacking a spreading cancer, Brennan told the president-elect: "You need to target the metastasizing disease without destroying the surrounding tissue." How to implement that strategy brought the discussion around to what Admiral McConnell had briefed the president-elect on days before and what would become the new administration's weapon of choice: weaponized pilotless aircraft, or drones.

In the end, Brennan did not become Obama's CIA chief. As soon as his name surfaced, left-wing bloggers railed against him for his supposed associations with the Bush administration's enhanced interrogation program, the use by the CIA of harsh techniques — torture, in the view of critics — to extract intelligence from high-level detainees. (Internally, Brennan had opposed those policies, but Obama did not want a partisan fight over such a controversial issue right off the bat.) Instead, Obama appointed Brennan his top counterterrorism adviser. From a windowless bunker in the basement of the West Wing, Brennan would come to have unrivaled influence with the president on matters of national security.

"Greg, it's Barack." It was the evening of November 12 and Greg Craig was at home with a house full of family and friends when the president-elect called. Handsome, with a boyish, open face and a mop of white hair, Craig had a resumé to match his central-casting looks. He'd worked at the intersection of politics, foreign policy, and law for most of his career, and at the age of sixty-three had attained considerable stature in the Democratic security establishment. Craig also had a strong sense of idealism, honed during the liberal ferment of the 1960s. A disciple of Allard Lowenstein, the liberal activist, Craig had registered black voters in Mississippi, tutored underprivileged kids in Harlem, and was a leading voice against the Vietnam War at both Harvard and Yale Law School. As a protégé of Edward Bennett Williams, the legendary defense lawyer, Craig firmly believed that the Bill of Rights provided the ultimate bulwark against government abuse.

Cheerful in the afterglow of the election, Craig was a little deflated when he began to hear, secondhand, what Obama had in mind for him. Now he listened to the president-elect make his pitch. "I want you to be my White House counsel," Obama said. For Craig the offer was a consolation prize; he'd joined the Obama campaign in its earliest days as a top foreign policy adviser and thought he had a serious shot at being national security adviser or maybe deputy secretary of state. But Craig had doomed that chance with a single act during the heated fight for the Democratic nomination. In March 2008 he issued a withering memo, under his own name, mocking Hillary Clinton's national security credentials and accusing her of vastly overstating her experience. As campaign memos went, it was unremarkable; but Craig had deep ties to both Clintons, dating back to their friendship at Yale Law School, continuing through the White House years, all the way to a late summer evening in 1998, when he and Bill Clinton sat together on the Truman Balcony for hours planning the forty-second president's impeachment defense. To attack Hillary in 2008 was to betray a lot of years together. Obama reserved a special place for those supporters who'd broken with the Clintons, especially people like Craig who did so early on; he knew that took courage.

But now Obama had decided to add Clinton to his "team of rivals" cabinet as secretary of state, a move aimed at unifying the party after a divisive election. If Clinton was in, then Craig was out—at least as far as a major foreign policy post was concerned. "Now I know your true love is foreign policy," Obama said soothingly. "But I want you to be with me in the White House and we'll find ways for you to be involved. You'll be in the room whenever you want it on foreign policy issues."

Though disappointed at first, Craig was buoyed by the president-elect's words. As counsel, he knew he would play a central role in rolling back the Bush legacy of coercive interrogation, black sites, and unchecked presidential power. He relished the opportunity to help Obama restore constitutional values to the war on terror. That night, he quietly celebrated with Derry Noyes, his wife of thirty-four years.

Craig showed up a few days later at the Obama transition office, a nondescript building in downtown Washington. He was situated in the national security corridor, sharing an office with Denis Mc-Donough, one of Obama's trusted advisers. There was a staggering amount of work to be done. Much of it would fall to Craig and the team of lawyers it was his job to assemble. There were hundreds of personnel appointments to be vetted, new ethics guidelines to draw up, and dozens of sensitive executive orders that needed to be drafted. Then there were the inevitable mini-crises that plague any presidential transition. After word leaked that New Mexico governor Bill Richardson, nominated by Obama to be commerce secretary, was a subject of a grand jury probe into corruption, Craig was called in to assess the damage. Richardson was quickly tossed overboard. Later, Craig oversaw the internal damage-control effort when news surfaced that Illinois governor Rod Blagojevich was under investigation by the feds for trying to sell Obama's Senate seat.

Craig delegated as much as he could during the transition in an effort to stay focused on national security. He believed Obama had to act swiftly and boldly. He needed to signal a clean break from the excesses of the Bush administration. No act would resonate more around the world than an executive order directing the military to shut down Guantánamo. To further underscore America's rededication to the rule of law, Craig urged Obama to issue an executive order dismantling the CIA's black sites and banning torture. Obama's instinct, however, was to proceed carefully. This was the first wartime transition in two generations. American soldiers and intelligence officers were engaged 24/7 in perilous counterterror operations around the globe. They were relying on rules of the game established by the Bush administration. You couldn't just unilaterally wrest these tools away from them in the middle of a war. So Craig began reaching out to the military and the intelligence community to solicit their advice and support.

One day he rode the subway out to the Pentagon to meet with Admiral Mike Mullen, the chairman of the Joint Chiefs of Staff. Mullen said he was not opposed to closing Gitmo, but he had one concern: he didn't want the debate over the military's detention policies to be burdened by the Guantánamo controversy. This was wartime, and the military needed the flexibility to take the enemy off the battlefield. Craig's solution was to draft a separate executive order establishing a task force to develop detention policy going forward.

No one had better downfield vision than Robert Gates, whom Obama had decided to retain as his secretary of defense. Gates had been an early supporter of closing Guantánamo, but saw potential problems that no one was yet focusing on. At one early transition meeting he raised those concerns directly with Obama. What would our criteria be for releasing or transferring prisoners? Gates wanted to know. They might not have all been the "worst of the worst," as former vice president Dick Cheney had darkly asserted. But nor were they all mountain shepherds mistakenly picked up as terrorists. "Our guys had risked their lives to capture these people," he said, according to participants at the meeting. "We need a rational way of explaining our decisions. We can't just cut them loose." There was no disagreement. Then Gates raised another concern: "What are we going to do if we capture Osama bin Laden or some other major terrorist figure in Somalia or Malaysia? Where will we detain him?" Layered beneath that deceptively simple question was a set of vexing challenges that the transition team was just beginning to seriously grapple with. Would terror suspects be brought to the mainland and prosecuted in civilian courts? Where would they be held? Would they be placed in brigs to be tried in military commissions? What authority did the United States have to detain terror suspects away from the more traditional battlefields of Afghanistan and Iraq? Could they be held indefinitely as enemy combatants? These decisions could not all be punted into the future. As the complex issues surrounding detainees cascaded through Craig's mind, he knew that Obama could dismantle the legal architecture of the Bush-Cheney war on terror with a stroke of the pen. But what would replace it? As for Obama, he was in "listening mode," as one participant recalls it, and said little.

While Gates was urging caution, another group was pushing for a "damn the torpedoes" approach: the so-called Gitmo bar. They were criminal defense lawyers, mostly from white-shoe law firms in Washington and New York, who had led the fight to grant legal rights to Guantánamo prisoners. They had been shut out by the Bush administration, which regarded them as little better than aiders and abettors of the terrorists themselves. But now they found themselves on the inside, with carte blanche access to lawyers on the Obama transition, including Greg Craig, though the press got no wind of it. The group's leader was Thomas Wilner, a courtly, well-connected litigator who had won two of the most important detainee-rights cases in the Supreme Court: *Boumediene* and *Rasul v. Bush*. In 2006 Obama had worked closely with Wilner and other lawyers to overturn the Military Commissions Act, a hated law that suspended habeas corpus rights for Guantánamo detainees. They ran their lobbying operation out of Obama's Senate offices. Now Wilner was working closely with the incoming administration to shut down Guantánamo altogether. He developed a PowerPoint presentation, circulated among the transition team, called "Close Guantánamo. It's Not Hard," arguing that shutting down the detention facility could be done in three to six months. Eight years before, Wilner had agreed to represent a group of Kuwaitis who'd been picked up by the US military in Afghanistan and shipped off to Guantánamo. The government fought him with everything it had. His own law partners at Shearman & Sterling shunned him for representing accused terrorists, refusing to let Wilner use the firm's name in court pleadings. Even his wife, Jane, was against his taking the case. Now, Wilner was advising the incoming administration on terrorism policy, even providing input on the executive order Obama was preparing to issue to close Guantánamo. It was government by lawyer, and not just executive-branch-appointed lawyers. Glenn Beck and Rush Limbaugh would have had a field day with the story.

CIA director Michael Hayden, a Bush appointee, wanted to push back on several fronts, and he knew he had his work cut out for him. No issue had been politicized more than enhanced interrogation — torture, as the left insisted on calling it. There was a lot of misinformation floating around, but he believed he could persuade fairminded people that the techniques were both humane and necessary for the safety of the American people. He got his chance on December 9 in a meeting with Obama and his top national security advisers at the Chicago transition office. Hayden had prepared assiduously, showing up with charts and slides. But his most unusual prop was David Shedd, the deputy DNI for policy, plans, and requirements. Not long into his presentation, Hayden called Shedd over. Suddenly, unexpectedly, Hayden slapped Shedd's face. Then he grabbed him by the lapels and started to shake him. He'd wanted to throw him up against the wall during this demonstration, but there were chairs in the way. Instead he explained to Obama and his aides about the interrogation technique known as "walling," in which detainees were thrown against a flexible artificial wall that made a loud noise on impact but caused little physical pain.

These were three of the remaining six techniques that made up the harsh interrogation methods the CIA had relied on since shortly after 9/11. (The most controversial practice, the simulated-drowning technique known as waterboarding, had not been used since 2003.) The others were the playing of loud music, keeping the lights on in the cell twenty-four hours a day, and sleep deprivation. What Hayden did not tell Obama was how interrogators kept detainees awake. Usually it involved severe physical stress, like hanging prisoners from ceiling hooks. Obama was respectful throughout the session, his face betraying no reaction. Hayden walked out of the meeting thinking it had been "a good day" and that he'd "mastered the brief." Perhaps he would be able to save the program — and maybe even his own job as DCI. At least one of the president-elect's advisers, on the other hand, felt like he'd just stepped off the set of a *Dr. Strangelove* remake.

About a week before Obama's inauguration, three éminence grises of the national security establishment — David Boren, the former chairman of the Senate Intelligence Committee; Republican senator Chuck Hagel; and Jeffrey H. Smith, the CIA general counsel during the Clinton administration — arrived at CIA headquarters at Langley, an austere, modern building nestled in the Virginia woods near

Washington. An agency staffer escorted them across the vast marble floor up to the director's conference room on the seventh floor, where a number of CIA officials were assembled. The men took their seats across the table from Director Hayden; Steve Kappes, his deputy; and the chief of the agency's Counterterrorism Center, a clandestine official. Obama had asked Greg Craig to organize the meeting; he wanted individuals with experience and bipartisan stature to hear the CIA's case for enhanced interrogation.

The atmosphere, at first, was businesslike, and both sides did what they could to defuse any tension. But some level of mistrust was inevitable. Obama had spent the better part of the past two years bashing CIA counterterrorism policies as an abdication of American values. Human rights groups were stepping up calls for criminal investigations, and Democrats in Congress were talking about truth commissions. Hayden, a friendly but tightly coiled man, made it clear from the outset that he had no interest in just going through the motions. "I am happy to give you this briefing," he told the group, "but if this is all theater then I can give your morning back to you." Craig answered for the group, invoking Obama: "This is a very serious inquiry for the senator. We want your views." So Hayden proceeded. This time there were no demonstrations, no slides or PowerPoints. But Hayden's advocacy of the interrogation program was just as fierce: it worked, and it was vital to America's national security, he said. Democrats had wildly mischaracterized the techniques, including California senator Dianne Feinstein, who, he said, made walling "sound like some kind of WWF steel-cage death match," when in fact suspects wore neck braces to avoid getting whiplash.

The meeting went on for almost three hours. Hayden boasted of the hundreds of leads they'd extracted from terror suspects. High-ranking detainees had cooperated, and obscure plots had been foiled.

Boren, seated directly across from Hayden, was beginning to fume. The CIA chief, he believed, was trying to "browbeat us into belief with his superior grasp of the detail." Then, Hayden told the group: "You might want to be careful about what you take off the table."

Boren had heard enough. Torture was a "stain on America's honor," he erupted. He chided Hayden for using euphemisms like "enhanced interrogation" when he was talking about torture. "We're all adults here," he said. "We can use the real words and then make our own judgments." Anyway, he went on, even if the tough tactics were taken off the table "and then something happened and the president called up and said, 'We have a situation, there's a dirty bomb in New York and it's going to go off in five hours,' the president could order you to use torture in that isolated instance." Hayden, sensing hypocrisy, fired back. "Wow, I've never even heard David Addington make that argument," he said, referring to Dick Cheney's zealous legal adviser, who had advanced a vision of near-monarchical presidential power during wartime. At that point the CTC chief spoke for the first time: "Even if he took the phone call, I would refuse to do it." And then one of his deputies, sitting against the wall, chimed in: "And if *he* agreed to do it, none of *us* would."

The career intelligence officers in the room were primed for a moment like this. America's spies had developed a weary cynicism toward their political bosses. Presidents always expected them to do whatever it took, however distasteful, to get the job done. But when those actions led to the inevitable investigative series in the *Washington Post* or to congressional hearings, the politicos were the first to call for accountability and the last to accept responsibility. These days, liability insurance was as essential a part of any spy's toolkit as listening devices or miniature cameras. Hayden thought about the dozens of Democrats on the Hill who'd been briefed on waterboarding in recent years. Some had even asked whether the techniques were harsh enough. So now, with the specter of criminal investigations looming as a new administration took power, Boren was blithely suggesting that, in the event the techniques were outlawed, the president could just, in effect, say "never mind" and reauthorize the CIA to take the gloves off. It was as predictable as it was troubling, Hayden thought.

There was one area where the two sides found common ground. Obama's advisers were fascinated by the CIA's targeted killing program and the ruthlessly effective use of drones. At a second meeting a few days later, they peppered their hosts with questions: How many al-Qaeda leaders had been neutralized? What was the civilian death toll? They were awed by the precision and lethality of the strikes — and by the successful recruitment of tribal spies in the badlands of Afghanistan and Pakistan. John Rizzo, a longtime CIA lawyer known for his bespoke tailoring and sardonic wit, came away from the meeting thinking Obama would keep the program, and might even step it up. "I guess they're not a bunch of left-wing pussies after all," he thought to himself.

In mid-January, with the inauguration only days away, the fledgling administration was preparing to make its first major policy switch from its predecessor: closing Guantánamo. By now Leon Panetta had been named the CIA director-designate, replacing Hayden. A veteran of the Hill and the Clinton White House, Panetta, at seventy, brought a measure of gravitas and political guile to the national security team. At a meeting to discuss the executive order mandating closure of the detention facility, Craig lightened the mood with a crack about Panetta's age: "I want Leon to be in every meeting I go to so I'm not the oldest guy in the room."

Craig, along with David Barron and Marty Lederman, lawyers

assigned to the Obama team at the Justice Department, was in the process of fine-tuning the language of the executive order. But the question that Robert Gates had raised about future detainees had not been answered, and the issue of where to place existing detainees had not been addressed. Obama's team needed time to sort these matters out, but wanted a symbolic statement. What kind of time frame were they looking at? Craig proposed one year. Janet Napolitano, tapped by Obama to be his director of Homeland Security, was piped in by video from Arizona, where she was tying up loose ends as governor. "How did we arrive at this deadline?" she asked skeptically.

"The groups said we could do it in six months," Craig said, alluding to the civil liberties and human rights organizations that had made closing Guantánamo their cause célèbre. "The military argued it would take at least eighteen months." Craig had simply split the difference. So much for the methodical analysis of national security and legal considerations. This was transactional politics, pure and simple. Craig needed buy-in from all of the stakeholders.

The key voice at the table belonged to Gates, and Craig knew it. Now, the defense secretary threw his considerable weight behind Craig. "A year is going to be an ambitious deadline," he acknowledged in his characteristic uninflected tone. "But it's the right one." Bureaucracies don't move without firm deadlines, the seasoned infighter noted. With that, the debate ended. It was an early sign of the respect, bordering on reverence, that Gates would command among the national security principals.

On Inauguration Day, January 20, the winter sun hung low under a cloudless blue sky. It was a bitterly cold day, but the glow of history seemed to warm the crowd spread across the National Mall to witness the swearing in of Barack Obama as the country's forty-fourth president. Yet even in the hours leading up to this exultant national moment, Obama's mood was tempered by the threat of terrorism. He seemed preoccupied when he showed up for a practice session to go over his inaugural address with aides. "He was wearing a running suit and he looked pretty withdrawn and sober," recalled David Axelrod, a top campaign adviser who was about to become his senior adviser in the White House. "You know what, guys, let's postpone this," Obama said. He had recently been told by Brennan and Mc-Donough about a potentially devastating plot that was still unfolding. Somali extremists, members of the al-Qaeda-linked Shabab, had slipped across the Canadian border and were planning to attack his inauguration with explosives.

He checked in regularly with his chief of staff, Rahm Emanuel, for updates. On the morning of the inauguration, as he and Michelle sipped coffee with George and Laura Bush in the Blue Room of the White House, his national security advisers huddled with Bush's outgoing team in the Situation Room. They worked through the crisis together, analyzing the intelligence and weighing their options. As reported by Martha Joynt Kumar, the presidential scholar who uncovered the episode while researching transitions, Hillary Clinton, with her unique ability to see the event from the president's perspective, asked the most incisive question: "So what should Barack Obama do if he's in the middle of his inaugural address, and a bomb goes off way in the back of the crowd somewhere on the Mall? What does he do? Is the Secret Service going to whisk him off the podium so the American people can see their incoming president disappear in the middle of the inaugural address? I don't think so." The group decided that Gates should not attend the inauguration. As the only Senate-confirmed cabinet secretary, he was the most logical candidate to take over the government in the event of the unthinkable.

In the end, the threat proved to be a false alarm. It was a poison-pen operation, in which one Somali group put out bogus information to harm a rival organization. But it was a sobering lesson — "a stark initiation into the responsibilities of the presidency," as Axelrod put it — that Obama's fight against the terrorists was at the mercy of dark and violent forces he would never be able to completely control. And that Bush's war was now his.

2

WHERE THE FUCK IS BIN LADEN?

A FEW MINUTES AFTER 11 A.M. on January 22, Barack Obama issued his first orders as commander in chief in the war on al-Qaeda. He didn't sign off on a missile strike, order a daring capture, or authorize a CIA covert operation. Instead he sat down at the *Resolute* desk, the ornate writing table that had been a gift from Queen Victoria to America in 1880, and picked up a black lacquered pen. Then, in front of a crowd of reporters and news photographers, he proceeded to sign a series of executive orders, all intended to roll back the worst abuses of the Bush administration's antiterrorism policies. In quick succession, Obama terminated the CIA's secret overseas prisons, banned coercive interrogation methods, and ordered the closing of the Guantánamo detention facility within a year. "There we go," the president said after the first signing, as if marveling at his newfound power to alter history.

Flanking Obama during the carefully scripted ceremony were sixteen retired generals and admirals, all of whom had fought passionately to end unlawful interrogation and other Bush-era excesses. Obama called them "flag officers," and they formed a protective ring around the anti–Iraq war president who'd ascended to the White House with no military background and negligible national security experience. Their presence subtly conveyed another message: that America was stronger — and safer — when it adhered to its constitutional values. "We intend to win this fight," Obama said. But "we're going to win it on our terms." With the signing of each order, the officers broke into applause.

David Axelrod strode across the Oval Office to congratulate Greg Craig on the initiatives. Clasping the White House counsel's hand, he said, "You did good, Greg. You did good." Indeed, crafting and shepherding the executive orders through to the signing ceremony was one of the proudest achievements of Craig's long career; he felt buoyant as he left the event. Later that day he told his staff, high-toned graduates of Harvard and Yale law schools, "This is a big victory." But it was just the beginning, he said. "We have to keep pushing our agenda." Even Obama, in the aftermath of the ceremony, momentarily shed his usual cool equanimity. Still learning his way around the labyrinthine West Wing, he wandered into the upper press area. Dan Pfeiffer, the newly installed deputy director of White House communications, was sitting in his office alone when the leader of the free world poked his head into the room. "We just ended torture," the president said. "That's a pretty big deal."

Across the river in Langley, Mike Hayden, the CIA's outgoing director, was discomfited by all the pomp surrounding the executive orders. He believed Obama would rue the day he gave up on the "program," as he called the Bush policy of coercive interrogation. And he resented the insinuation that CIA officers, who had sacrificed so much to protect the American people, had somehow degraded the country's moral position. He had lost those battles, but he still believed he could be of service to the new president. Mike McConnell, the DNI, had squeezed him out of the daily presidential intelligence briefings. But just one day after the executive-order ceremony, Hayden pushed his way back in. The CIA was launching its very first drone strikes of the Obama era.

On the morning of the twenty-third, Hayden advised the president of a missile strike scheduled to take place in the FATA, Pakistan's Federally Administered Tribal Areas, near the Afghan border. The targets were high-level al-Qaeda and Taliban commanders. Hayden, accustomed to briefing the tactically minded George W. Bush, went into granular levels of detail, describing the "geometry" of the operation, the intelligence it was based on, and the risk of collateral damage. He prided himself on his briefing skills. "I tell a good story, even in the Oval," he'd told colleagues. The president listened attentively but began to grow impatient as Hayden rambled on. Obama was a big-picture guy; he trusted his advisers to manage the details. He wanted the essentials, boiled down and preferably on paper. It was an awkward moment. Later that day word got back to Hayden from the White House: he was "never" to brief the president like that again.

Meanwhile, a world away in the tiny village of Karez Kot in South Waziristan, tribesmen heard a low, dull buzzing sound from the sky. The CIA had followed a group of suspected militants to a compound "of interest." It was a frigid evening and the men entered a large mud and brick house. They gathered around a radio, a nighttime ritual in the isolated region. Moments later, at about 8:30, a Hellfire missile from a remotely operated drone slammed into the compound, obliterating a room full of people.

During the transition and in the days after the inauguration, the CIA's drone program had continued to operate, uninterrupted, under protocols established by the Bush administration. Most of the time, the drone strikes succeeded in killing terrorist targets. But as the pilotless aircraft lingered high above Karez Kot on that evening, relaying live images of the fallout to its operators, it soon became clear that something had gone terribly wrong. Instead of hitting the CIA's intended target, a Taliban hideout, the missile had struck the compound of Malik Gulistan Khan, a prominent tribal elder and member of a pro-government peace committee. The strike killed Khan and four members of his family, including two of his children.

It fell to John Brennan to tell the president about the incident. Obama was disturbed, and he grilled his counterterrorism adviser for answers. How could this have happened? What about the pinpoint accuracy of these weapons, which he had heard about all through the transition? Obama had vowed to change America's message to the Muslim world. After the election, he gave his first formal interview as president to Al Arabiya, the Arabic-language news channel, offering the Arab and Muslim worlds "a new partnership based on mutual respect and mutual interest." He banished from his administration the use of sweeping and alienating Bush-era phrases like "war on terror" (although the latter would remain in common parlance). Obama even showed a willingness to publicly acknowledge his own Muslim ancestry, using his middle name, Hussein, during the swearing-in ceremony. Yet here he was, in his first week as president, presiding over the accidental killing of innocent Muslims.

As Obama briskly walked into the Situation Room late that afternoon, his advisers could feel the tension rise. "You could tell from his body language that he was not a happy man," recalled one participant. Obama settled into his high-backed, black leather chair. Hayden was seated at the other end of the table from him, summoned back to the White House to walk the president through the incident and explain how it had gone so badly awry. The conversation quickly devolved into a tense back-and-forth over the CIA's vetting procedures for drone attacks. The president was learning for the first time about a controversial practice known as signature strikes, the targeting of groups of men who bear certain signatures, or defining characteristics associated with terrorist activity, but whose identities aren't necessarily known. They differed from "personality" or "high-value individual" strikes, in which a terrorist leader was positively identified before the missile was launched.

Sometimes called crowd killing, signature strikes were deeply unpopular in Pakistan. Obama struggled to understand the concept. Steve Kappes, the CIA's deputy director, offered a blunt explanation. "Mr. President, we can see that there are a lot of military-age males down there, men associated with terrorist activity, but we don't always know who they are." Obama reacted sharply. "That's not good enough for me," he said. Kappes respectfully tried to convey that a counterterrorism campaign in a place like the FATA was by definition a messy enterprise. Drone operators could misidentify head scarves associated with particular militants, or mistakenly characterize a group of men going outside for a smoke as a gathering at a terrorist compound. As precise as drone technology was, the fog of war could never be entirely lifted.

Hayden forcefully defended the signature approach. You could take out a lot more bad guys when you targeted groups instead of individuals. And there was another benefit: the more afraid militants were to congregate because of the threat of a drone attack, the harder it would be for them to assert command and control — to plot, plan, or train for attacks against America and its interests. Obama understood the arguments but remained unsettled by the tactic. "The president's view was 'OK, but what assurances do I have that there aren't women and children there?'" according to a source familiar with his thinking. "'How do I know that this is working? Who makes these decisions? Where do they make them, and where's my opportunity to intervene?'"

Obama left it for others to spar with the CIA. Tom Donilon, the deputy national security adviser and a favorite of Obama's, took on Hayden. "We have to review how we do this stuff," Donilon said. "I'm not sure I'm comfortable with how we're doing it." It wasn't stated explicitly, but Donilon's implication was that the White House might want a bigger role in managing individual strikes. For Obama, holding a tighter grip on the program was a natural impulse, underscored by the botched strike the day before. He was intent on fighting a surgical war in Pakistan. He knew how easily "kinetic" operations could spin out of control, causing diplomatic blowback and other problems. But for Hayden, maintaining "delegation authority" within the CIA was a red line. The president had broadly authorized the continuation of the program under a covert finding, and the tempo of the attacks (at the time, the CIA was firing roughly ten strikes a month) made it impractical for the White House to review each individual operation. Hayden didn't want to have to call up a White House official in the middle of the night for strike approval.

In the end, Obama relented on both signature strikes and delegation authority — for the time being. The White House did tighten up some procedures: The CIA director would no longer be allowed to have his deputy or the head of the counterterrorism division act as his proxy in signing off on strikes. Only the DCI would have sign-off authority. And the White House reserved the right to pull back the CIA's signature authority in the future — as it would do after an errant attack killed civilians, or to settle the churn in diplomatic relations between the United States and Pakistan. According to one of his advisers, Obama never seemed entirely comfortable with the CIA's signature strikes. Intellectually, he appreciated the arguments for them, but he remained unsettled. "He would squirm," recalled the source. "He didn't like the idea of kill 'em and sort it out later." Still, Obama's willingness to back the program represented an early inflection point in his war on terror. Over time, the program grew exponentially, far beyond anything that had been envisioned by the Bush administration.

Rahm Emanuel was unequivocal in his support for kinetic power — whether it was targeted killings from the air or raids on the ground. For all the handwringing among the lawyers and civil libertarians, Obama's chief of staff understood the political upside to a program that took out high-level terrorists. That's what the vast majority of Americans wanted. And there was one target in particular who had the potential to be a game-changer for his boss: Osama bin Laden. Eight years into the war on terror, the intelligence community was no closer to determining bin Laden's location. In early February, Emanuel took Bruce Riedel aside outside the Situation Room and pressed him on the issue. "Why the fuck don't we have any clue where Osama bin Laden is?" he asked with characteristic invective. Riedel, a former CIA analyst with a mild, academic manner, had been asked by Obama to chair a strategic review of policy toward Afghanistan and Pakistan. His response to the chief of staff's question was blunt: "There's nobody in charge." The intelligence and counterterrorism communities had so many overlapping and intersecting layers, he explained, and "there needs to be a sheriff in charge of this posse." Later, Riedel followed up with Donilon, telling him that there needed to be somebody in the government who "went home every night and asked himself, 'Am I any closer to fulfilling my primary mission, which is bringing Osama bin Laden to justice?'" That spring, on June 2, 2009, Obama signed a memo telling CIA Director Leon Panetta that, "in order to ensure that we have expended every

effort, I direct you to provide me within thirty days a detailed operation plan for locating and bringing to justice Osama bin Laden."

As far as Dick Cheney was concerned, whatever might have been
happening with drone strikes or plans to kill or capture Osama bin
Laden, Obama's honeymoon was over as soon as he signed the executive orders. On February 4, Cheney gave his first post-inauguration
interview, to Politico. He was characteristically gloomy — and partisan. He warned of a "high probability" that al-Qaeda would attempt
a catastrophic nuclear or biological attack in the coming years, and
that Obama's policies would increase the organization's chances of
success. "When we get people who are more concerned about reading the rights to an al-Qaeda terrorist than they are with protecting
the United States against people who are absolutely committed to do
anything they can to kill Americans," he added, "then I worry."

Two days later, on February 6, Obama met with the victims of the
USS *Cole* bombing. It was a potentially awkward encounter. With the
Cheney broadside lingering in the air, Obama had to explain why, in
one of his first acts since taking office, he had ordered the suspen-
sion of charges against Abd al-Rahim al-Nashiri, a mastermind of
the October 2000 attack on the *Cole,* which killed seventeen US sail-
ors docked in a Yemeni port. Even before he had signed the executive orders, Obama had ordered a halt to military commissions. The
administration was weighing whether to continue the controversial
military proceedings.

The president's aides were nervous. It was never a good thing to
be ambushed by the families of terror victims. They were particularly
leery of Kirk Lippold, the retired commander of the *Cole* and the informal leader of the families. Lippold had been a fierce Obama critic,
and Craig worried that he would use the occasion to "hold forth and
attack the president." But when Obama walked into the Eisenhower
Executive Office Building, the families rose and gave him a stand-

ing ovation. Most disagreed with his plan to close Guantánamo. And they remained unhappy that al-Nashiri's trial had been suspended. But Obama had done one thing that neither Bill Clinton, George W. Bush, nor, for that matter, Dick Cheney had ever done: he met with the *Cole* families. Obama promised them "swift and certain" justice and then exchanged hugs with the family members, many of whom clutched pictures of their dead loved ones.

On February 9, Douglas Letter, a career Justice Department official, walked into a stately federal courtroom in San Francisco. Letter was defending the government in an appeal filed by five terrorism suspects who, under the CIA's extraordinary-rendition program, were transported to secret detention sites in other countries, where they'd been subjected to harsh interrogations. The Bush administration had argued to dismiss the case, invoking the "state secrets" doctrine, claiming that to go ahead with the trial would do irreparable harm to US national security. To the surprise of the judges on the federal appeals panel, Letter advanced the same state-secrets argument as the Bush administration had.

"Is there anything material that has happened that might have caused the Justice Department to change its legal position?" Judge Mary Schroeder asked — obviously referring to the recent election.

"No, Your Honor," Letter replied. And he went further, noting that these were "authorized positions" that had been "thoroughly vetted with the appropriate officials within the new administration."

There was nothing especially new about invoking the state-secrets privilege to shield sensitive intelligence; Republican and Democratic administrations had done so often over the years. But Obama had campaigned to make government more transparent and to show more deference to Congress and the courts. Now he seemed to be embracing the Bush-Cheney agenda of secrecy and maximalist executive power. The move provoked an uproar among liberals and civil libertarians. To make matters worse, Obama only learned about it after the fact, from the front page of the *New York Times*. He was furious. The story contained a biting statement from Anthony Romero, the head of the ACLU. "This is not change. It's more of the same," Romero charged. "What the fuck," Obama squawked, in one of his earliest "whisky tango foxtrot moments" (National Security Adviser Jim Jones's code for Obama's use of "WTF.") "This is not the way I like to make decisions," he icily told an aide. At a February 20 Oval Office meeting, Obama pushed his lawyers to find a commonsense middle ground: "There should be a way to let cases go forward without revealing state secrets," he said, prodding them to "think proactively" and be "surgical."

But it was increasingly clear that this was the way he would be making decisions over the next few months — on the fly, with little notice, in response to deadlines in court cases challenging the Bush administration's counterterrorism policies. The rickety legal structure that the Bush administration had built was under heavy stress from multiple lawsuits. Judges moving their dockets along wanted to know what the new administration's positions would be. There were a dizzying number of issues being raised, all of them legally and politically fraught — all of them having potentially significant national security consequences. What authority did the government have to kill or capture suspected terrorists? Should the so-called "torture memos," opinions issued by the Justice Department's Office of Legal Counsel between 2002 and 2005, detailing techniques used for interrogating terrorism suspects, be released? What about photographs of prisoner abuse at Abu Ghraib? Was it legal to hold terror suspects indefinitely? For Obama it seemed that not a single day passed without one of his lawyers stopping by to present him with some new legal crisis that had to be decided on the spot. On one occasion his secretary, Katie Johnson, walked into the Oval Office and told the president that someone from his legal team needed to see him about some urgent matter. Obama turned to the people gathered in the room and began venting. "It's another one of these damn litigation decisions they want to talk about, and I'm tired of it," he said, scowling. "I'm tired of being jammed this way."

To avoid future snafus, the Justice Department's Donald Verrilli stayed up until 3 A.M. one night devising an elaborate litigation calendar intended to help the president's lawyers keep track of the many national security cases wending their way through the system. It was an oddly clerical assignment for one of the most respected lawyers at Justice, someone whom Obama would later appoint to be US solicitor general.

Stumbles are typical in the early weeks of a new administration, and the day-to-day routine would smooth out over time. But early miscues had already started to give Greg Craig a reputation, particularly with Rahm Emanuel, for being disorganized and politically tone-deaf. White House counsels are expected to see around corners and anticipate looming legal issues before they turn into damaging political problems. Obama aides began blaming Craig for failing to defuse the legal IEDs before it was too late. But the truth was more complicated. Emanuel had begun marginalizing Craig from the outset of the administration. Cut out of the all-important "senior advisers" meeting, Craig's exposure to the president was limited from day one. The evidence suggests that Craig — or his office — dropped the ball on the state-secrets issue. But there were also times when Craig sounded the alarm, warning the White House political staff of looming problems.

One such time was when Craig found out that the Defense Department, complying with a court order in a Freedom of Information Act case, was getting ready to release a cache of photographs depicting the abuse of suspected terrorists held in US custody. Emanuel and other members of the president's political team were notified in a meeting, but Craig went even further. In an April 16 memo to Emanuel, Axelrod, and others, Craig expressed concern that the issue had not received "enough attention." He went on, "The purpose of this memo is to lay out this situation in greater detail and ask you to focus on it during the day today." The administration soon announced it would release the photographs, which caused a political uproar. But the more serious problem was internal. General Ray Odierno, commander of US military forces in Iraq, pleaded with Obama not to release the pictures, which he feared would inflame Muslim passions and endanger the lives of US service members. The president abruptly — and very publicly — reversed course. It was an embarrassing flip-flop for which Craig would be unfairly blamed.

Emanuel and his team had other problems with Craig. They thought he was more interested in pursuing a sexy policy agenda than dealing with the legal drudgery — analyzing obscure legislation or interpreting the fine points of ethics regulations — that is the mainstay of the counsel's office. But that criticism, which had some validity, also obscured the fact that the source of Emanuel's frustration was that Craig's more liberal policy objectives conflicted with the chief of staff's more centrist political course. In the end, however, the problem was more elemental: Emanuel and Craig, ideological and temperamental opposites, just didn't like each other. And it is axiomatic of any White House that the tougher the politics become, the harder the president's aides search for useful scapegoats. Craig became Emanuel's.

Obama was elected, in part, to wind down the wars of 9/11, to reduce America's global footprint, and to refocus national energies on challenges at home and core interests abroad. But when he took office, he inherited a military molded by George Bush, Dick Cheney, and Donald Rumsfeld that was still very much on the offensive in the global war on terror (GWOT), as it had come to be known in the later years of the previous administration. In March 2009, a chance arose to bring that war deep into Somalia.

The military had been itching to take the fight to the African state in a more aggressive and sustained fashion. The desperately poor, chaotic country, beset by clan rivalries, piracy, and humanitarian disasters, was a perfect breeding ground for terrorists. Taking advantage of these chronic conditions was the radical Islamist insurgency al-Shabab. An offshoot of the Islamic Courts Union, which controlled Somalia until US-backed Ethiopian forces invaded the country in 2006, the Shabab had loose but growing affiliations with al-Qaeda. The military saw Somalia as a time bomb — the next Afghanistan — and it wanted to act before it was too late.

In March, the chairman of the Joint Chiefs of Staff, Admiral Mike Mullen, briefed the president and his national security advisers on a "kinetic opportunity" in southern Somalia, the Shabab's stronghold. There was intelligence that a high-level operative associated with the group would be attending a "graduation ceremony" at a Shabab training area. The target seemed to be a genuine bad guy, connected to an attack on a safe house in Ethiopia that had been used by US special operations forces. But the military couldn't pinpoint his precise location. So why not just take the whole camp out? The only people there would be "military-age males." The Pentagon had prepared a "strike package" that could devastate an entire series of training areas. A ship off the Somali coast would fire as many as fifteen Tomahawk land-attack cruise missiles (TLAMs) or, alternatively, B1 bombers could drop two-thousand-pound bombs. This was a military signature strike of major proportions. Obama was skeptical, but he listened without showing his doubts. At the end of Mullen's presentation, Obama said, "OK, let's go around the table." He wanted to hear from his entire national security team.

It was a subtle challenge to the military. The Department of Defense had "nominated" the target. If the State Department or another agency wanted to object, "they could raise their hand," recalled one source who was in the room. But to go around the table like that, inviting dissent with Admiral Mullen, was a different way of doing business. Yet the principals raised no objections.

Then Obama pointed to one of the uniformed men sitting behind Mullen, against the wall: James "Hoss" Cartwright, a four-star Marine general and the vice chairman of the Joint Chiefs. "Mr. President, generally the wars we've been prosecuting have had these rules," Cartwright said in a low-key, midwestern manner. "They did something to us, we went in and did something back — and then we had a moral obligation to put back together whatever we broke.

"In these places where they have not attacked us, we are looking for a person, not a country." Cartwright was now beginning to veer off from Mullen, his superior officer. Then he laid it on the line: "If there is a person in the camp who is a clear threat to the United States we should go after him. But carpet-bombing a country is a really bad precedent." Some of the military men began to shift in their chairs. Cartwright had chosen the term carefully; he knew that "carpet-bombing" would pack an emotional punch with a president who wanted to be surgical in his approach to the war on terror — especially in countries where the United States was not officially at war.

Cartwright had already established a comfort level with his new commander in chief. He had given Obama his "midnight hour" briefing during the transition, laying out for him all of the frightening scenarios he might have to face as president, from a sudden nuclear strike to a catastrophic cyber-attack. A few days after that first meeting Obama asked one of his aides to summon Cartwright for another visit. "I need to see that guy that scared the hell out of me," he said. But the real source of his connection to the general was philosophical and strategic. Drafted into the army in 1970, Cartwright had made a highly unusual rise through the ranks to his current position. He had a conservative and deliberate approach to war fighting that appealed to Obama. He also had a bit of a rebellious streak, which was on display during the Somalia briefing: "I ask you to consider: where are we taking this activity? Because the logical next thing after carpet-bombing is that we go there and open up a new front."

Obama seized on Cartwright's words to lay down his own marker. "That's where I am," he said. He told his assembled advisers that he was committed to getting bad guys, terrorists who posed a clear and demonstrable threat to Americans, but that he wanted "options" that were precise. Obama once again rejected the "mow them all down" approach that he and John Brennan had talked about in Chicago. Instead, he wanted a new litmus test for military operations outside conventional theaters of war, like Somalia and Yemen, that would single out targets as true threats to the United States.

The Shabab strike was a no-go.

What emerged in early 2009 was an unusual alliance that would serve to guide Obama through the shadow wars: Hoss Cartwright would join John Brennan in advising the president about terrorist targets, the three forming a kind of holy trinity of targeted killings.

By this time, Brennan had established himself as a prepossessing figure in the White House. Massively built, with closely cropped hair, a ruddy complexion, and deep-set eyes that could appear menacing at times, "Mr. Brennan," as he was referred to deferentially by White House staffers, was seen as "the real thing," a bona fide terrorist hunter who had been on the trail of Osama bin Laden for a decade. "He is like a John Wayne character," David Axelrod would remark. "I sleep better knowing that he is not sleeping."

In the coming months and years, Brennan and Cartwright would find themselves pulling the president out of state dinners or tracking him down on a secure phone to discuss a proposed strike. Obama could be known to muster a little gallows humor when Cartwright or Brennan showed up at the Oval Office unannounced. "Uh-oh, this can't be good," he would say, arching an eyebrow. One of Brennan's least favorite duties was pulling Obama away from family time with his wife and daughters for these grim calls.

Obama's approach to kinetic activity tended to be deliberative and careful, but it was also supple; "he was willing to change his mind," in the words of one military source, occasionally even "widening the aperture" based on new intelligence or the recommendations of his field commanders. On one evening in late 2009 Cartwright and Brennan met with Obama in the Oval Office to consult with him on a target in Yemen that the president had previously declined to approve. The two men had General David Petraeus, at the time head of US Central Command, on the phone. Petraeus wanted to add the target, for whom they unexpectedly had a clear shot, to an operation in mid-execution. To Cartwright's surprise, Obama, after assuring himself that the man in question was a legal target and the operation had been suitably vetted, reversed himself and gave his approval for the hit. The operation was a success. But such calls took their toll. Obama would sometimes later reflect on whether they knew with certainty that the people they were targeting posed a genuine and specific threat to American interests.

The three men were making life-and-death decisions, picking targets, rejecting or accepting names put forward by the military, feeling their way through a new kind of war — Obama's war.

On March 9, the Justice Department was buzzing with excitement. Name cards were being printed, fine points of protocol studied, aides were scurrying around worrying about logistics and security. Eric Holder was hosting the first meeting of the president's Guantánamo Review Task Force. No one could remember a meeting with so many "principals" at the department. All the big guns would be there: Gates, Clinton, Panetta, Dennis Blair (the director of national intelligence, succeeding Mike McConnell), and Mullen. Normally, cabinet members in status-conscious Washington observed "cabinet rank." When two secretaries got together for a meeting, the official lower in the pecking order would travel to the other's department: from State to Defense to Justice, and so on. Thus, the attorney general would go to the Pentagon to meet the secretary of defense, but the secretary of state would host the defense chief at Foggy Bottom. On this day, however, the entire Obama war cabinet had come to the Justice Department. Obama's January 22 executive order had designated the attorney general as coordinator of the Guantánamo review. His mandate was to lead a government-wide process to sort through all of the remaining Guantánamo detainees to determine their proper disposition. Should they be released? Transferred to another country? Prosecuted?

Greg Craig had argued that "fresh eyes" were needed for a case-by-case examination of the evidence that was being relied on to detain the prisoners. The executive order had been crafted almost exclusively by civilian lawyers, who were intuitively more comfortable with the Justice Department's law- and evidence-based judgments than the Defense Department's intelligence-based assessments. Moreover, for the idealist Craig, the symbolism of giving the attorney general responsibility for Guantánamo was appealing. It established a clean break with the old order and restored constitutional protections to a prison camp that had become infamous around the world as a legal black hole. Or at least it seemed to.

Some of the Bush holdovers were offended by the hubris they sensed in the Obamaites. Didn't they know that for most of Bush's second term they were trying to shut down Guantánamo? In fact, they'd transferred more than five hundred detainees out of the camp — more than twice as many as remained. It had taken years of diplomacy. "A lot of them were shaking their heads when they saw the executive order and the one-year deadline," recalled one incoming Obama Justice Department official. "'You have no idea how hard this is going to be,' they'd say. 'We left you the hardest cases.'"

The principals took their seats in the attorney general's conference room. With its high, vaulted ceilings, dark wood paneling, and dramatic murals, it seemed particularly steeped in history that day. Looming over the group was a portrait of Robert Jackson, another wartime attorney general and an icon of the rule of law. Holder opened the meeting with the hope that the group would unanimously decide the fate of each individual detainee. That would give the process legitimacy, he argued. Unstated was his hope that it would spread some of the responsibility (or blame) for the eventual decisions around.

Panetta, the shrewdest legislative tactician in the group, asked about congressional strategy: Which committees had jurisdiction? Who could they count on as allies and who would be trying to sabotage their efforts? As he well knew, congressional politics could trump anything that might happen at this meeting. Secretary Clinton, meanwhile, said that there was a lot of diplomatic heavy lifting to be done to persuade Europe and other allies to resettle detainees.

But she also stated that she and her team were "in it to win it." Gates said little.

Sitting among the policy titans was Matthew Olsen, a mild-mannered Justice Department lawyer whom Holder had appointed to run the review. A little awed by the group, Olsen stuck to process. He showed a few slides that described the Guantánamo population and passed around a one-page memo he'd prepared for the principals, an introduction to the roughly 240 hard cases that stood in the way of closing the prison. After the meeting ended, Gates turned to Olsen and, with a barely perceptible smile, said, "Good luck." Olsen wondered what the defense secretary knew that he didn't.

Olsen, forty-seven, was a veteran prosecutor who'd made his bones going after drug kingpins and murderers in federal court. Later, he investigated terrorism and espionage cases, eventually rising to be the top career official in the Justice Department's national security division. Despite his thinning brown hair, Olsen had more than a passing resemblance to the actor Tom Cruise. He kept a basketball in his office, which he would roll around in his hands as a way of channeling nervous energy, just as Cruise's character had done with a baseball bat in the movie *A Few Good Men*. In many ways, Olsen was a perfect choice for the Guantánamo job. He was smart, self-effacing, and, with his background in both law enforcement and intelligence, able to smooth relations on his fractious team. How hard could it be to relocate 241 men?

One day in early March, Olsen walked into his task force offices, located at a secret address in Tysons Corner, Virginia, an edge city on the outskirts of Washington. The CIA had loaned his team a floor of a nondescript building that blended seamlessly into the local commercial district. There was nothing visibly whiz-bang about the office, yet it was wired into the government's most sensitive national security databases and hardened against terrorist attack. Working with a team of about a dozen prosecutors and intelligence analysts, Olsen had to establish the profiles of the 241 detainees. Of those the government wanted to prosecute, how many cases were potentially tainted by torture, relying on confessions gained under coercion? Were there any detainees who were too dangerous to transfer or release, because they had trained in al-Qaeda camps or swore allegiance to bin Laden, even though there was insufficient or no evidence to charge them with any crimes? Guiding them was the broad and rather vague dictate of the executive order: everything they did had to be "consistent with the national security and foreign policy interests of the United States and the interests of justice."

There were logistical challenges. For one thing, the detainee files were in a state of disarray, spread throughout the government. It took weeks to collect them in a centralized place. Olsen had to fight through red tape simply to get his staff password access to key databases. But the far greater hurdles were cultural rather than bureaucratic. From the start, there was a vast divide between the lawyers and the intelligence analysts. Prosecutors are trained to make binary judgments about guilt or innocence. They rely on evidence, the law, and the adversarial system to ferret out the "truth." Intelligence analysts assemble disparate strands of information to detect patterns and form judgments about national security threats. They were not preoccupied with legal standards like "preponderance of the evidence" or "reasonable doubt" — and they were generally predisposed to believe that most of the detainees were, in fact, dangerous terrorists. On the task force's first day, one analyst raised his hand and asked Olsen, incredulously, whether the administration really planned to close Guantánamo. "What are we going to do with all of the terrorists?" the agent wanted to know. Olsen suppressed his frustration.

At the White House, on the other hand, policy on Guantánamo was being driven by the lawyers, and they were keeping a close watch on Olsen. Closing the prison was a major presidential promise and the clock was ticking toward the one-year deadline established in the executive order. At an early Situation Room meeting, Olsen started to feel the pressure: When would the review be complete? What was taking so long? Olsen explained that it would take time to methodically go through the case files, analyze the evidence, interpret the intelligence, and make responsible judgments. "What's so hard?" Daniel Meltzer, the deputy White House counsel, asked impatiently. "Just do one and then multiply by 240." Olsen had enormous respect for Meltzer, a brilliant law professor and onetime president of the *Harvard Law Review* who had written scholarly articles about terrorism and the law. But Meltzer was a pure product of the academy, with little government experience and no hands-on national security experience. Olsen was beginning to realize what he was up against.

The March 5, 2009, edition of the *New York Times* had reported that Obama was beginning to show some gray in his hair. There were just a few flecks in his closely cropped cut, but the bloggers had a field day. "Are his gray hairs a sign of life-shortening stress?" *Slate* asked. The truth is that Obama was under unimaginable pressure, facing a global economic meltdown, two wars, and massive unemployment. At 2:30 that day, he met with Treasury Secretary Timothy Geithner. Major financial institutions, including Citibank, were still in danger of collapsing, weighed down by the toxic assets on their balance sheets. Obama's financial advisers were telling him that if they couldn't break the trend, the economy would fall into a depression later that year. That same day, Obama received one of the bleakest and scariest briefings of his young presidency. Bruce Riedel, the counterterrorism expert heading Obama's strategic review of Afghanistan and Pakistan, gave him his preliminary assessment: "Afghanistan is a disaster, and we're losing," Riedel told Obama. "Pakistan is worse: it's falling apart and has over one hundred nukes."

Late that afternoon, a group of administration lawyers led by Holder and Craig met with Obama in the Oval Office. The administration was facing another court deadline, habeas corpus cases brought by lawyers for Guantánamo detainees, and, once again, the president was forced to make a series of quick, difficult, and highly consequential decisions. Under what theory could Obama justify holding the detainees—and who could be held? US District Court Judge John Bates was inviting the administration to articulate its own positions in a brief due in seven days. Layered beneath those basic questions was a host of others, the answers to which would shed light on how much of a change maker Obama would be in the fight against al-Qaeda. Among them: Were we at war? If so, could detainees be held indefinitely without trial? What was the geographic scope of the battlefield—did it extend beyond Afghanistan?

As the group gathered, Obama began shaking his head. "As tough as these issues are, they're not the hardest ones I've had to deal with today," he told his advisers, with an air of bemused disbelief. Munching on an energy bar, the president and his lawyers got down to business. First, Obama wanted to know whether he could get more time. But the judge had already granted one extension and he would not indulge them further. One of the Justice Department lawyers, Amy Jeffress, noted that it was risky to come up with a new definition for who could be detained before they'd completed the review of who was actually in Guantánamo. Litigating against a new standard could mean more detainees winning release. Jeffress suggested they stick with the Bush administration's definition until they could carefully develop their own. But Obama immediately rejected that idea; after the state-secrets debacle, he was not going to needlessly open himself

up to attacks from the left. And he said he didn't want his adminis-
tration relying on any of the extreme legal arguments concocted by
John Yoo, the former Justice Department lawyer and author of the
Bush administration's most controversial opinions.

The discussion continued for close to two hours, with Obama
often asking pointed questions and occasionally interjecting legal
and tactical points of his own. There was one issue he was adamant
about: he would not, as George Bush had, rely on his own inherent
authority as commander in chief to detain suspects at Guantánamo.
"I don't think it makes sense for me alone to decide, just because
I'm the president, who should be detained," he told his lawyers, according to several participants. "I'm not comfortable exerting that
authority." At around 7 P.M. the lawyers left the Oval Office with their
assignment, daunting as it was: rewrite the legal parameters of Barack
Obama's war on al-Qaeda.

David Barron, a brainy, reserved law professor who'd recently
joined the Justice Department's Office of Legal Counsel, led the effort. Powering through eighteen-hour marathon sessions fueled by
greasy Chinese takeout and sodas, they produced a draft brief in five
days. Obama signed off on it March 11, and two days later Justice
Department lawyers filed it with Judge Bates. Though at the time it
garnered little attention in the press, it is a foundational document
in Obama's war on terror. Did Obama embrace a law-enforcement
model that, as conservatives argued, would make the country more
vulnerable to attack? Or was his position effectively "Bush Lite," ex-
hibiting some tonal changes with respect to his predecessor but few
if any substantive reforms?

A careful reading of the March 13 brief suggests that neither narrative is quite right. The document reflected an Obama-like search for
middle ground rather than an ideologically driven approach. Obama
embraced the legal proposition that the United States was at war with

al-Qaeda. Flowing from that, the government could detain terrorism suspects at Guantánamo indefinitely. At the same time, administration lawyers announced that they would abandon the term "enemy combatant," one of the iconic designations of the Bush war on terror. But it was more a symbolic statement than a substantive reversal of policy. Still, the administration limited the open-ended detention of prisoners to those who were already in custody on the Cuban island. The brief promised a "forward-looking multi-agency effort . . . to develop a comprehensive detention policy with respect to individuals captured in connection with armed conflicts and counterterrorism operations." Moreover, the United States could pursue the enemy outside the traditional battlefield, in places like Yemen and Somalia. At the same time, the administration accepted the applicability of the international law of war, including the Geneva Conventions, in the conflict, and it narrowed the class of individuals who could be detained without trial to members of al-Qaeda or its affiliates, or to "substantial supporters" of those groups. Finally, the brief stated that Obama would not rely on his inherent authority as commander in chief to exercise those powers. Instead, detention authority would be grounded in the authorization granted by Congress to use military force against al-Qaeda after the 9/11 attacks.

Two days later, former vice president Dick Cheney went on the attack in an appearance on a Sunday-morning news show, stating, "Now he [Obama] is making some choices that, in my mind, will, in fact, raise the risk to the American people of another attack." Obama, Cheney said, was "returning to the Clinton approach of treating terrorism as a law enforcement matter rather than a war." That same day, as if on cue, Craig had more unwelcome news for Obama. The Justice Department was slated to release the Bush torture memos in three days in response to a judge's order in an ACLU Freedom of Information lawsuit. In Craig's estimation, this was actually a good thing. It would strike a blow for transparency while further distancing the Obama White House from the previous administration's extralegal practices. But the intelligence community was dead set against releasing anything that wasn't almost entirely redacted, arguing that the opinions would allow al-Qaeda to train its fighters to resist even brutal interrogation techniques. Moreover, releasing the memos to the public would devastate CIA morale. Rahm Emanuel was dead set against it. Obama pleaded for more time. The administration managed to get an extension until April 16.

Holder and Craig were the earliest and most passionate voices in favor of making the memos public. Holder told the president that "if you don't release the memos, you'll own the policy." John Brennan initially agreed. But a CIA lobbying campaign ginned up by former director Hayden persuaded Brennan to reverse his position. Panetta also started out in favor but changed his mind. As a brand-new director, with no background in intelligence, he was viewed suspiciously by the career spies. But Panetta listened carefully to the arguments made by his new constituents. He knew he needed their support. Emanuel backed Panetta. The last thing he needed as he was moving forward to implement the president's domestic agenda was a fifth column at Langley. The debate went back and forth for weeks, with different players changing their minds, sometimes more than once in the course of the same meeting. Dennis Blair, the DNI, was on the fence, perhaps because he was trying to read the president's opaque, vacillating mind. The CIA had given him the same talking points Panetta had received, and most observers expected him to side with the intelligence community. But when called on by the president at one meeting, he put the talking points aside. "Release them, Mr. President," he said. "Lance the boil. It'll be a one- or two-day story."

There was sometimes a finger-to-the-wind quality to these meetings. Obama began one by asking the principals to state where they were on the issue. At the time, the internal betting was that Obama would back Emanuel and his CIA chief. As they went around the table, the president's aides tacked with the prevailing winds: don't release the memos. But then Obama signaled that he was now leaning the other way, and back around the table came a series of "on-the-other-hand" pronouncements.

Panetta suppressed a smile. His erstwhile allies, profiles in courage, were abandoning him on a dime. Emanuel, by contrast, was not able to muster any ironic detachment. He abruptly got up, excused himself to the president, and began to walk out of the Situation Room. Obama, somewhat startled, said: "Rahm, I was going to let you say your piece, I wanted to hear your point of view." "You know my opinion, Mr. President," Emanuel replied.

The debate eventually transformed into a full-blown argument on the merits of coercive interrogation procedures. Blair had carefully examined the reports and was convinced that waterboarding and other harsh techniques had yielded important intelligence. What he did not know was whether that evidence could have been obtainable through noncoercive methods. He scoured the government and academia for any reliable research that established whether enhanced interrogations actually worked. At the next principals' meeting he revealed the results of his inquiry. "There's no body of knowledge that says here's the right way to do it," he told the group. Then, turning to Obama, he said, "Mr. President, we do not know if we could have gotten that information in other ways. We do know that we got valuable information using those techniques, but that's as far as we can take it." Obama, who was now leaning toward releasing the memos, said: "Well, if we don't have any evidence that it works, you might as well stick with your principles."

On the evening of April 15, after dinner with his family, Obama called his chief of staff. "I've been thinking about the memos." Emanuel informed the president that a group of his advisers were meeting on the subject right then. A few minutes later, Obama was in Emanuel's West Wing office listening to about a dozen national security and political aides hash it out. He then spontaneously convened a moot-court debate, asking Craig and Denis McDonough to take opposite sides. Craig asserted that releasing the memos was consistent with the administration's pledge to restore the rule of law and reclaim America's moral standing around the world. He might as well have been quoting Obama directly. The president came off the fence and sided with Craig. He began to dictate a public statement that would be released the following day along with the memos.

For his part, Blair issued a letter to the intelligence troops, seeking to cushion the blow. "Today is a difficult one for those of us who serve the country in its intelligence services," he wrote. He pointed out that the tactics were deemed legal by the Justice Department and that they had been approved by senior policymakers. Then he expressed something that had been taboo since the start of the Obama administration: "High-value information came from interrogations in which those methods were used and provided a deeper understanding of the al-Qaeda organization that was attacking this country." A few hours later a raging Rahm Emanuel was on the phone. "What did you mean we gained valuable information from those techniques?" he demanded to know. Blair, a four-star admiral who commanded a destroyer when Obama's chief of staff was barely out of college, responded: "I meant exactly what I said."

"Well you shouldn't have put that in your memo."

3

TORTURE DEBATES AND MURDER BOARDS

AROUND THE TIME the administration began debating the release of the Bush torture memos, Holder received a call from Senator Sheldon Whitehouse, a Democrat from Rhode Island who sat on both the Judiciary and Intelligence Committees. "Eric, we need to talk," Whitehouse said in a quietly urgent tone. "I can't tell you what it's about because it's classified," he continued. He asked Holder to arrange a meeting in a secure, soundproof room where they could safely discuss national security secrets. At first, Holder's aides were skeptical and weren't sure if they should even schedule the meeting. Whitehouse had been one of the more pugnacious — some would say hyperpartisan — critics of the Bush administration. A Yankee in the tradition of Rhode Island senators, he possessed a stern New England moralism that rubbed some of his colleagues the wrong way. But Holder liked and respected Whitehouse. They'd served together as US attorneys during the 1990s, and they shared a love for the Department of Justice, along with a desire to reclaim what they viewed as its rightful mission.

A few days later they met in the department's Command Center, each accompanied by one aide. Holder greeted Whitehouse warmly, but the senator went straight to the point. The Senate's Select Committee on Intelligence was close to completing a yearlong investigation into the CIA's enhanced interrogation program. Its findings were deeply disturbing, he told Holder. "Eric, this is awful," Whitehouse said. "You have to see what our government has done, what has been done in the name of the United States." The broad outlines of the program had leaked to the press, including specific techniques, like waterboarding, sleep deprivation, and stress positions. But the public accounts were incomplete and sanitized. Only the raw intelligence reports could convey the full horror of what had happened in the CIA's interrogation chambers. With the change in administrations it would finally be possible to hold people accountable, Whitehouse believed. Yet the senator could read the signals coming out of the White House as well as anybody. He knew there was no appetite for opening a criminal investigation into the previous administration. He had called Leon Panetta and urged the new CIA director to take a fresh look at the allegations, but concluded that Panetta would be captive to his own agency, which was adamantly opposed to a torture inquiry. So now he was turning to Holder.

Only the attorney general had the stature and the independence to set aside politics, to pursue the facts and the law impartially. "Eric, you need to take a hard look at this program," Whitehouse said. "You need to know what really happened." He began reading out loud from the classified reports he had brought with him. In detailed but clinical language they described an interrogation regime whose psychological brutality and moral depravity went beyond anything Holder had imagined. He knew about the waterboardings, but not about their duration or intensity—that Khalid Sheikh Mohammed had been subjected to the grim procedure 183 times, and Abu Zubaydah, the terrorist operative who worked with al-Qaeda, 83 times. There had been mock executions in which detainees were made to believe that prisoners in nearby cells had been shot to death. Others were told their children would be killed or their wives raped if they didn't cooperate. One detainee had a gun and then a power drill waved in front of his head.

For the first time, Holder learned about a place called the Salt Pit; a secret CIA prison outside Kabul where detainees were harshly interrogated in the aftermath of the American invasion of Afghanistan. A massive windowless bunker, the facility was not formally part of the CIA's enhanced interrogation program. It was a kind of way station for detainees, some of whom were later transferred to the agency's secret prisons. One CIA official likened the Salt Pit to "Triple-A ball" for interrogators who might one day get the chance to put the screws to high-value detainees in the big-leagues black sites. In the early hours of November 20, 2002, Gul Rahman, a suspected militant, had died in the Salt Pit after he was left shackled and hanging naked from the waist down in a cold, dark cell. During the night, the temperature plunged to thirty-six degrees. An autopsy later indicated that he had frozen to death. The supervisor of the Salt Pit at the time was a relatively junior CIA officer. Like so many others after the September 11 attacks, he was given the responsibility of overseeing harsh interrogations despite the fact that he had virtually no relevant experience. Rahman's was the only known fatality inside a CIA-run detention facility after 9/11. No one had been prosecuted for it.

Holder's mood grew visibly somber during the meeting. "I could see that something changed in him," Whitehouse later recalled. Sensing this, the senator made his pitch in stark, unequivocal terms: "Eric, right now the Bush administration is responsible for what happened," Whitehouse told him. "But if we don't do what's right and investigate these allegations, we will be responsible."

Holder was shaken when he left the Command Center. His sense of outrage and shock spilled out in a meeting later that afternoon with Kevin Ohlson, his chief of staff, and national security counselor Amy Jeffress, who, with Matt Miller, his communications director, made up the troika of close advisers he referred to as his ExCom, named after the team of national security aides who advised JFK during the Cuban missile crisis. Whitehouse's call to action had resonated with the attorney general. "It's not enough that we stopped doing these things," he told Ohlson and Jeffress. "If we don't look into this and hold people responsible, then we become morally culpable." At the same time, Holder knew that the political consequences of an investigation would be severe; Republicans would surely accuse the administration of a witch hunt aimed at the men and women who risk their lives every day to protect the country. Holder also had concerns about the impact on the CIA, whose operatives would be at the center of any probe. As a prosecutor and a former judge, he had always felt close to the cops and agents on the front lines. He had attended too many funerals not to appreciate their sacrifice. And he knew that President Obama didn't want to see the CIA dragged through a morale-sapping grand jury investigation. It had not taken long for Obama to understand how central America's spies were to the war on al-Qaeda, which he now viewed as his top national security priority.

A few days after his meeting with Whitehouse, Holder was at home catching up on his reading when he came across an article in *Vanity Fair* magazine by Christopher Hitchens, in which the writer and critic described what it was like to be waterboarded. Hitchens had arranged to be "abducted" by a team of security contractors in a rural part of North Carolina. They hooded him, placed him in a dark room, and strapped him to a sloping board, positioned so that his head was lower than his heart. They placed a thick towel over his hooded face and proceeded to pour water into his nostrils, a managed-drowning technique. After reading the article, Holder viewed the accompanying video online, at *Vanity Fair*'s website. He sat in his study, engrossed in the macabre spectacle. Hitchens lasted for fewer than ten seconds before asking for mercy, sputtering and gagging as the cloth used in the demonstration was removed from his mouth. Watching the video, Holder was both mesmerized and repulsed.

Over the next few weeks he plunged into classified reports and briefings on the CIA's interrogation program. He was increasingly convinced that he would need to launch an investigation, or at least a preliminary inquiry to determine whether a full-blown probe was warranted. One avenue of investigation had already been foreclosed by the administration. It had been decided that any conduct that had been authorized by the Bush Justice Department's controversial legal opinions would be off-limits to prosecutors. If CIA officers had acted in good faith on the basis of Justice Department advice, then they should be left alone. But Holder and his advisers had identified at least ten instances in which interrogators had gone far beyond what had been sanctioned by the prior administration's legal team.

On April 7, he met in his office with Jeffress and Ohlson to begin considering the contours of such a probe. The strategy session began with a cautionary note. Jeffress emphasized to Holder that career lawyers in the Bush Justice Department had already looked at each of these cases and declined to prosecute. The allegations even then were several years old, so relying on witnesses' memories would have been problematic. That had been the conclusion of prosecutors in the Eastern District of Virginia. Furthermore, they had not been able to clearly establish criminal intent.

Now, several years further into the distance, for an incoming administration to reinvestigate allegations that had been dismissed by professional prosecutors would be controversial, opening Holder up to charges of political motivation. Holder acknowledged Jeffress's point but quickly moved on. Neither the attorney general nor anyone on his staff had read the Eastern District's declination memos, which laid out the legal rationale for the decision not to prosecute. Instead, Holder and his team batted around potential special prosecutors for the job, including big-name lawyers like Patrick Fitzgerald as well as more anonymous insiders who would draw less attention to the case. "You need to appoint someone who is really regarded as apolitical," Jeffress told Holder. "But you're going to be criticized either way," she added.

A few days later Holder and his wife, Sharon Malone, attended a small dinner party in a leafy corner of Washington. The couple cut an elegant swath through the city's social circuit. Holder was so mild mannered and comfortable in his own skin that he could instantly put people at ease. He was "Eric" to everyone, yet he possessed none of the false humility that often signaled vanity in Washington players. Malone, by contrast, was at first more restrained than her husband. Immaculately turned out, even at home on the weekends, she was more likely to offer a polite smile than a warm embrace upon initial meetings. She was more intense than Holder, often revealing a steely resolve. She had grown up in the Deep South under Jim Crow—her sister, Vivian Malone Jones, had integrated the University of Alabama, becoming its first African American graduate in 1965. Sharon Malone had a fierce sense of right and wrong.

The dinner that night was with a group of Washington journalists and lawyers, all eager to hear intimate details of Obama's Washington. They pumped the attorney general for information, hanging on his every word, by turns solicitous and prying. Holder was discreet,

mostly dancing around opportunities to criticize the Bush administration. He acknowledged the climate of fear that had led the previous administration to take some extreme positions, and praised it
for setting up an "effective antiterror infrastructure." Malone, after
settling in and relaxing, was less reticent. She had been reading a
book about a dark and little-known chapter in American history, the
virtual reenslavement of hundreds of thousands of black Americans
in the South between the end of the Civil War and World War II.
(According to Douglas A. Blackmon's *Slavery by Another Name,* African Americans were arbitrarily arrested for trumped-up crimes, hit
with huge fines, and then sold into industrial servitude to pay back
their "debt.") The book's underlying message was that a nation unwilling to confront its sins was fated to repeat them. Malone drew a
direct line between America's shameful racial history and the abuses
of Guantánamo and Abu Ghraib. "Both are examples of what we
have not done in the face of injustice," she said, her Alabama-in-
flected accent more discernible as her voice rose with indignation.

The two were a study in contrasts. "Eric did not marry a shrinking violet," Malone would sometimes tell friends, with a chuckle. She
traced their differences to divergent upbringings. "His parents are
from the West Indies . . . he experienced a kinder, gentler version
of the black experience." Holder had grown up in East Elmhurst,
Queens, a lower-middle-class neighborhood that had been a step-
pingstone for immigrants and blacks who had relocated to the North
during the Great Migration. Bright, athletic, and good-natured,
Holder had led a largely happy, drama-free childhood. His father,
Eric Sr., was in real estate and owned a few small buildings in Harlem. His mother, Miriam, stayed at home and doted on her two boys.
Holder didn't dispute the idea that his happy upbringing had led to
a sunny view of the world. "I grew up in a stable neighborhood in a

stable, two-parent family," he would claim, "and I never really saw the reality of racism or felt the insecurity that comes with it."

Malone's family had been farmers in rural Alabama, though by the time she was born they had moved to Mobile. Her father painted boats in the shipyard and her mother was a housekeeper. "We never had that 'we're rolling now' feeling," she recalled.

Malone found it ironic that her husband had stumbled into a racial controversy in his first weeks in office. In his third week on the job as Obama's attorney general, Holder gave a speech on race relations in honor of Black History Month. It was a largely anodyne address, but the night before delivering it he'd slipped in the infelicitous phrase "nation of cowards" to describe the hair trigger Americans are on when it came to race. The speech churned through a couple of cable news cycles, infuriating Rahm Emanuel. He had an "every day is election day" mentality; unforced political errors, when he was trying to guide the president's domestic agenda, drove him to distraction.

Holder generally had a more upbeat view of race than Malone. But he was not immune to occasional flashes of passion on the emotional subject. Either way, he misjudged how his "nation of cowards" comments would be received. Even in progressive Washington — even in the administration of Barack Obama — successful blacks were perpetually navigating the tricky shoals of race. Malone instructed Holder to be "bicultural and bilingual." "It doesn't matter how aggrieved you feel," she told him. "You have to suppress that angry tone because it's the surest way of not getting your message across." And yet she also encouraged him to stand up forthrightly for what he believed in. For those who knew the couple well, it was clear that Malone played a spine-stiffening role in their marriage. "Eric sees himself as the nice guy," she observed. "In a lot of ways that's a good thing. He's always saying 'you get a lot more out of people with kindness than meanness.' But when he leaves the 'nice guy' behind, that's when he's strongest."

Soon after that dinner party, the Bush torture memos were released. The left hailed the move as an important shift toward transparency and government accountability. And yet one could not help but notice the defensive tone of both Obama's and Holder's statements at the time. Most of the president's press release was devoted to upholding the need for secrecy in the national security arena and to defending the "men and women of the intelligence community" who "serve courageously on the front lines of a dangerous world." Obama's principal rationale for disclosing the opinions was that their contents had already largely been reported. The latter half of his statement was aimed at deflecting calls for investigations. "This is a time for reflection, not retribution," he asserted. "Nothing will be gained by spending our time and energy laying blame for the past." In a separate statement, Holder echoed the president's conciliatory message. He bent over backwards to assure that CIA officers who "acted in good faith on authoritative legal advice from the Justice Department" would not be prosecuted. And he went further, vowing to aggressively defend their legal interests, providing lawyers to represent them in "any state or federal or administrative proceeding." Holder even promised to indemnify CIA employees for any monetary judgments imposed against them. It was a classic straddle.

Holder hoped the revelations graphically described in the legal opinions would stoke national outrage, reframe the debate, and help build support on Capitol Hill for an investigation. The public had been only generally familiar with the harsh techniques employed by CIA interrogators. The opinions, written in chillingly detached legal prose, revealed disturbing specifics. Abu Zubaydah had been placed in a dark "confinement box" and told that a "stinging insect" would be placed inside. He and Khalid Sheikh Mohammed were waterboarded hundreds of times. Others were subjected to eleven straight days of sleep deprivation or doused with water as cold as forty-one degrees.

Yet the outrage never materialized. The broad public just didn't seem to care. Instead, Holder faced ferocious opposition to any probe from the intelligence community. On more than one occasion, Panetta took him aside after a cabinet meeting and warned him against investigating the agency's enhanced interrogation program, once again asserting that such a move would "devastate morale." Holder liked Panetta, and listened to his arguments solicitously. But he was undeterred. Other than predictable calls from liberals like Vermont senator Patrick Leahy and Wisconsin's Russ Feingold, there was no groundswell for an investigation—yet Holder could not let it go. Emanuel did his part to try to deflect the issue, going on the Sunday-morning news programs to declare that it was time to put the dark chapter behind us. But Holder could not just walk away.

Open warfare threatened to break out in late April, when David Axelrod summoned Holder to the White House for a meeting on "media training." As Obama's senior adviser and top communications guru, it was Axelrod's job to make sure that the administration's public messaging was aligned with its political and policy agendas. In an age of warp-speed news cycles, ideologically driven bloggers, and a Washington press corps ready to pounce on the slightest gaffe, "message discipline" was an obsession bordering on mania. White House officials—especially the chief of staff—were trying to maintain a laser-like focus on the economy and health care. There was always some cabinet secretary going off the reservation, popping off on TV or straying from the White House–supplied talking points, and Emanuel worked with Axelrod to keep them in line. The chief of staff was like a political commissar in the Soviet Army, warily prowling the government for renegades, ruthlessly enforcing loyalty. He even once lit into Bo, the Obamas' Portuguese water dog, whose household accidents he deemed "off message."

Now Emanuel had his sights set on Holder. The attorney general had gotten off to a rocky start with the White House with his "nation of cowards" speech. One week later, Holder stepped into it again. On February 25, Jim Messina, Emanuel's deputy, walked into his boss's office to inform him of Holder's latest "gaffe." At a press conference earlier that day, Holder had told reporters that the administration would push to reinstate the assault-weapons ban, which had expired in 2004. The comment roused the powerful gun lobby and its water carriers on Capitol Hill. "Senators to Attorney General: Stay Away from Our Guns" read a press release issued by Senator Max Baucus of Montana — a Democrat, no less.

Emanuel was furious. He slammed his desk and cursed the attorney general. Holder was only repeating a position Obama had expressed during the campaign, but that was before the White House needed the backing of pro-gun Democrats from red states for their domestic agenda. The chief of staff sent word back to Justice that Holder needed to "shut the fuck up" on guns. In the span of seven days, Holder had stumbled into controversies over two culture-war issues, race and guns, that Team Obama was desperate to avoid. It was time to rein in the attorney general, bring him in for "media training" — the political equivalent of the vaudeville hook.

"Why do I have to do this?" Holder peevishly asked Matt Miller. Holder thought of himself as a loyal member of the president's team and was beginning to chafe at the White House's meddling. He wasn't some junior official to be ordered around by high-handed aides. He was the attorney general. Moreover, Holder resented the insinuation that he was a political bumbler in need of remedial training. He was also distrustful of Axelrod's motives, and he suspected that

Emanuel was behind the meeting. Holder knew that his early stumbles, however minor, were flash points in a much larger war that was breaking out over substantive policy issues, including torture, detention, and the fate of Guantánamo detainees. It pitted idealists like Greg Craig and Valerie Jarrett, who had become personally invested in Obama's promise to roll back the Bush legacy in the war on terror, against cold-eyed pragmatists like Emanuel and Axelrod, who feared that the politics of national security represented a growing threat to Obama's domestic agenda.

Maintaining his position above the fray, the president straddled both camps. Obama was a civil libertarian by instinct and legal training, but he wasn't doctrinaire about it. He believed, as he had once written, that tensions arise not always because one side is wrong and the other right, but because "we live in a complex and contradictory world," which makes it difficult to find the proper balance between competing values. He had grown up, as he had famously written in *Dreams from My Father,* uncertain of his identity, moving between racial and cultural worlds like a double agent. Yet now he was operating in a zero-sum political environment where those representing the extremes in each side of any given argument saw no point in compromise. He could be scornful of ACLU absolutists who saw the slightest loosening of their agenda as an inevitable slide toward authoritarianism, and he found it maddening that even his most principled critics on the right, like South Carolina senator Lindsey Graham, too often refused to acknowledge the validity of the other side's positions. Yet he could not stop taking fire from both sides, and it was hard to tell which side made him crazier. No criticism seemed to sting more than when liberals accused him of selling civil liberties down the river. When the ACLU ran an ad campaign in 2010 that featured a picture of Obama morphing into George W. Bush, the president was more than a little irritated.

Many presidents have been artful straddlers. The question that would haunt this president was, did he have fire in his belly? Obama often took the path of least resistance, opting for passivity. He bobbed and weaved among his own advisers, endlessly adjusted tactics, and played for time in the ever-diminishing hope that the politics might eventually turn his way. His tepid approach to congressional opposition, however, only made things worse. Each time he backed away from a fight, Republicans on the Hill hit him harder. Within his own administration, the president's elusiveness created confusion about who was in control of policy, what strategy should be pursued, and ultimately, what Obama really wanted or believed. In this vacuum his advisers fought brutally, each side invoking the president in support of its cause.

Holder became a pivotal figure in this drama. As attorney general he occupied one of the most sensitive jobs in the government, perched at the intersection of law, national security, and American values. Lawyers under his command exercised enormous influence in the war on terror. Simply by signing a classified Justice Department legal opinion they could restrain or unleash enormous power. And, crucially, the obligations of Holder's office required him to operate with independence from the White House. Obama, steeped in the traditions of the American legal system, understood the value of having an independent attorney general. But like Obama, Holder labored under his own set of internal conflicts. Like the best of his predecessors, he struggled to find the proper balance between faithfully serving his president and faithfully serving the law. The line between loyalty and independence is a murky one. Lean too far one way and you risk corrupting the office, too far the other way and you marginalize yourself.

In the chaotic last days of the Clinton administration, nine years earlier, Holder had found himself on the wrong side of that line. As deputy attorney general he had blessed the controversial pardon of Marc Rich, the fugitive financier charged with massive tax evasion and fraud, whose socialite wife was a major Clinton donor. Holder was widely criticized in the press and on Capitol Hill, accused of doing the president's bidding and of placing his own personal ambition above principle. It was a searing experience in an otherwise unblemished career. Consciously or not, the trauma of the Rich pardon would profoundly shape Holder's relations with the Obama White House.

Any White House tests an attorney general's strength. But the one run by Rahm Emanuel required a particular brand of fortitude. A legendary enforcer of presidential will, Emanuel relentlessly tried to anticipate political threats that could harm his boss. To the chief of staff, the Justice Department, with its independent mandate, was an inherently nervous-making place. As a White House staffer during the Clinton administration, Emanuel had tangled endlessly with Justice. He had done everything he could to marginalize Attorney General Janet Reno, whom he saw as an annoyingly prudish figure whose rigid independence often thwarted the White House's political goals. He was famous for blitzing Justice officials with phone calls, obsessively trying to gather intelligence, plant policy ideas, and generally keep tabs on the department. Ironically, Holder, then serving as Reno's deputy, had been Emanuel's main backchannel to the White House. But things were different now. Emanuel had one of the highest profiles in the administration and he couldn't afford to be perceived as meddling in the Justice Department's affairs. Holder now had the burden of maintaining institutional autonomy. In Washington as in the private sector, sometimes a new title changes everything.

At a National Security Council meeting in early spring, Holder laid down a marker for his independence. With some heat in his voice, Holder told the principals that he was contemplating launching an investigation into the Bush administration's brutal interrogation practices. The Situation Room revelation was greeted with an awkward silence. Nobody openly objected; the last thing the White House wanted was word to leak that the attorney general was being pressured to back away from a politically sensitive investigation.

Holder was not a natural renegade. His first instinct was to shy away from confrontation. If he disagreed with you, he was likely to compliment you first before staking out an opposing position. "Now, you see, that's interesting," he'd begin gently. It may have been unconscious, but it wasn't guileless. Holder's solicitous approach had smoothed his rise to power, winning him friends across the political spectrum. But he mostly stuck to his guns, diplomacy notwithstanding. He hadn't stuck to them at the time of the Rich pardon, and now that he was back at Justice, he had a chance to redeem himself.

Emanuel and Axelrod were uninterested in Holder's quest for redemption. They considered it narcissistic and self-aggrandizing at the expense of the president. Inside the West Wing, a narrative was developing that Holder had "overlearned" the lessons of Marc Rich, that he was on a crusade to assert his own independence. But there was something more visceral at the heart of the animus between Holder and the White House. Holder was personally closer to Obama than almost anyone else in the cabinet, a dynamic that over time bred resentment inside the West Wing. Preternaturally calm and studiously above the fray, Obama was the administration's adult in chief. But a White House managed by the agitative Emanuel could sometimes feel like an extension of the high school cafeteria, with aides acting out personal jealousies and vying for the attention of the big man on campus. Obama prided himself on his ability to separate his friendships from his professional responsibilities. When he offered Holder the attorney general's job, Obama had warned him that doing their jobs responsibly would require personal and institutional distance. "Things are going to be different between us," he told Holder on the Saturday after the election. "It's not just going to be Barack and Eric any more." But that was easier said than done.

It irritated Emanuel that, despite repeated efforts, he could not get Obama to discipline his errant attorney general. When Agriculture Secretary Tom Vilsack or EPA Administrator Lisa Jackson screwed up, alienating a key constituency or going off-message on a talk show, Obama would pick up the phone himself to deal with the problem. Or he would dispatch the chief of staff's deputy, Jim Messina, to administer a woodshedding on his behalf. But despite Emanuel's pleading, Holder was untouchable. "Eric's doing a good job," the president would say. Emanuel would walk out of the Oval Office exasperated.

It was even more maddening for Emanuel that Holder was able to circumvent him on highly sensitive Justice Department matters. A key role of any White House chief of staff is controlling the flow of information in and out of the Oval Office. Emanuel guarded that power jealously. But he couldn't control private conversations between Holder and the president in social settings. At key moments, whether it was on the decision to investigate Bush-era torture or try Khalid Sheikh Mohammed in civilian court, Holder had critical "pull-asides" with Obama, out of Emanuel's earshot.

Obama and Emanuel had a strong professional relationship. In Emanuel, the president had a brilliant legislative tactician with an instinctive feel for the interplay between politics and policy. The president knew he was lucky to have a chief of staff who brought such intensity to the job. But the two men did not have a strong personal connection. They didn't socialize with each other. Emanuel wasn't invited to Camp David on the weekends and he didn't hang out with the Obamas on Martha's Vineyard in the summer.

Obama's relationship with Holder operated on different levels. The president respected Holder professionally, impressed by his achievements and his rise in official Washington. When Obama was an obscure state senator in Illinois, Holder was serving as the country's first black deputy attorney general, at a time when Obama had many friends and colleagues from Harvard and the University of Chicago law schools who worked at the Justice Department. Holder also had earned Obama's political loyalty by walking the plank for him during the primaries, turning against Hillary Clinton and joining his campaign. Holder was the highest-ranking Clinton official to have endorsed Obama during the primaries, and he did so early on.

But ultimately their bond was built on personal affinities more than professional or political kinship. The chemistry was clear from their first meeting at a Washington dinner party in 2004. It was at the home of Ann Walker Marchant, a former Clinton administration official and the niece of Washington power broker Vernon Jordan. Obama, recently elected to the US Senate, was being shown off to the city's power elite. Seated next to each other, Obama and Holder shunned the usual Washington chatter about politics and policy. Instead they talked sports, razzing each other about their local teams — Obama was a die-hard Chicago fan and Holder was "all New York." Living away from his family, who'd remained in Chicago, Obama was still trying to make his way in Washington. Holder gave him advice about how to find normalcy amid DC's strange tribal customs. He offered to take him out to get some soul food and watch a ball game. "I'm South Side," Obama said, grinning broadly and referring to the best part of Chicago for southern fare.

There was another factor that explained the rapport. Obama could genuinely relax around Holder, who was disarmingly laid back and didn't possess any of the high-octane intensity or neediness typical of presidential aides. Hanging out with Holder may not have amounted to "escaping the bubble," something Obama was forever trying to do. But he could loosen up with his friend in ways that he could not with others. When Obama gave his "race speech" in Philadelphia in March 2008, addressing the controversy surrounding his longtime pastor, Jeremiah Wright, a rare moment of high anxiety during the campaign, he asked Holder to be there. But as they waited offstage, Obama didn't solicit Holder's political advice or ask him to go over the address. Instead they bantered about the NCAA basketball tournament, which was just getting under way.

Holder could hardly claim a background as exotic as Obama's. Still, Holder and Obama had common cultural attributes that shaped similar worldviews. They were both black men raised outside the conventional African American tradition who'd worked their way to the top of the meritocracy. They had succeeded spectacularly in a largely white world in part because they betrayed little, if any, racial anger. And yet they lived lives that reflected authentic commitments to racial justice and empowerment. Obama had worked as a civil rights lawyer, taught seminars on race and the law at the University of Chicago Law School, and spent years as a community organizer. Holder rose to the top of the American legal establishment as a prosecutor and a District of Columbia judge. But his notions of justice and public service went far beyond the courtroom. As US attorney in Washington at a time of high racial tension in the city, Holder was a regular at evening community meetings, and he sometimes could be found talking to the mother of a wayward teen on her inner-city stoop.

More strikingly, both men had married formidable wives who exerted powerful influences in their lives. Michelle Obama and Sharon Malone were smart, beautiful, and principled women, deeply attuned to their African American ancestry, who kept their husbands "real." The two quickly became close, strengthening the relationship between Obama and Holder. The couples socialized frequently, attending each others' birthday parties at swanky Washington restaurants, or getting together at small, informal dinners at the home of Valerie Jarrett, the Obamas' oldest and most trusted friend in the White House, where they might also take in a football game. Michelle and Sharon's get-togethers were even more down-home and intimate. Malone sometimes dropped by the White House residence for drinks or a meal with Mrs. Obama. The First Lady would come over to the Holders' for "pizza night," a near-inviolable family tradition, or Sunday brunch. Holder would often retire early to read in his upstairs office or watch TV, while the wives continued talking for hours. For Michelle, it was a chance to escape the bubble, to speak unguardedly with a girlfriend who shared a common background and a similarly ironic perspective on official Washington.

The Obama-Holder alliance was nurtured and strengthened by Jarrett. Jarrett had gotten to know Holder during the campaign and was fond of him. Sometimes during campaign conference calls, they'd mischievously email each other offline to mock the windbags advising the presidential hopeful. In Washington she served as his sherpa, leading Holder through the West Wing's tangled politics and personal dynamics.

Emanuel, not surprisingly, felt threatened by Jarrett's close relationship with the Obamas. He worried that she would emerge as a kind of shadow chief of staff, undermining his authority. During the transition he even tried to nudge her out of the White House, suggesting to the president that she fill Obama's vacant Senate seat. Later, they fought over office space, always a symbolic stand-in for power. The Obama-Holder-Jarrett axis only fueled the perception inside the chief of staff's Tammany Hall that the attorney general was untouchable. When word of Holder's appointment leaked to *Newsweek* before Inauguration Day, Emanuel suspected him of being the source and told the president-elect so. But Obama and Jarrett rejected that theory, instead deflecting the blame onto two unlikely staffers of the vice president–elect, Joe Biden.

Emanuel had reason to be suspicious of Jarrett. Obama's senior adviser often served as Holder's inside source, feeding him key bits of intelligence and playing back critical comments from White House aides, revealing Emanuel's private counsels. Emanuel began to suspect Jarrett's subterfuge during one 7:30 morning meeting. When he laid into Holder, he noticed Jarrett pick up her BlackBerry and begin typing. Later, when Holder was at the White House on other business, he went to see Emanuel in his office. He closed the door and laid into the chief of staff for criticizing him in front of White House staff. Emanuel gave as good as he got. When Holder returned to the West Wing hallway, he told his deputy chief of staff, James Garland, "I think I might have dropped a few too many f-bombs."

The fraught interpersonal dynamics were complicated further by race. It wasn't that Emanuel suspected a sinister black cabal of trying to thwart him. It was more subtle and benign than that. He knew that Obama and Jarrett, for all the right reasons, wanted the country's first African American attorney general to succeed.

Emanuel's normal routes to maintaining discipline were blocked. He couldn't call Holder directly, for fear of getting caught politicizing the Justice Department. Nor could he lean on Obama to discipline Holder. Yet Emanuel was able to draw on his years of experience in the dark arts of bureaucratic subterfuge to work around these barriers. When Janet Reno had been hopelessly out of sync with the Clinton White House, he had installed a trusted White House aide on her staff who deftly guided the Justice Department back into the fold. Why not run the same play? He hatched the plan with Axelrod and Jim Messina, the deputy chief of staff. They selected Chris Sautter for the operation. A politically savvy lawyer from Indiana, Sautter had once run the Washington office of Axelrod's media consulting firm. Messina quietly reached out to Holder's deputy, David Ogden, to lay the groundwork with the attorney general.

May 8, 2009, was a typically frenetic day for the attorney general, with a mix of serious policy meetings and ceremonial duties. In the afternoon, he presided over the "investiture," or formal swearing in, of Ogden. With his grace and humor, Holder was a gifted master of ceremonies at such events. But this time he was going through the motions. The two had quickly developed a toxic relationship. Ogden thought Holder was hoarding the department's national security responsibilities and should have delegated more authority to him. Holder considered Ogden presumptuous and comically self-important. After a brief reception, Holder drove over to the White House with Ohlson, Miller, and Garland for the Axelrod meeting. As they walked into the Roosevelt Room, just steps away from the Oval Office, they could feel the tension rise.

Seated behind a massive cherry table were Axelrod, White House Communications Director Anita Dunn, and Ben LaBolt, a feisty press aide who was close to Emanuel. Press Secretary Robert Gibbs came in for part of the meeting. Axelrod instructed Holder to sit across from them. Leaning forward, striking a prosecutorial tone, Axelrod began firing questions at the AG. He pointedly asked Holder about race and guns before the others piled on with a barrage of other questions.

It was a "murder board," a rehearsal session to prepare top aides for press conferences or congressional testimony. Ohlson, Holder's loyal chief of staff, saw it as an ambush, and he was outraged. He thought the White House was trying to knock Holder down a peg; the questions and the coaching were belittling and condescending, in his estimation. "Nation of cowards," Axelrod intoned. "Do you regret using that phrase?" "Don't venture into social policy questions," Holder was advised. On terrorism, the attorney general was told to "focus on the simple statement, like 'we're working to keep the American people safe.'" Holder seethed, but kept his anger to himself.

After about ninety minutes of rapid-fire questions, Axelrod stood up and asked everyone to leave except for Holder. The attorney general pushed back. He was with his most trusted aides, and anything Axelrod had to say to him, they could hear. "These are my guys," he said. Axelrod warned that he was going to speak bluntly.

"Eric, you're the attorney general," he said softly. "You have to consider the consequences of what you say." He told him that the White House needed better communications with Justice and more coordination on policy and messaging. Holder fumed, but again said nothing. Then Axelrod revealed the real reason for the meeting: "We need someone working closely with you, someone who has finely tuned political instincts. We need someone who can serve as an early-warning system," Axelrod told him. "Messina has talked to Ogden about this."

Holder couldn't believe it: the White House wanted to assign a minder to him and they'd plotted with his deputy behind his back. "We can play this little game, but it's not going to happen," he thought to himself. But he still didn't punch back. He told Axelrod he'd take the suggestion under advisement.

The meeting ended abruptly and Holder headed back to Justice. Humiliated, feeling betrayed by his deputy, Holder was in a slow burn. His aides in tow, he headed straight to the fourth floor, blew past the secretaries, and confronted Ogden in his conference room, where he was holding a meeting. "I understand you've had some interesting conversations about me with David Axelrod," Holder said sarcastically. Ogden, flustered, suggested they go into his private office. There, he picked up a piece of paper on his desk and gave it to Holder. It was Chris Sautter's resumé. "I had been planning to give this to you," Ogden said. Holder scowled as he and his aides swept out of the deputy attorney general's office.

Ogden would be pushed out of the Justice Department six months later. But his fate had been sealed on that Friday afternoon in May, the same day that Holder had presided over his swearing in.

A few days after the murder board, Holder was back at the White House for a cabinet meeting. After the session ended, Axelrod made a beeline for the attorney general. Obama's senior adviser was incensed. It had gotten back to him that Holder and his aides were spreading the word that he was trying to improperly influence the Justice Department. Axelrod, who knew all too well that even the hint of White House meddling with Justice Department investigations could detonate a full-blown scandal, had been careful not to come close to that line. "Don't ever, ever accuse me of trying to interfere with the operations of the Justice Department," he warned Holder after confronting him in the hallway. "I'm not Karl Rove," he added, referring to George Bush's political consigliere who had been accused of pressuring Justice to fire politically unpopular US attorneys. Holder did not appreciate being publicly dressed down by the president's most senior political adviser. Determined to stand his ground against Tammany Hall, the AG ripped into him in full view of other White House staffers. "That's bullshit," he replied vehemently. The two men stood chest to chest. It was like a school yard fight back at their shared alma mater, Stuyvesant, the elite public high school for striving kids from New York City. White House staffers caught in the crossfire averted their eyes. Jarrett, whose office was nearby, materialized as things got hot. Petite and perfectly put together as always, she pushed her way between the two men, her sense of decorum disturbed, ordering them to "take it out of the hallway."

Uncomfortable with open conflict, Holder later made attempts to mend his relationship with Axelrod. For his part, Axelrod's dealings with the attorney general were civil, but from then on he refrained from speaking to Holder about substantive issues.

By the midway point of Obama's first year in office, the White House's thermostat had swung toward Tammany, away from the idealists. The prospects for torture investigations seemed to be losing momentum. Congress was growing restive about Guantánamo and the fate of its detainees. The fault line between the White House and Justice was deepening. Soon after Holder's murder board, Emanuel exploded when a Justice Department official gave a speech announcing tougher antitrust-enforcement rules. It was an unremarkable policy pronouncement from a Democratic administration, but a few days earlier Emanuel had issued an administration-wide edict that nobody, upon pain of death, was to create "any bad headlines" interfering with health care reform. The White House had carefully staged a series of health care events for the president on May 11. So when, that morning, the *New York Times* prominently reported the speech by Obama's top antitrust lawyer, Christine Varney, set for later that day, the chief of staff was apoplectic. Just as the administration was courting corporate America's support for its signature legislative priority, the Justice Department seemed to be launching an aggressive new offensive against big business. Emanuel sent word back to Justice that Varney needed to be "muzzled." As Varney was making her way to the Washington think tank where she was scheduled to deliver her speech, White House aides frantically tried to get the address called off. But when they finally reached Kevin Ohlson, Holder's chief of staff, it was too late. Varney was making her way up to the podium.

Holder resented the interference. But he also understood that he could ill afford a war of attrition with the White House. As important as it was to maintain his independence, he could not accomplish anything if he were completely marginalized. It was time to recalibrate. Later that afternoon, the attorney general gathered his senior advisers and told them that they needed to coordinate better with the White House. "We must be independent," he said, choosing his words carefully. "But we can't let the White House get blindsided on things we can share appropriately." One participant at the meeting translated: "Don't Bigfoot the president." A few days later Holder delivered the message at a White House meeting. Varney won't be making any more "bad headlines," he told Larry Summers, Obama's chief economic adviser. Holder, the reluctant insurgent, was offering a cease-fire. But his peace offensive would be short-lived.

By early June, Emanuel could see that the administration was losing Congress over detainee issues. Both the House and the Senate had passed appropriations bills that placed restrictions on the transfer of detainees from Guantánamo to the US mainland. The Senate vote was 90 to 6, a lopsided tally that sent shock waves through the administration. All but six Democrats had effectively voted against Obama's promise to shutter Guantánamo. It was one of those telling moments when airy idealism was subsumed by raw politics. Democrats could all too easily imagine the negative ads their opponents would run, accusing them of voting to "bring the terrorists back home."

Emanuel decided it was time to cut the White House's losses. On June 3, without any input from Holder or his department, he negotiated a deal with Senate Democrats. The total ban on transfers would be lifted, but the administration would have to give the Hill forty-five days' notice before any prisoner could be moved. As Emanuel well knew, that was plenty of time to stir up opposition, effectively blocking detainee transfers from Cuba to the United States. "It was not a compromise," Holder fumed to his staff. "It was a capitulation." Adding to the humiliation, Emanuel directed Holder to attend a Democratic caucus meeting later that evening where he was to give the deal his seal of approval. Holder refused. Instead, he dispatched Ogden, an intentional snub in hierarchy-minded Washington. That evening, Deputy National Security Adviser Tom Donilon and John Brennan joined Ogden to meet with Democrats in the ornate LBJ Room inside the Capitol building. The administration officials nearly got their heads taken off, as anxious senators demanded to know how the White House planned to manage the exploding politics of terrorism. "Where's your plan?" they shouted over and over again. Among the most agitated were liberals like Barbara Boxer and Barbara Mikulski, who were up for reelection. These were the same representatives who had pilloried the Bush administration for its fear-mongering tactics in the war on terror, but behind the grand doors of the LBJ Room, all politics were local. We're going to get clobbered back home, the Democrats protested. An adviser to Ogden, watching the drubbing unfold in horror, handed a note to Ronald Weich, the Justice Department's assistant attorney general in charge of congressional relations. It simply read: "I fear for our Democracy." Weich, who knew the Hill as well as anybody in Washington, turned the piece of paper over and scrawled on the other side: "Welcome to my world."

Holder was livid about Emanuel's end run. He and his aides drafted a stiff-necked protest memo to the president, complaining that the White House had totally blocked Justice from pressing its case in Congress. Their hands were being tied behind their backs, the memo said. How would the administration ever be able to close Guantánamo if it could not build support on the Hill and with the American people? At the last minute, however, Holder decided to address the missive to the chief of staff instead of to the president. He worried that, otherwise, the memo would be perceived as an effort to "jam" Obama, a breach of etiquette cabinet members were instructed to avoid at all cost. Sending it to Emanuel was aggressive enough.

The chief of staff reacted scornfully, immediately accusing Holder of writing it so that he could leak it and embarrass the White House. Axelrod caustically called the move "not helpful." Even Greg Craig, an ideological ally of Holder's, thought the attorney general had gone too far, calling the communication "angry and untimely."

4

ESCAPE FROM GITMO

ONCE MATT OLSEN'S GUANTÁNAMO TASK FORCE began its work, it rapidly became clear to insiders that closing the detention center would be a herculean task. The problem of where to put its 241 inmates seemed to grow more intractable by the day.

The Obama team began its relocation efforts with some one hundred Yemeni detainees. The largest national group in the facility, the Yemenis made up close to half the Gitmo population. Returning them to Yemen was a nonstarter. The desperately poor country was on the brink of becoming a failed state. The US-backed regime was struggling to contain a civil war in the north involving Shiite rebels, and secessionists in the south with ties to al-Qaeda. President Ali Abdullah Saleh had such a tenuous grip on his country, counterterrorism officials in the United States had little faith he could hold the Guantánamo Yemenis securely in his prisons. They had good reason to worry. In 2006 twenty-three prisoners — thirteen of them al-Qaeda members, some of whom were responsible for the deadly attack on the USS *Cole* in 2000 — had escaped from a high-security prison in the capital city of Sana'a. Using only broomsticks and broken bits of a fan, they had improbably tunneled their way out of the prison and into a nearby mosque. American officials had dubbed it "the Great Escape" — with irony, since no one had any doubt that the caper was an inside job. An FBI agent stationed in Sana'a wryly asked what the prisoners had done with all of the dirt they'd dug up.

But there was one group of roughly twenty Yemenis at Gitmo that seemed to present a special opportunity. All had strong ties to Saudi Arabia; some were born in the desert kingdom, which bordered Yemen. John Brennan admired the Saudi government's rehabilitation program for returning jihadis — its recidivism rate was low, about 10 percent, compared with 50 percent in the American criminal-justice system — and he thought that the administration might be able to get a "foot in the door" with this initial group and eventually transfer the remaining Yemeni detainees to the program. But President Saleh was opposed to the plan, considering the transfer an infringement on Yemen's sovereignty. The Yemenis had long resented what they viewed as patronizing treatment by their neighbors to the north.

Brennan tried anyway, working the diplomacy largely himself, cutting out the State Department. He knew Yemen well. He had spent time there in the 1990s when he was the CIA's man in Saudi Arabia. He had fond memories of camping out with local Bedouins in the Arabian Desert. Over the years he had developed a comfortable, if fractious, relationship with the mercurial Saleh, whom he was able to approach directly. After much cajoling and flattery on Brennan's part, Saleh finally relented, traveling to Riyadh to personally seal the deal with King Abdullah, a diplomatic flourish the Americans regarded as a formality. But the agreement blew up when the Yemeni president haughtily told the Saudi leader, "I will allow you to take a few of my citizens." Abdullah could not allow the insult to Saudi pride to stand. "You were not doing me a favor," he fumed. "It is I who was doing you the favor." It was a breach of desert honor. Now, nobody was doing the Yemeni detainees any favors: they would remain in Guantánamo.

It was a discouraging blow to the Obama team. If they failed in their efforts to transfer 20 Gitmo detainees, how would they manage springing 241? And within the president's timeline?

As tough as the Yemeni case was, an even more perplexing challenge awaited the administration.

It was an odd quirk of history that Obama's efforts to reform the war on terror foundered over an obscure Turkic-speaking people from the far reaches of central Asia. Gitmo's "Camp VI" had been built later than the other facilities at the prison (it opened in November 2006), and it was meant to be the most humane of the cellblocks, housing the least dangerous of the detainees. Among those transferred to Camp VI were seventeen Muslim dissidents, ethnic Uighurs from the restive region of Xinjiang in the far northwest of China. Little known to most of the rest of the world, the Uighurs had a contentious history with China's rulers and the Han Chinese, the country's dominant ethnic group.

The Uighurs practice a moderate form of Islam, but they are fiercely protective of their cultural identity. For decades they had chafed under Communist restrictions on their religion and resented the influx of Han Chinese immigrants that the government had helped settle in predominantly Uighur cities, including Gulja, near the Kazakh border. The more the Chinese government cracked down on political and cultural expression, the more assertive the Uighurs had become. And though relatively rare, there had been bombings and other acts of violence aimed at the government by Uighur separatists, or "splittists," as the Chinese called them. In the late 1990s, as a form of collective punishment, government authorities held mass execution "rallies," requiring thousands of Uighurs to attend. The official media explained the gruesome rituals as "killing one to frighten thousands." In 1997 nine Uighur men were executed in Gulja for separatist activities. Protests ensued, which led to a massive police crackdown in which thousands of Uighurs were arrested and many were tortured by government agents.

It was in this climate of fear and repression that young Uighur men began looking for ways to escape China in search of better lives, and in some cases to train to strike back at their oppressors. Among them were Abdul Sabour and Abdul Semet. Sabour grew up on a farm near Aksu, along the Northern Silk Road. As he came of age and learned that he could practice his religion and cultural traditions freely outside China, he looked for a way out. Inspired by covert US radio broadcasts, he set off for America. He made it as far as Kyrgyzstan before being robbed by the local police. Semet left his home in the rugged mountains of Xinjiang, hoping to tell the world "what is happening to the Uighurs." He ended up in Pakistan, where he was threatened with deportation back to China.

By the summer of 2001, Sabour, Semet, and others of their countrymen had found their way to a ramshackle Uighur camp in Afghanistan's remote White Mountains. There they did manual labor, studied the Koran, and helped build a mosque. According to US intelligence, the camp was run by a shadowy figure named Abdul Haq, a Uighur separatist who fed their imaginations with romantic tales of rebellion and liberation. They received rudimentary training, learning to assemble and disassemble the camp's lone, aging AK-47. They had limited target practice with limited ammunition. It was a spartan existence, but the men shared a natural camaraderie and were largely left to themselves. That changed in mid-October, when American warplanes began their air assault on Afghanistan.

On October 12, American bombs rained from the sky, destroying the camp and much of the surrounding area. In the chaos and confusion, a number of the camp members fled into the mountains of Tora Bora. For nearly a month they took shelter in caves, foraging for food, and trekked through snowy mountain passes searching for safe havens. They eventually followed a group of Arab men across the border into Pakistan, where they were taken in by local villagers. The Uighurs were welcomed as guests; tribesmen slaughtered and roasted a sheep in their honor. But it was a ruse: the men were soon lured to a nearby mosque, where they were sold to the US military for $5,000 a head, bounties the Americans had promised in leaflets dropped all over the region. Six months later, they were sent to Gitmo.

It didn't take long for American officials to realize that the twenty-two Uighurs held at Guantánamo posed no threat to the United States. By late 2003 the US military had determined that at least fifteen of them could be released. But the Uighurs presented a unique challenge. They could not be sent back to their homeland because, although China had called for their repatriation, the Chinese government had branded them terrorists, and they would face almost certain imprisonment, torture, and possibly execution upon return to the country. The Bush State Department tried, largely without success, to resettle the Uighurs in more than one hundred countries, but US officials could not overcome the diplomatic and commercial clout wielded around the world by China. (Albania accepted five of the detainees for resettlement in 2006.)

Shortly after arriving at Guantánamo, many of the men had been told by their interrogators that they were innocent, and that they'd soon be free to go. "Congratulations, your interrogation is complete, you are innocent, you will be leaving soon," a military interrogator told Abdul Semet in April 2003. And yet by the time Obama took office, not only did the seventeen Uighur detainees remaining at Guantánamo continue to endure their nightmarish imprisonment, the conditions of their confinement had gotten much worse. The loneliness, endless tedium, and the feeling of abandonment by the world were soul crushing, according to one of their lawyers.

For Obama, the Uighurs represented an opportunity. To his core, he believed that the fear-mongering approach of the previous administration had diminished America's ability to fight a smarter, tougher, and more just war on terror. Could he roll back the "color-coded politics of fear," as he had vowed in 2007? In closing Guantánamo, the United States would have to admit at least some prisoners into the country. How could America expect its allies to accept detainees if we were not willing to do so ourselves? Why not the Uighurs? They had no history of violence against the United States. Moreover, by the time Obama was elected, they had all been ordered released by the US courts.

For Greg Craig, all of these practical considerations were important. But as he learned about the Uighurs' saga he became driven by more elemental concerns: basic justice and human rights. The more Craig thought about the Uighurs, the more he began to see them as a solution rather than a problem. Legally, their cases had been resolved by the courts; they represented at most a minimal threat to US security; and as for the politics, Craig thought that resettling them in America, integrating them into some leafy suburban community, could drive a knife through the myth that all of the detainees at Guantánamo were dangerous, hardened terrorists — the worst of the worst, as Dick Cheney had put it.

The idea of resettling the Uighurs in the United States had been percolating at lower levels since the transition. But it wasn't until a snowy morning in early March that Matt Olsen, head of the Guantánamo task force, learned that the idea had a powerful advocate in the

West Wing of the White House. Summoned to a breakfast meeting by Craig, Olsen at first wondered whether he was in trouble. Lately he'd had some sharp exchanges with White House aides who were frustrated that his team hadn't begun clearing detainees for release or transfer. The clock was ticking on the Guantánamo deadline, and the White House wanted action. Olsen thought the White House didn't yet grasp the complexity of the detainee decisions. There were some pretty bad dudes down there, after all.

As they walked into the elegant dining room of the Hay-Adams hotel, Olsen, who grew up in Rockville, Maryland, felt as out of place as the patrician Craig seemed at home. But Craig, with his bonhomie and avuncular manner, quickly put Olsen at ease. He asked how the task force was going and whether he had all the resources he needed. Then he turned the conversation to the Uighurs and the prospect of bringing them into the country. Craig outlined the pragmatic policy arguments for the plan, but his voice rose with conviction when he talked about what the Uighurs had endured in the name of America's war on terror. He thought they had been grievously wronged. Craig told Olsen: "You need to go down and meet with the Uighurs. You need to have looked them in the eye." Olsen's first reaction was mildly scornful; was Craig one of those defense lawyers who operated on intuition, who thought you could peer into the soul of a man to determine whether he was good or evil, innocent or guilty? But on reflection he realized that Craig was thinking strategically. He understood that resettling Guantánamo detainees in an American community carried political risks. When the inevitable questions arose, they'd better be able to tell the Republicans or the press that they'd personally interviewed prisoners up for release.

Back in the task force offices at Tysons Corner, Olsen's team was sharply divided over the Uighur detainees. The rank-and-file agents assigned from Homeland Security and the FBI were especially opposed to bringing them in. They viewed their mandate narrowly: keep terrorists out of the country. They were not impressed with the highfalutin foreign policy and diplomatic arguments that Obama officials were making. Moreover, they knew it would be their asses on the line if one of these men attacked American citizens or blew up the Chinese embassy. Still, Craig forged ahead, quietly putting in motion a plan to transfer the Uighurs to Northern Virginia, where there was a large expat community.

On March 31, 2009, Andrew Tannenbaum, a Justice Department lawyer on the Olsen task force, stepped off a C-17 transport plane onto the Guantánamo airstrip. Accompanied by two FBI agents, Tannenbaum had flown down to interview the Uighur prisoners individually. The task force had already assembled detailed threat assessments for each detainee. But now, FBI interrogators, trained to bond with their subjects, wanted to discern the Uighurs' state of mind and whether they were, in any way, prone to violence. Did they, for example, harbor hostility toward America after seven years of wrongful imprisonment, and might that make them vulnerable to recruitment by terrorists? The agents, in effect, were trying to peer into the souls of the detainees, as Craig had instructed.

The interviews took place in a sparsely furnished prefabricated trailer. Tannenbaum began each one-hour session with a short introduction: "As you know, President Obama has ordered the closure of Guantánamo," he would explain. Then the FBI agents commenced their questioning of each detainee. There was little about the men that seemed threatening. What stood out, though, was how apprehensive the Uighurs were about coming to the United States. Could they go to Europe or Canada instead, they wanted to know. America had branded them as terrorists. The military had even allowed Chinese security agents to interrogate the Uighurs at Guantánamo. If they came to America, they feared they'd be attacked in the streets. Only one of the detainees had exhibited any serious behavioral problems. Before his interview, he sheepishly warned the agents that he was given to outbursts he could not control. It was a Tourette's-like condition that the Uighurs called "Jin," a Muslim concept akin to being possessed by evil spirits. As predicted, in the middle of the interview he let loose with a torrent of profanities. "Fuck fuck fuck you, Osama bin Laden," he erupted, before being pacified by his lawyer.

Even as planning for the Uighurs' transfer progressed, the task force remained splintered. The dispute would have to be resolved by the Principals Committee, the president's top national security advisers. A meeting was set for April 14, and as with the inaugural meeting of the Guantánamo task force, it was to take place in the attorney general's conference room, with Holder presiding. But on the morning of the fourteenth, Olsen and his DOJ colleagues were directed to come to the White House instead. Justice Department officials suspected Rahm Emanuel was behind the move. It seemed to grate on White House staffers that Holder was presiding over a meeting of the Obama war council at Justice. Was the AG being sent a message — that the White House was the ultimate decider where sensitive national security policies were concerned?

Before heading over to the meeting, a Holder aide called the White House Counsel's office to remind staff that the executive order designated the attorney general chair of the president's task force and that it was his meeting to run; at the risk of pettiness, the attorney general's aides insisted that he sit at the head of the table. They understood the importance of optics, that once you start losing the perception of power, real power begins to slip away. A White House staffer said not to read anything into the venue change. It was a matter of convenience; there was another important White House meeting immediately following the Uighur session. But when they arrived in the Situation Room, Holder and his aides noticed a new name card on the table, and it was in the head position: "Mr. Emanuel."

Among the top security officials there to discuss the fate of seventeen Chinese Muslims were FBI Director Robert Mueller; Janet Napolitano, the director of Homeland Security; Dennis Blair, the director of national intelligence; and John Brennan, the White House counterterrorism adviser. When CIA Director Leon Panetta ambled into the room, he shrugged and said with a certain world-weary bemusement, "Boy what a mess this is going to be." Panetta, whose career in government stretched back to the Johnson administration, sensed intuitively that the polarized politics of terrorism could overwhelm the Uighur plan.

Other than Panetta's sardonic observation, the meeting was almost entirely free of overt political considerations. There were, however, strong institutional agendas on display. Mueller, whose agency would surely be held accountable if the Uighurs defied all expectations and turned to violence, was opposed to resettling the detainees in the United States. Mueller raised the remote possibility of an attack on the Chinese embassy. But the more persuasive argument in bureaucratic-minded Washington had to do with funding. Mueller asserted that the bureau would have to keep the Uighurs under surveillance "24/7." That would require a huge expenditure of FBI resources, millions of dollars per detainee, he claimed. Greg Craig marveled at the FBI director's chutzpah. Panetta, a former budget director under Bill Clinton, merely smiled and said, "I have to question your numbers, Bob." Mueller jokingly backpedaled: "It's not fair having a former budget director in the room." Napolitano, like Mueller, was preoccupied with parochial concerns. The Uighurs, admitted into the country under the immigration laws, would technically be under Department of Homeland Security supervision. During the debate about the numbers, she said, "One would be better than two." But the clear implication to everyone in the room was that "zero would be better than one." Holder, on the other hand, was strongly in favor of the plan, making the pragmatic argument that resettling the Uighurs in the United States was the key to persuading other countries to take in detainees.

Risk averse and bureaucratic minded, no one at the table made the argument that the Uighur resettlement plan was a matter of decency and justice. Until John Brennan spoke: "They're not US [citizens], but let's face it, they spent seven years of their lives at Gitmo and we have an obligation to them." He continued: "Every day, people are released from prison, with risk. But we do it because we're a country of laws. We own a piece of this and it will be costly but we have to step up to our obligations." It was an early sign that Brennan, the dour and tough-minded spy, would prove to be one of the most committed civil libertarians in Obama's inner circle. Napolitano, an expert at reading the prevailing political winds, muted her concerns. Mueller, who believed that his role was to give his best advice if asked, not to make policy, also relented. At the end of the meeting, Emanuel reviewed the bidding: None of the principals would oppose the transfer of at least a small number of Uighurs to the United States. In the chief of staff's formulation, they would be allowed in "two by two, up to eight." The lawyers from Justice and Homeland Security were dispatched to Guantánamo to seal the deal with the first two Uighur detainees.

Around this time, two lawyers representing the detainees, Sabin Willett and Susan Baker Manning, met with attorneys at the Department of Homeland Security to begin discussing the outlines of an agreement. David Martin, a senior lawyer at DHS, informed the attorneys that the government would be willing to accept just two of the

Uighur detainees for resettlement in the United States. "If you guys are up for that, we need to talk about the conditions," he told the Uighurs' representatives. Willett, a Boston bankruptcy lawyer who had taken up the Guantánamo case as a personal cause, pushed for the release of four of his clients, but ultimately accepted two, figuring the government needed to start slowly. Martin then laid out the conditions of the men's resettlement: they would be prohibited from going to any government locations; they'd have to wear electronic monitoring bracelets; they would be required to check in on a daily basis with parole officers, and they would not be allowed to possess firearms of any kind. Willett thought the conditions were absurd. But again, he understood that the administration needed the political cover. Meanwhile, he began thinking about a public relations strategy to present his exotic clients in a favorable light. He'd start with a media blitz, perhaps even profiles on *60 Minutes*. "If people saw these guys working at some suburban dry cleaner, they'd say, 'What's the big deal?'"

The White House understood that the plan to bring Muslim detainees into the United States — even a small number of men who had been ordered released by the courts — was rife with political danger. Every step had to be planned, every public statement carefully vetted; the timing of the announcement was crucial. Schedules were scoured to find out whether there were any other announcements or public appearances that could threaten the administration's control of the narrative. At an April 16 planning session, White House, Justice, and Homeland Security officials went through the political calendar looking for a clear day. Justice wanted to move as quickly as possible, to avoid leaks that could scuttle the operation. Dan Pfeiffer, the deputy White House communications director, suggested Wednesday, April 29, but that day was quickly set aside when staff were reminded that it was Obama's one hundredth day in office. Although Press

Secretary Robert Gibbs had dismissed the milestone as a "Hallmark holiday," White House aides were acutely aware of its symbolism, especially for a president who had drawn comparison to FDR. Matt Miller mentioned that Holder's first congressional appropriations hearing was coming up. The immediate consensus was that nothing should be announced with respect to the Uighurs before Holder had got past the hearing. The last thing the White House wanted was for the attorney general to be bombarded with questions about a plan to bring Guantánamo detainees into the country.

There was good reason to worry. On April 22, a wet, dreary Wednesday afternoon, Olsen and representatives from two other Justice Department task forces trekked up to Capitol Hill to meet with Frank Wolf, a Republican congressman from Virginia who sat on the key subcommittee that controlled the Justice Department's budget. For weeks, Wolf had been badgering Justice for a briefing on Guantánamo. Under strict White House orders, Justice officials had been putting him off. It was another example of the White House's skittishness toward Congress on terrorism policy: Obama's desire to do the right thing was a political challenge, and White House aides just didn't want to face it. But Holder was scheduled to testify before the congressman's panel in the coming days, so his aides decided they could not wait any longer. In a ritual commonly practiced before executive branch officials go up to testify, they responded to Wolf's letters, scurried around researching his pet issues, and finally gave him his Gitmo briefing.

A cantankerous and volatile thirty-year veteran of Congress, Wolf was not easily mollified. Olsen could barely get through his boilerplate introduction before the congressman laid into him. "How are you going to close Guantánamo? Where's your plan?" Then he zeroed in on his real concern. He didn't want any terrorists tried in his district, which was near Alexandria, where the federal courthouse was located. "There are people who work and live down there," he pointed out, yelling now and naming individual shop owners and merchants, who also happened to be his constituents. "We're not going to shut that part of town down. That's not going to happen."

At that moment one of Wolf's aides leaned over and reminded him about the Uighurs. Wolf perked up. He had heard about the administration's plan, most likely a leak from the FBI, which had assiduously stroked him for years, since he controlled its budget. He asked Olsen about the proposed resettlement. Anticipating the question, Olsen had prepared a careful answer: "Sir, we are working very hard on the Uighurs," he said. "I'm not prepared to talk about any specific decisions about any of the detainees." That sent Wolf into a full-blown diatribe. "They're terrorists," he spluttered. "They're not coming to Northern Virginia, they're not coming to the United States." His face red with rage, Wolf vowed to "go to the floor" of the House every day to denounce the Uighurs — and Olsen.

Olsen staggered out of the House office building into the damp, chill air. He'd never gotten a lashing like that from a member of Congress. A White House lobbyist attended the meeting, so word of the Wolf debacle spread quickly among Obama's top political advisers. They were not pleased. The ban on congressional briefings on Guantánamo was reissued.

On April 24 Obama and his top national security advisers gathered in the Situation Room for a status report on Guantánamo. Facing a looming deadline, the president wanted to know: when would they shut down the prison? Only forty-eight hours after his collision with Wolf, Olsen now had to brief the commander in chief.

As Olsen began his carefully prepared presentation, Vice President Joe Biden swiveled away from him and began kibitzing with an aide seated against the wall. Olsen tried to stay focused on his talking points, but Biden was a famous motormouth. Obama had seen it before, sometimes in the gravest settings, including his weekly "Terror Tuesday" counterterrorism briefings. Now, the president, who often took notes during his briefings, put down his pen and said, "Wait a minute. Wait a minute. Wait a minute," each time with more irritation in his voice. He turned and glowered at the vice president, saying nothing, waiting for his constitutional successor to notice — as a school teacher might handle a puerile child. Biden kept yakking. Finally, Obama slapped him on the arm. "Joe, the guy's trying to talk. Pay attention." Nervous laugher echoed in the room.

Olsen quickly got back on track and started breaking down the numbers for Obama — how many detainees could be resettled in other countries, how many could be released, and how many could be prosecuted either in civilian courts or military commissions. "What about the Europeans?" Obama asked. "How many detainees will they take?" At the opposite end of the table, Ambassador Daniel Fried was looking at his own numbers. They were not encouraging. Fried, as the soon-to-be-named Special Envoy for Guantánamo Closure, had the unenviable job of trying to persuade the Europeans to accept detainees for resettlement. He'd anticipated the president's question and used it as an opportunity to make a point he believed was the linchpin to closing the detention facility. "If we're willing to take a small number of detainees, I can resettle sixty or sixty-five. If we don't take any we'll be lucky to get between thirty-five and forty," he told the president. A lot depended on the Uighurs. Phil Schiliro, the president's liaison to Congress, suggested Olsen tell Obama about his meeting with Frank Wolf. Obama looked up and asked: "Who's Frank Wolf? I've never head of him." Biden, with a wave of his hand, dismissed Wolf as insignificant.

Later that week, Eric Holder traveled to London, Prague, and Berlin, nominally for a series of ministerial meetings. His real agenda was pressing the Europeans to take some Guantánamo detainees, including a number of Uighurs. In a speech at the American Academy in Berlin on April 29, Holder declared a bright new day in the transatlantic alliance, darkened during the Bush years. Then he made his pitch. "To close Guantánamo, we must all be willing to make sacrifices and we must all be ready to make unpopular choices . . . The United States is willing to do its part and we hope that Europe will join us — not out of a sense of responsibility but from a commitment to work with one of its closest allies to confront one of the world's most pressing challenges."

Earlier in the day, Fried and Olsen had made the rounds at the German Foreign Office. The Germans had known Fried well from his days as assistant secretary of state for Europe during the Bush administration. In London, Paris, and Rome, European policymakers had haughtily lectured him about Guantánamo and America's disdain for human rights and international law. Now, Fried thought, let the Europeans strike a blow for the rule of law by agreeing to resettle some of the Uighur detainees. But European moral outrage only went so far. Behind the scenes, Beijing was applying intense counterpressure, warning that any nation taking in Uighur detainees would place a "heavy burden on bilateral relations," according to a cable revealed by WikiLeaks. That was diplospeak for putting at risk lucrative commercial contracts and military deals. The Germans heeded the warning and refused to take a single Uighur.

On that same day, thousands of miles away, Sabin Willett and Susan Baker Manning were meeting with Abdul Semet and Huzaifa Parhat in Guantánamo. The two detainees had been approved for resettlement in the United States, their lawyers told them. Semet and Parhat had to agree to monitoring, surveillance, and certain restrictions on their movements in exchange for being resettled in Virginia. Willett handed them the agreements, which had been authorized by two government attorneys. After at first balking, the Uighur prisoners agreed to the terms and signed the documents.

Back in Washington, news of the administration's plan to bring in the Uighurs had begun to leak to the press. Frank Wolf seized the moment, first in a May 1 letter to President Obama registering his "grave concerns" about the plan. Three days later Wolf took to the floor of the House and reminded his colleagues that all politics are local, even when it comes to the scourge of global terrorism: "Let me be clear," Wolf bellowed. "These terrorists would not be held in prisons, but they would be released into your neighborhoods. They should not be released into the United States. Do members realize who these people are?" Mitch McConnell, the Republican majority leader, smelled blood. For two weeks, he attacked the administration nearly every day, echoing Wolf. Nor was the wildfire contained to the GOP caucus. Eventually, the Democrats' leader in the Senate, perhaps Obama's closest ally in Washington, joined the uprising in a true nightmare for the White House political staff. "We don't want them around," Harry Reid declared. A week before, Barack Obama had no idea who Frank Wolf was. Now Wolf was leading a fear-induced insurrection in Congress that threatened one of the president's most high-profile campaign promises. On terrorism, it was becoming increasingly clear, the politics of fear were as strong as ever. How hard would Obama fight? How much political capital was he willing to expend to push back against Congress?

In early May, Obama wasn't in a fighting mood; he was just peeved. How could he have been so badly sandbagged? he asked incredulously at a meeting of his senior advisers. Obama understood that terrorism was a wedge issue and that Republicans, much in the way they'd exploited urban crime in the '70s and '80s, would use it for all it was worth. He was perfectly aware of the trap that was being laid for him, and yet he cared about these issues and wanted to strike a balance between security and liberty, and also meet his timeline as laid out in the executive order. Moreover, as a black man, in the debate about the Uighurs he surely heard echoes of the civil rights struggles of the past. His favorite quote from Martin Luther King Jr. acknowledged that the march toward progress is slow and deliberate: "The arc of the moral universe is long but it bends toward justice."

Rahm Emanuel had a decidedly less nuanced view of the matter: "It's not a move forward issue. It's a clean up the last guy's mess issue," he told one West Wing colleague. Emanuel wasn't a lawyer, and he had little patience for pesky legal issues, especially ones that were politically risky. His job, as he saw it, was keeping the president focused on the Main Chance, reforming health care while fighting two wars and staving off a depression. Guantánamo was just a pain-in-the-ass distraction, he told Craig. "We are trying to bring in two 747s [the wars in Afghanistan and Iraq] at the same time we are trying to reform our national health care system, and right in the middle you want to send up a flock of Canadian geese, which is Guantánamo, which could take down one of those 747s."

The shrewd chief of staff knew how best to frame presidential choices. The Uighurs provided a case study for how he operated. In the spring of 2009, a supplemental appropriations bill to keep the government running was working its way through the House and Senate just as the Uighur issue was exploding. There were two versions in the works, but both restricted funding to bring detainees into the United States. Both also included a $1.1 trillion loan package for the International Monetary Fund that Obama had promised the Group of 20, the international body comprising the world's biggest industrial and emerging economies, in London a few weeks before. Emanuel framed the choice starkly: You can secure funding for the IMF in the midst of a global economic crisis. Or you can have your detainee funding. "You can't have both," Emanuel said emphatically.

Framed that way, Obama had little choice but to save the world from financial doom.

By May 2009, Greg Craig was a badly diminished figure within the White House. He was cut out of meetings, and his access to the president was practically nonexistent. Craig's efforts on behalf of the Uighurs drew derision from Emanuel and David Axelrod, who thought it had grown into an obsession. He only learned about the president's souring on the Uighur plan through chance encounters. One day, Craig bumped into Axelrod in the hallway near the senior adviser's West Wing office. When Craig raised the subject of the Uighurs, Axelrod began shaking his head. "The president is against it," he told Craig. "He doesn't want it to happen. He hates it."

Craig was stunned. Less than a month before, the Principals Committee had unanimously endorsed his plan. Now, in its first confrontation with Congress over detainees, the White House was folding without any resistance. If they don't have the stomach to take two innocent Uighurs, where would they find the political will to shut down Gitmo? he wondered. But Craig had a more immediate problem: on his watch, the United States government had signed a formal agreement with two Guantánamo detainees, allowing them to enter the country. Craig realized the disastrous implications. The Uighurs had a potentially enforceable contract. Their lawyers could go into court and force their transfer to the United States. At the very least, it would be a PR nightmare. At the same time, Craig realized that Obama had been poorly briefed on the matter. Did he know about the agreement? Did he know that his national security team had carefully considered the pros and cons of bringing in the two Uighur detainees, and had reached consensus? Craig decided to draft a memo to the president, laying out the background. To refresh his own memory he called Matt Olsen, pulling him out of a meeting in the Justice Department's secure Command Center. His tone was urgent and agitated. He wanted a timeline of the Uighur decision-making process and he wanted it fast. "A lot depends on this," he told Olsen. And then, more as if to reassure himself than Olsen, he proclaimed it "a good process." Olsen figured out what was happening: the Uighur plan was cratering.

The next morning, Craig drafted a two-page memo to Obama, laying out the timeline that had led to the Uighur decision. "As you think about what should be done about the Uighurs, it might be helpful for you to be familiar with the history and the process that has brought us to where we are," the memo said. Craig consciously did not want the memo to be an advocacy document; but that did not mean it wasn't meant to advance an agenda. Throughout the memo Craig carefully pointed out that at virtually every step of the way, consensus was reached and that all of the key decisions were made in the presence of the president's top advisers. To underscore the point, Craig cc'd the memo to Emanuel, Axelrod, Denis McDonough, White House Deputy Chief of Staff for Policy Mona Sutphen, Phil Schiliro, Robert Gibbs, and John Brennan. Then, after attaching the signed Uighur agreements, Craig sent the memo on to the president.

Soon thereafter, Craig was invited to attend Obama's senior advisers meeting for the first time. This was the president's inner sanctum, made up of hardcore Obamaites like Emanuel, Axelrod, Valerie Jarrett, and Robert Gibbs. In an uncharacteristic loss of composure, Obama snapped at Craig about the Uighur situation. "Greg, you put me in a jam," he said. "How could you have given them this contract without my approval?" Craig responded that Obama's inner circle had all known about and signed off on it. But it was too late. The narrative about Craig had already been written: it was another legal and political mess that he should have headed off before it landed on the president's desk. Craig would last in the White House for another eight months, but after a presidential dressing-down in front of the staff, the stench of death was all around him. It was a matter of weeks before the first anonymous leaks forecasting Craig's departure began appearing in the newspapers. There were undoubtedly other reasons for Craig's eventual demise, but the prevailing story would be that he sacrificed his White House career for the freedom of a handful of Uighurs.

On May 19, Sabin Willett was in Washington on other business when he got an urgent message from Craig asking him to come to the White House. Sitting with Willett in his stately, wood-paneled office, Craig got to the point quickly. "Sabin, we can't do it. We can't bring in the Uighurs." Willett couldn't believe it. "What do you mean? I've got a contract. I've got an agreement. I've got Martin's [David Martin, deputy general counsel for the Department of Homeland Security] name in ink on a deal that says you're doing it." It was playing out just as Craig had feared. "I've got ninety-eight senators against this; we can't do it," Craig shot back. The two trial lawyers went into heavy sparring mode. "I'm going to sue you," Willett threatened. "I'm going to court." Craig bluffed back: "You're not going to win. This would be a terrible mistake." Willett conceded the point, but then showed he could play politics as well. "I'm going to go to court because your boss is going to have to say that these people don't threaten anybody; that's why he approved this deal. Why else would he do it?"

The next day, Craig was approached by Michael Strautmanis, from the White House's Office of Public Engagement. Earlier that morning Strautmanis had met with Ewart Brown, the premier of Bermuda, who happened to be visiting Washington. He indicated that Brown, unprompted, had offered to take some of Guantánamo's Uighur detainees. Did Craig want to talk to him? Strautmanis asked. "Absolutely," Craig said, thunderstruck by this unlikely bit of divine intervention. The following day, Brown met with Craig at the White

House, and the two men began hammering out a deal. That began a cloak-and-dagger operation that became known to the small group of participants as "the Wild Ride." Knowledge was limited to a tiny contingent that included Obama, Emanuel, Hillary Clinton, Robert Gates, Craig, and Fried. Brown insisted they move quickly, under a heavy blanket of secrecy. As a British colony, Bermuda does not have autonomy over its foreign policy and national security. Brown was sure that if word got out, the British government would pull the plug on the plan in order not to alienate China. Keeping London out of the loop was a serious diplomatic breach, but Brown was willing to take the risk — especially for the chance to ingratiate himself with America's rapturously popular new president.

Craig turned to Fried to work out the diplomatic and security details with David Burch, Bermuda's interior minister. The plan was finalized on June 10 at Cabinet House, the colonial government building in Hamilton, Bermuda's capital. Craig was there, along with Fried, Burch, Willett, and Susan Baker Manning, the attorney representing the Uighurs. The Bermudans wanted Craig in attendance, so that if something went wrong he could mobilize the White House. There was one other key figure present: Art Collins, a Washington lobbyist-cum-fixer, who represented Bermuda, brokered the negotiations. Discreet, efficient, and action-oriented, Collins essentially ran the operation. The fate of the four Uighur detainees Bermuda agreed to take in now would be determined by a single lobbyist, under cover of darkness, without the knowledge of Bermuda's governing body.

The plan was to fly down to Guantánamo that evening in a plane chartered by the Bermudans. But there was a problem: the pilot lacked the necessary certificate to make the harrowing nighttime landing on Gitmo's sliver of an airstrip. That was when Collins snapped into action. "Goddamnit, I'll find a plane," he growled, grabbing his cell phone. Within a few hours, a Gulfstream V executive jet was on its way from Teterboro, New Jersey. The group was "wheels up" by 1 A.M. They landed in Guantánamo a little before 3, in pitch darkness, save for some runway edge lights and a floodlight trained on the US soldiers waiting to greet them. Twenty minutes later, a bus rolled onto the tarmac and four Uighur detainees got off—Abdul Semet, Huzaifa Parhat, Abdul Nasser, and Jalal Jaladin. Baker Manning, who had been restrained throughout the legal proceedings, let out an enormous whoop. With that, the formal military handover, dutifully filmed for posterity, got under way.

An officer held up massive photographs of the four detainees for identity confirmation. A guard then snipped the men's plastic cuffs and told them they were free to go. As the Uighurs climbed up the gangway, Craig told their lawyers they were to sit in the back of the plane; the Americans would sit up front between the Uighurs and the cockpit. After all this, Willett thought to himself, there was still September 11 resonance. On the plane, the mood was buoyant. The Uighurs ate sandwiches, drank Cokes, and practiced their broken English. Craig sacked out in the aisle. Two hours later, as the morning light broke over the Atlantic Ocean, the G-V banked hard toward Hamilton airport. The Uighurs looked down at the turquoise waters. "Are those dolphins?" one of the men asked in broken English. "Is that the ocean?" Stepping off the plane, the newly free men each kneeled down and kissed the earth.

In the months to come, the former Guantánamo detainees would thrive in Bermuda. They worked at the Port Royal Golf Course, where they tended the greens and fairways, went fishing on the weekends, and played soccer with the locals. Their biggest preoccupation seemed to be finding Uighur women to marry. The Brits were furious, having been hoodwinked by their island territory. Foreign Secretary David Miliband called Hillary Clinton to register his government's protest, and in a personal aside, promised to "strangle"

Fried. The British governor in Bermuda launched an investigation to determine whether the Uighurs posed a security threat of any kind. It came up empty. For their parts, Craig and Fried felt vindicated. But the experience also left them with a sense of foreboding: "The Uighurs were a hinge point of history," Craig would say later, somewhat grandiosely. "It was a demonstration that we did not really have the political will to deal with Guantánamo." Fried, whose puckish humor helped him navigate the crosscurrents of politics and principle in his work, quoted a line from the sci-fi send-up *Men in Black* to make the point: "There's always an Arquillian Battle Cruiser, or a Corillian Death Ray, or an intergalactic plague that is about to wipe out all life on this miserable little planet." Fried then gave the Washington translation: "You always have people against you. You always have unfair editorials from somebody. Fight, don't run. You've got to mean it."

5

KILL OR CAPTURE

WHILE WASHINGTON WAS erupting in partisan fury over Guantánamo and detainees, the war on terror was accelerating in quiet, distant, yet deadly fashion.

Barack Obama's ferocious campaign of targeted killings was for many the central paradox of his war on terror. While running for president, he had railed against waterboarding, illegal detentions, and the Bush administration's penchant for secrecy. In lofty speeches, he promised to restore America's reputation as a benign superpower, a paragon of international law and human rights. But a year into his presidency, the most noticeable strategic shift in his fight against al-Qaeda was the unrelenting use of hard, lethal power in the form of the CIA's covert drone program. By the time Obama accepted the Nobel Peace Prize in December 2009, he had authorized more drone strikes than George W. Bush had approved during his entire presidency. (There were only 9 strikes conducted in Pakistan between 2004 and 2007. In 2010 there were 111.) By his third year in office,

Obama had approved the killings of twice as many suspected terrorists as had ever been imprisoned at Guantánamo Bay. There was little doubt that the program was effective as a tactic; drone strikes routinely killed high-value targets on the CIA's hit parade. And the scores of lower- and midlevel militants that were being eliminated devastated al-Qaeda's morale and seriously diminished its ability to train terrorists and plan operations. "We're killing these sons of bitches faster than they can grow them," the *Washington Post* quoted a CIA veteran relaying the boast of the agency's counterrorism chief.

Less clear was the strategic value of the program. Drone strikes alone would not roll back what Obama called in one campaign speech "the tide of hopelessness" that drew Pakistani boys to radicalism. By 2010 Brennan and Panetta would make the case to Obama that the punishing strikes in Pakistan would lead to the "strategic dismantlement" of al-Qaeda's core organization. Still, people who have spoken to Obama about the drone program say he was under no illusion that it would "win" the war on al-Qaeda. But Obama believed he had to stay focused not only on the big picture but also on the individual terrorist who might slip US defenses and attack the homeland. What Americans did not see was how much time the president spent dealing with potential threats. "You live in that office every minute with the realization that you have lives that are depending on your judgments," recalled David Axelrod. Drones may not have been a panacea, but they were an awfully seductive tool. "The president is skeptical that kinetic strikes will end the war on terror," said one of his closest counterterrorism advisers. "But he is not skeptical that they can stop a terrorist who is planning to kill Americans in Times Square."

The targeted killing program has been heavily criticized among human rights groups and international organizations, which question both the wisdom and legality of the strikes. The UN's rapporteur for extrajudicial killings called the operations potential "war crimes." And although the number of noncombatant deaths was hotly contested, the perception that drone attacks were indiscriminately targeting civilians in Pakistan inflamed anti-American sentiment throughout the Muslim world. Top US law enforcement officials worried that Muslim Americans would turn their rage on their own country. By 2010, there was evidence to support their concerns: both Najibullah Zazi, the Afghan coffee vendor who plotted to attack the New York subway system, and Faisal Shahzad, the failed Times Square bomber, said they were, in part, motivated by drone strikes in their ancestral homelands.

Still, anyone who had listened carefully to what Obama said during the campaign should not have been surprised about his administration's embrace of the drone program. "I will not hesitate to use force to take out terrorists who pose a direct threat to America," he said in August 2007. "I will ensure that the military becomes more stealthy, agile, and lethal in its ability to capture or kill terrorists." If capturing was proving to be difficult, killing was much easier.

For much of his first year in office, Republicans persisted — and often succeeded — in portraying Obama as weak and bumbling in his approach to counterterrorism. What was less perceptible was how quickly and intuitively Obama had taken to the shadowy world of intelligence and special operations. Obama had not served in the military; he didn't don bomber jackets when he visited the troops as routinely as George Bush had; and early on in his presidency he looked self-conscious saluting as he stepped off Air Force One. (It took some time for him to master the art of the crisp presidential salute.) But nor was Obama, the first US president to have come of age after the Vietnam War, plagued by chronic self-doubt about the use of force. During the transition, he'd explored the morality of drone strikes with John Brennan and Denis McDonough, both Jesuit-educated Catholics who opposed the death penalty. But there were few signs that he had serious qualms about the program. One columnist called Obama the "covert commander in chief" for his proclivity to operate under the radar and, when necessary, with lethality.

Obama did not enter office in thrall to the CIA. The botched January 23, 2009, strike in South Waziristan that had killed an innocent tribal elder and several of his family members had made him wary at first. But he learned quickly that the agency's operational capabilities were well suited to his strategic goal — taking high-ranking al-Qaeda and Taliban operatives off the battlefield while shrinking America's footprint in the region. For its part, the CIA took great care to make sure Obama was up to speed on its latest successes and capabilities. In early 2009, Panetta, accompanied by undercover officers from the agency's counterterrorism division, continued the president's crash course on kinetic operations, giving Obama a detailed Oval Office briefing on the drone program. The elaborate presentation was designed to highlight successful kills, but also to show the care and precision with which the operations were carried out. Obama learned about the intricate set of permissions that were required before the trigger could be pulled on a strike. Panetta explained to him how CIA operators watch potential targets for hours to determine their "patterns of life," helping them distinguish between suspected terrorists and civilians. In one video shown to the president, a missile was fired at a militant only to be diverted at the last minute when a noncombatant suddenly appeared in range. The operators called the trick "going cold."

Obama would often take Panetta aside after national security meetings and ask for details about particular strikes. Occasionally he'd call the CIA director in for a full-blown briefing when the CIA had taken out a particularly high-value target. They were an unlikely pair of shadow warriors. Panetta was a garrulous former congressman with no intel background who had left Washington to work his family's walnut farm in California's Carmel Valley. Obama was the onetime community organizer who'd seized the hopes of a war-weary nation with the promise to end American wars of choice. But they were both deeply pragmatic men who quickly came to see the drone program as a potential strategic game-changer in the war on terror.

Though initially skeptical of Panetta's appointment as CIA director, agency veterans learned to appreciate his close ties to Obama. In October 2009 Panetta brought a CIA wish list of counterterrorist requests to a White House Situation Room meeting. He asked Obama for ten items, thinking he might get half of them. At the end of the meeting Obama said: "The CIA gets what it wants." Panetta got everything, including more Predator drones, authority to go after larger "target boxes" in Pakistan (the designated areas in the tribal regions where the CIA was permitted to operate), and increased resources for the agency's secret paramilitary forces. "We're conducting the most aggressive operations in our history as an agency," Panetta would comment. "That largely flows from this president and how he views the role of the CIA."

Obama followed the CIA operations closely, but the program became a quasi obsession for Rahm Emanuel. The White House chief of staff kept tabs on the hunt for high-value targets with an avidity that left even some CIA veterans uncomfortable. He was especially attentive during the summer of 2009 when Predator and Reaper drones were prowling the skies high above the Hindu Kush on the lookout for Baitullah Mehsud, the bloodthirsty leader of the Pakistani Taliban who was believed to be behind the assassination of former prime minister Benazir Bhutto and scores of suicide bombings. The CIA had taken more than a dozen shots without striking their quarry. Emanuel repeatedly called Panetta or his chief of staff, Jeremy

Bash, to see if they'd had a successful hit. When they finally took Mehsud out in August 2009, Emanuel celebrated. He had a hawkish side to him, having volunteered with the Israeli Defense Forces as a civilian during the 1991 Gulf War. But above all, Emanuel recognized that the muscular attacks could have a huge political upside for Obama, insulating him against charges that he was weak on terror. "Rahm was transactional about these operational issues," recalled a senior Pentagon official. "He always wanted to know 'how's this going to help my guy,' the president."

Though the program was covert, Emanuel pushed the CIA to publicize its kinetic successes. When Mehsud was killed, agency public affairs officers anonymously trumpeted their triumph, leaking colorful tidbits to trusted reporters on the intelligence beat. Newspapers described the hit in cinematic detail, including the fact that Mehsud was blown up on the roof of his father-in-law's compound while his wife was massaging his legs.

The question remained: Could the shadow warriors capture terrorists? Or could they only kill them? Around the time of the Mehsud strike, US Special Operations Forces had a bead on a major al-Qaeda terrorist. For years the CIA and military had been hunting Saleh Ali Saleh Nabhan, a senior member of al-Qaeda's East Africa branch and a critical link between al-Qaeda and its Somalia-based affiliate, the Shabab. Nabhan had been implicated in a number of deadly terrorist attacks in East Africa, including the bombing of an Israeli-owned resort in Mombasa, and he was a suspect in the US embassy bombings in Kenya and Tanzania. Taking him out would have been a major victory in the war on terror. But capturing him would have been an even bigger coup, a potentially huge intelligence windfall that could have helped counterterrorism officials understand the connections between al-Qaeda and its offshoots. After months of patiently watching him, intelligence suddenly indicated that Nabhan was preparing to travel along a remote coastal road in southern Somalia. It was time to act.

Highly classified PowerPoint slides were transmitted to key national security precincts around the government, providing background on Nabhan and laying out a series of detailed options for neutralizing the al-Qaeda leader.

Early one September evening, more than three dozen officials assembled by secure videoconference to consider options for the sensitive operation. The meeting was chaired by Admiral Mike Mullen, chairman of the Joint Chiefs. After a short introduction, Mullen called on Vice Admiral William H. McRaven, head of the Joint Special Operations Command and one of the military's most experienced terrorist hunters. Nabhan had been under close surveillance for months. He'd stayed mostly in heavily populated areas, where the risk of casualties, either to civilians or American soldiers, was too great to launch any kind of raid. But now it looked like they had the narrow window of opportunity they had been hoping for.

Nabhan's convoy would soon be setting out from the capital, Mogadishu, on its way to a meeting of Islamic militants in the coastal town of Baraawe. McRaven, a square-jawed Texan and former Navy SEAL, crisply began laying out the concepts of operations that had been developed in anticipation of this moment. Each one specified the military hardware that would be required, as well as collateral-damage estimates. Tomahawk cruise missiles could be fired from a warship off the Somali coast, the least dangerous option in terms of US casualties. Such missile strikes had been a hallmark of the Bush administration. For all of its "dead or alive" rhetoric, the Bush White House was surprisingly risk-averse when it came to antiterrorist operations in lawless areas like Somalia. But the missile strikes were not always effective. Sometimes the missiles went astray, killing civilians, and even when they hit their targets they didn't always take them out. McRaven and the other military men remembered the story a few years back when the navy had fired a cruise missile to take out an al-Qaeda operative sleeping in a shack. The missile struck nearby, but the suspected terrorist "just walked out from under it," according to one participant in the operation.

The second option on the table was a helicopter-borne assault on Nabhan's convoy. There was less chance of error there. Small attack helicopters would allow the commandos to "look the target in the eye and make sure it was the right guy," according to one military planner involved in the Nabhan operation. After the strike, the American commandos would touch down on the ground just long enough to confirm the kill. The final option was a "snatch and grab," a daring attempt to take Nabhan alive. From a purely tactical standpoint it was the most attractive alternative. Intelligence from high-value targets was the coin of the realm in the terror wars. But it was also the riskiest option, requiring significant boots on the ground.

And there was another problem: where would Nabhan be taken if the military succeeded in capturing him? Nine months into its own war on al-Qaeda, the Obama administration had no detention policy for terrorists captured outside established war zones like Afghanistan or Iraq. The CIA was out of the interrogation business, its secret black sites shut down by Obama's executive order. Moving Nabhan to Guantánamo was out of the question, since the administration's committed policy was to transfer detainees out of there, not in. The detention facility at the US air base in Bagram, Afghanistan, wouldn't work either; the White House didn't want the prison to become the new Guantánamo. Turning him over to the host government, as they might have done in Pakistan or Afghanistan, was also not an option in anarchic Somalia. Finally, bringing Nabhan to the United States for prosecution or prolonged detention was a political nonstarter for the Obama White House. Some weeks earlier, Hoss Cartwright, the vice chairman of the Joint Chiefs, had raised with Obama the conundrum they were facing. He warned the president that the military could not afford to be "trapped in a no-quarters environment." Obama did not understand the military idiom. Cartwright explained that under the laws of war the military was required to take the target of an operation into custody if he surrendered or was wounded. "We do not have a plausible capture strategy," Cartwright told the president.

Despite the challenges, the group continued to war-game the possibility of a capture operation. Cartwright said the military's elite forces could execute a "vehicular interdiction." Helicopters would swoop in, allowing a sharpshooter to shoot through the engine block of Nabhan's jeep. The vehicle would die, helicopters would land, and commandoes would grab Nabhan. Then they would stash him on a ship at sea while figuring out what to do with him — "pretty much making it up as we went along," as one participant put it.

Unstated but hanging heavily over the group that evening was the memory of another attempted capture in Somalia. Many on the call that day had been in key national security posts in October 1993 during the ill-fated attempt to capture a Somali warlord, a debacle that left eighteen dead Army Rangers on the streets of Mogadishu and inspired al-Qaeda leaders in thinking that they could defeat the American superpower. Black Hawk Down, as the debacle became known, was a searing event for a generation of military officials and national security policymakers. Bob Gates, who was head of the CIA when US troops first entered Somalia, was now firmly opposed to putting boots on the ground in that chaotic, godforsaken place. As Daniel Benjamin, the State Department's coordinator for counterterrorism, said during the meeting, "Somalia, helicopters, capture. I just don't like the sound of this."

In the end, the president was given a kill option and a capture option. (There was also a contingency plan: dropping a 500-pound bomb from a fixed-wing aircraft, but that possibility was obviated because of cloud cover.) But as everyone left the meeting that evening, it was clear that the only viable plan was the lethal one. That night, Obama signed off on Operation "Celestial Balance." The next morning Somali villagers saw several low-flying attack helicopters emerging over the horizon. Several AH-6 Little Birds, deployed from US naval ships off the Somali coast, approached the convoy, strafing Nabhan's jeep and another vehicle. Nabhan and three other militants were killed. One of the helicopters landed long enough for a small team of commandos to scoop up some of Nabhan's remains — the DNA needed to prove he was dead.

The mission was a success of a sort — a bold daylight raid that showed Obama was willing to take risks to track down and obliterate the enemy. But it also masked deeper concerns. Rumors swirled through the Pentagon that Nabhan had been killed because the White House didn't want to face the tangled and politically fraught detention issues. Jeh C. Johnson, the military's top lawyer, was so concerned, he conducted his own inquiry to satisfy himself that that was not the case. In the end, no direct evidence has ever emerged showing that the decision to pursue a kill over a capture in the Nabhan case was dictated by the lack of a long-term detention policy. Yet participants in the conference call that day realized that over time, the lack of a policy would foreclose important tactical avenues in the war on terror. The inability to detain terror suspects was creating perverse incentives that favored killing or releasing suspected terrorists over capturing them. "We never talked about this openly, but it was always a back-of-the-mind thing for us," recalled one of

Obama's top counterterrorism advisers. "Anyone who says it wasn't is not being straight."

It is a truism that in Washington, policymaking is driven by crisis. The hardest questions get put off until external events force a decision. This is especially the case in national security policy. The Nabhan case was a seminal moment for the administration, spurring more than a year of factious debate about detention policy. At one principals meeting not long after that episode, General Cartwright succinctly summarized the conundrum the government had found itself in. "We shouldn't incentivize kills over captures," he told the group. It was a sentiment echoed by Tom Donilon, the deputy national security adviser who had taken on the unenviable assignment of trying to forge a detention policy. "We can't be left in a situation where the only option for someone who has valuable intelligence is to kill him," he said plaintively at another meeting. "It's just unacceptable to be left with the idea that that's lawful but that a lesser step is not."

The detention dilemma had tugged at Obama from the outset of his presidency. The knot of national security, legal, and political challenges made it one of the most insoluble policy problems in his war on terror. At some level, it was widely accepted within the administration that some form of long-term detention, at least for a subset of Guantánamo prisoners, would be necessary. It was even contemplated in the Guantánamo executive order, which had divided detainees into several distinct categories. Some would be transferred to other countries, some would be prosecuted, and still others, like the Uighurs, would be released. But close readers of the document also noticed Greg Craig's artful use of the phrase "other dispositions," which signaled that some number of detainees would almost certainly have to be held indefinitely. A few weeks after the executive order was signed, in its March 13 brief, the administration's foundational legal document in its war on terror, Obama claimed the authority to hold detainees in prolonged detention without trial. And yet throughout much of his first year in office, the president remained deeply reluctant to embrace such a policy.

Law-of-war detention had been part of the American legal landscape since the country's founding. The principle that combatants can be detained until the end of hostilities to prevent them from returning to the battlefield is as old as warfare itself. And yet to Obama it was not axiomatic that you could simply graft the traditional laws of war onto an unconventional conflict like the war on terror. For one thing, ascertaining who the enemy was and who could be legally detained was a challenge. And how would one determine the end of hostilities against an unconventional, metastasizing force unlikely to ever sign a formal peace treaty? All of these factors vastly increased the chances of accidentally detaining innocents.

In the spring and summer of 2009 Obama was worried about precedent and politics. He knew that as a Democrat, his embrace of more controversial tactics would be harder to roll back once the threat receded. He also knew that preventive detention was a red line among his liberal base, who viewed the policy as fundamentally at odds with basic notions of American justice. So for months, the president stalled. Obama would tentatively embrace long-term detention only to backtrack a short while later. He pushed and prodded his advisers to explain why preventive detention was necessary. Over and over again he asked the same question: "If these guys are so dangerous, why can't we prosecute them?"

On May 14, 2009, the president and his aides had just put the finishing touches on yet another carefully crafted statement on a contentious terrorism issue. This time it was his decision to revive military commissions, another legacy of the Bush-Cheney policies reviled by liberals. It was only one day earlier that Obama had stood in the Rose Garden, reversing his administration's decision to release the new batch of photographs depicting US military personnel abusing captives in Afghanistan and Iraq. The sudden about-face provoked a liberal firestorm. The ACLU's Anthony Romero issued a statement accusing the Obama administration of "complicity" with Bush "in covering up" the photos. So when word leaked on the fourteenth that the administration was reviving military commissions, Romero let loose again, slyly telling the *New York Times* that he had coined a new slogan for an ad campaign that his organization was preparing: "The Bush-Obama doctrine" on terrorism.

Romero's broadsides had by now become an irritatingly familiar refrain to the president. Obama's bouts of self-pity were rare, but he could be forgiven for wondering where his supporters were on terrorism — or if indeed he had any. While the ACLU and others on the left were castigating Obama as Bush Lite, Dick Cheney was accusing him of being soft on terror and leaving the country vulnerable to attack. It was galling to Obama that Cheney was still able to sow fear in the public, not to mention intimidate feckless Democrats in Congress. The revolt over the Uighurs was just the latest example. The very next day, May 15, the House of Representatives would pass legislation restricting the administration's ability to transfer detainees from Guantánamo to the US mainland.

Obama had spent four months seeking the middle path, a Buddhist approach to governing that could seem naive and self-defeating in a smashmouth, winner-take-all political culture. Now he was feeling like a pinball, getting knocked around from every direction. When speechwriter Ben Rhodes walked into the Oval Office with the final version of the statement on military commissions, Obama began to fulminate. "I'm tired of dealing with these issues in a one-off way," he said. "What we need to do is just give a speech where we lay out our position on all these issues, standing behind the Oval Office." The president wanted to establish a counternarrative, one that could reframe the debate and begin to turn around the politics. This was classic Obama, a set piece address—his advisers called them "framing speeches"—that would provide an overarching vision and context for his policy decisions. As new issues came up, they would fit neatly into this framework and he wouldn't be forced to react defensively to all the incoming fire. At least, that was the theory: one speech would change Washington.

The assignment went to Rhodes, a talented thirty-one-year-old speechwriter with quiet confidence and an understated demeanor not always common in young White House aides. It was a little intimidating for Rhodes. He was already working on an address Obama was scheduled to deliver in Cairo in early June, seeking a "new beginning" in America's relationship with the Muslim world, perhaps the most highly anticipated speech of Obama's young presidency. Now he had a matter of days to draft a major domestic address to guide the public through a thicket of complicated legal and national security issues, while avoiding the political land mines embedded across counterterrorism policy.

At the end of the day on Friday, May 15, he walked upstairs to the Oval Office from his cramped basement warren to see if he could catch Obama. Rhodes was hoping for a few minutes of guidance—broad strokes to help him think through the speech and identify its major themes. Obama beckoned him in. "Here's what I want to do with this speech," the president said, rising from his seat. He began dictating without notes, pacing around the Oval Office in wide circles. Rhodes scribbled quickly as Obama unfurled a remarkably detailed outline of the address. He spoke continuously for an hour, interrupted only once, when House Speaker Nancy Pelosi called about an unrelated matter. After hanging up five minutes later, Obama picked up the thread exactly where he'd left off. Rhodes had debriefed Obama many times before, but he'd never experienced anything like this. "All of these complicated issues were churning in his mind," he later recalled.

Obama began by explaining some of his decisions since becoming president, like banning torture and closing Guantánamo. On torture, he didn't want to appear starry-eyed, he told Rhodes. He wanted to say that as commander in chief, he now saw the intelligence and he was "convinced" that such harsh tactics were not the most effective means of interrogation. On Guantánamo, Obama wanted to lay the blame where he believed it properly belonged, with the Bush administration. "The problem wasn't my decision to close Guantánamo," he told Rhodes. "It was the decision to open it in the first place." Then Obama dove into his plan to shut down the detention facility and how his administration would dispose of the individual cases in a way that promoted both security and the rule of law. Off the top of his head, he divided the detainees into five separate categories. First, he said there would be a presumption in favor of trying terror suspects in civilian courts. The second group, Obama acknowledged, would be tried in revamped military commissions. A third category were those who had been ordered released by the courts. Another group included detainees who could be safely transferred to other countries.

As Rhodes was struggling to get every word down, Obama mentioned the fifth and final category: "those who are going to continue to have to be detained" because they cannot be prosecuted but are too dangerous to release. Then he looked up at Rhodes and paused for a moment. He knew this would be the most controversial part of the speech. "We're going to have to continue working on the language for that category. We're going to have to sit down with the legal team and the national security team to think through precisely what we're going to say here." He cited the example of a suspected terrorist who'd received extensive bomb-making training in an al-Qaeda camp or one who'd sworn allegiance to Osama bin Laden. They were people who had not necessarily committed crimes for which they could be prosecuted, but they were bent on killing Americans. Obama was adamant that detainees who were subject to preventive detention would have to be given the chance to have their cases reviewed over time to ensure they were not being held mistakenly. And finally, the chief executive would not be the sole arbiter of who could be detained without trial. He used a phrase that would appear word for word in the final speech. "In our constitutional system, prolonged detention should not be the decision of any one man," Obama said. Denis McDonough had suggested that Obama deliver the speech at the National Archives, where original copies of the Constitution, Declaration of Independence, and Bill of Rights were kept. The symbolism was clear — that America could fight this war without sacrificing the rule of law. Obama loved the idea.

On May 20, the day before the Archives address, Obama met with a group of prominent civil libertarians, human rights activists, and liberal law professors. He wanted to escape the White House policy bubble. He was eager to speak to experts who were deeply immersed in these issues. He also knew that there were some things in the speech that would not please the left. The meeting was a chance to assuage a key pressure group and, perhaps, preemptively take the edge off their inevitable criticism.

Obama walked into the Cabinet Room alone. His most senior political advisers were already there, seated in chairs along the wall: Emanuel, Axelrod, Jarrett, Craig, and Brennan. Seated at the table with the civil libertarians was Eric Holder. Obama took his seat and told the group he had skipped lunch so that he could extend the time allotted for the meeting. Then, leaning into the massive mahogany table, Obama began to describe his overall philosophy toward counterterrorism. It was another long, careful monologue. Obama's mastery of detail and nuance impressed his guests. Throughout the seventy-five-minute session, none of his advisers said a word. Only Obama spoke with the White House visitors. Some of the president's positions would have been familiar to anyone who had listened to him during the campaign: "American values and security are complementary, not contradictory." Yet he acknowledged that the concept was not yet gaining traction with the American people. With former vice president Dick Cheney "running around" giving fearmongering speeches, he said, Americans still believed they had to accept "tradeoffs" between liberty and security. The Archives speech, Obama now said, was a chance to reposition the debate and regain momentum. He offered a ray of hope, citing a White House poll that showed 50 percent of Americans believed he was doing a better job of protecting the country than Bush. Only 25 percent believed that Bush had done more to protect the country.

Obama then made a remarkable statement for a still-new president. According to several participants and contemporaneous notes from the session, he told the group that he wanted to create a series of institutions and laws that would limit the scope of presidential action in the global fight against terrorism — a framework that would be binding not just for himself but for future presidents. He said he was especially concerned about the dangers of unfettered presidential powers in the panic that would follow a future terrorist attack. Obama's words were soothing to his audience, but also astonishing. It was the president as constitutional lawyer, arguing for restraints on his own power.

As they delved deeper into the specific policy decisions, the meeting got more contentious. The toughest questions revolved around preventive detention. Kenneth Roth, the head of Human Rights Watch and a former federal prosecutor, asked Obama about the precedent that the United States would be setting around the world. "Do we want [Russian prime minister Vladimir] Putin declaring enemy combatants in his global war against the Chechens?" he asked. "And once you're named a combatant in such a war, the opposing side has the power not only to detain you but to shoot you." Did Obama want to legitimize Putin's "assassination campaign"? It was a point that Obama himself had addressed in his 2006 book, *The Audacity of Hope*. "When we detain suspects indefinitely without trial," Obama wrote, "we weaken our ability to pressure for human rights and the rule of law in despotic regimes." Obama parried the point with a question of his own. Did his guests see any alternative to preventive detention, for terror suspects captured on unconventional battlefields? They did: prosecute them in a civilian court of law, or release them.

Obama betrayed his irritation only twice, and both times he directed it at the ACLU's Romero. Relatively early in the conversation, Romero had launched into a soliloquy that struck a few in the room as off-key: "As a gay, Puerto Rican kid who grew up in the Bronx, I never thought I'd ever believe in a politician like I believe in you," Romero said with emotion in his voice. "But now I'm troubled by what I'm seeing." As Romero spoke, Obama looked visibly annoyed, shifting in his chair and staring impassively at him. Obama kept his temper in check when he answered. "I profoundly respect your role and you need to respect mine," he said, according to participants. "I have a broader set of responsibilities." But he seized the moment to register his displeasure with the ACLU's rhetoric equating his policies with those of George W. Bush. "They erase all nuance," Obama complained. And they give ammunition to the Republicans. Romero pushed back. "No one questions your values," he began. "But when your substantive policies are not substantively different from your predecessor's, then the comparisons are fair, accurate, and they are likely to continue." Obama didn't bother to respond.

Toward the end of the meeting, Obama came back around to preventive detention one more time. It was clearly still eating at him, and he appeared to be looking for some kind of modus vivendi with the activists. He tested an idea with the group that his advisers had begun to think about among themselves: establishing a prolonged detention system only for those fifty or so Guantánamo detainees whom the administration had deemed too dangerous to release and not eligible for prosecution. There would be a different set of rules for anyone picked up in the future, who would either be charged or released. He suggested the congressional authorization for the use of force, the legal basis for long-term detentions, could be interpreted to apply to people picked up for a proscribed period only. In other words, Obama was trying to draw a line separating the "legacy" cases he'd inherited from new cases under his own watch. Perhaps with an eye on posterity, Obama said he saw this as a way of limiting the damage of whatever negative precedent he might set.

The proposal split the civil libertarians. The more pragmatic among them were sympathetic to Obama's dilemma. He had inherited a mess. Some of the Guantánamo detainees could not be prosecuted because they had been tortured, tainting the evidence that would be key to winning convictions. Tom Malinowski, director of the Washington office of Human Rights Watch, on the other hand, thought it would be a mistake to single out any group of Guantánamo detainees for indefinite detention. But he promised not to issue a press release accusing Obama of "trampling on the rule of law and being as bad as George Bush." Others, like Romero, were absolutist, ceding no ground. None of them was happy about where Obama appeared to be going.

At one point during the meeting Romero urged the administration to identify a single case of Bush-era torture to investigate, "to hunt one head," as he put it, a kind of show prosecution that would send a strong message of accountability for such lawless behavior. The president waved Romero off in midsentence, conveying that he was utterly uninterested in, even contemptuous of, the idea. "Well, that's one man's view," Obama said coldly. Abruptly rising from his chair, he curtly thanked the group for coming and walked out of the room. "He looked pissed," recalled one participant.

The morning of the speech, Obama met in the Oval Office with Emanuel, Axelrod, Donilon, and other key aides. They were still line-editing some of the basic arguments and adding last-minute rhetorical points. Someone remembered that Lindsey Graham had argued that the idea that the United States could not safely house 240 or so detainees in its supermax prisons was irrational. Rhodes tracked down the exact quote and wove it into the speech. They were still not done when Obama arrived at the Archives later that morning. He had to be placed in a "hold" while Rhodes inserted final edits, transmitting them electronically to the teleprompter even as Obama was walking up the stairs to the dais.

Finally, "the speech" began, and Obama's oratorical presidency was put to the test. In the majestic limestone and marble rotunda of the National Archives, Obama gave an impassioned defense of his policies. He believed he could reboot an agenda that was faltering in Congress and losing luster with the American people. He still promised to close down Guantánamo and to transfer dozens of detainees to secure facilities in the United States, where many of them would be tried in civilian courts. And, yes, some detainees would have to be held without trial. But there would be "clear, defensible, and lawful standards" for anyone who fell into that category. Ultimately, he said, the terrorists can't succeed "if we stay true to who we are, if we forge tough and durable approaches to fighting terrorism that are anchored in our timeless ideals."

For Obama, more was at stake than just his policy against terrorists. It was a test of his active approach to governing: float above the fray, reframe debates, convince lions and lambs to follow the shepherd.

Romero and some of the other civil libertarians had been invited to sit in the audience, but they declined to attend. They didn't want to be political props in a policy address they could not fully embrace. Dick Cheney, meanwhile, was watching the speech from the American Enterprise Institute, his conservative redoubt in downtown Washington. As soon as Obama finished, the former vice president delivered a harsh rebuttal. Carried live by the cable stations, it created a split-screen face-off that dramatized the wide gulf between Obama and his adversaries on the right over how best to protect the country while safeguarding its liberties. In the end, Obama's speech accomplished little beyond diminishing the idea that "framing speeches" were a powerful tool of governance.

After the Archives address, Tom Donilon, the deputy national security adviser, moved to consolidate control of detention policy within the White House. Donilon was a favorite of Obama's for his policy smarts, political savvy, and his lawyerly skills at managing the bureaucratic process. He began a series of high-level policy meetings to achieve some measure of consensus before the issue went before the national security principals. By mid-July there seemed to be agreement on at least one aspect of the policy: the forty-eight Guantánamo detainees who had been deemed too dangerous to release, transfer, or prosecute would be held indefinitely under the laws of war. Even Greg Craig had come to realize that there was no alternative. Indeed, it was Craig and Jim Jones, the national security adviser, who drafted a detailed memo for the president recommending the policy and laying out an elaborate set of rules governing preventive detention for the Guantánamo detainees. The memo had been signed off on by all of the national security principals before it was given to Obama for his signature.

In mid-July Obama and his national security advisers gathered in the Roosevelt Room. Donilon began the meeting by reminding the president that, at least for now, they were only discussing the existing Guantánamo population. Obama leaned back in his chair. He began by praising all of the hard work and careful thought that went into the memo. But then he said he was not prepared to accept their recommendation. "Look, I haven't decided to do long-term detention at all," Obama said. "I'm just not convinced we need to do this." Some in the room were perplexed. Hadn't he signed off on this in the Archives speech? Does he have an alternative plan up his sleeve? But there was an oddly repetitive quality to the debate. The president came back to the same question he had been asking for months. "Why can't we just transfer the ones who are not a big deal and then prosecute the others in Article III courts [federal courts established by Article III of the Constitution] or in military commissions which we have reformed?" he asked. It was another instance of president as Hamlet. He was facing an excruciatingly hard decision and he wanted more time. That meeting became known as "the meeting that launched a thousand memos," because so many Justice Department lawyers were tasked with justifying preventive detention in its wake.

A few days later, Harold Koh received a call from Greg Craig. His presence was requested at a meeting with the president later that day. The topic was detention policy, and he would be briefing Obama. As the State Department's top lawyer, it was Koh's responsibility to ensure that American foreign policy complied with international law, making him a kind of informal ambassador to the human rights community. As the former dean of the Yale Law School and a respected expert in international law, his academic credentials were impressive. Nevertheless, it was unusual, if not unprecedented, for the general counsel of a government agency to be summoned to brief a president. Koh dropped everything and began preparing for the briefing.

The invitation stirred excitement in Koh's office. His German secretary kept saying "Oooobamaaa" in her strong Teutonic accent, while others gathered around asking Koh what he would tell the president. Dutifully observing department protocol, Koh alerted Secretary Clinton's office about the meeting. Word came back that it would be fine — so long as he made it clear that he was speaking for himself and not representing the institutional interests of the State Department or the secretary herself. Clinton liked Koh, but his reputation as a liberal bomb-thrower preceded him. Just to be sure, a State Department official would be dispatched to the meeting as a note taker — in case Koh said anything that would have to be cleaned up later.

Greg Craig had organized the meeting. By now he was badly marginalized within the administration, sidelined from important discussions, his voice on policy matters greatly diminished. But he had not lost any of his convictions, and he was determined to try to influence the process any way he could. Koh was his weapon. When Craig urged the president to meet with him, it was not lost on anybody that Craig shared Koh's ideological perspective; both were strong advocates of civil liberties. Craig stacked the decks by not inviting Koh's counterparts in the other national security agencies, like the Defense Department or the CIA, a departure from protocol that ruffled some feathers.

Koh was a unique character in government policy circles. He was a sharp advocate for his positions, even in the face of overwhelming opposition. And his views ran considerably to the left of most senior Obama officials. From his perch at Yale he had railed against the Bush administration's 9/11 policies, once asserting that the United States would find itself on the "axis of disobedience" along with North Korea and Iraq for its brazen disregard of international law. His views that US courts should pay more deference to international law had invited conservative charges that he was a radical "globalist" willing to surrender American sovereignty. Critics had even charged, absurdly, that Koh's support for an international convention on the "elimination of all forms of discrimination against women" would have led to the abolition of Mother's Day in the United States.

Koh started his job in June, after a grueling confirmation battle. Many of the important legal decisions in the war on terror had already been made, but that didn't stop him from trying to roll them back. Issuing memos from his State Department office, Koh challenged key interpretations of the Authorization for Use of Military Force, the principal statutory authority that both the Bush and Obama administrations relied on in their war on al-Qaeda. He questioned whether the battlefield extended beyond Iraq and Afghanistan to Yemen and Somalia. Koh also pushed for narrower definitions of who was covered by the AUMF and, therefore, who could be detained or targeted by drone strikes. Koh was generally tilting against windmills, but his sheer relentlessness, and his assiduous preparation, occasionally wore his rivals down. Not exactly a happy warrior — he had a brooding side — Koh could charm his colleagues with a sardonic wit. "This isn't exactly change we can believe in," he said dryly at one interagency meeting on military commissions. Koh may have inherited his stubborn streak from his father. Kwang Lim Koh had been South Korea's ambassador to the United Nations and later was chargé d'affaires in Washington during a time of great political turmoil in his country. After a military coup in South Korea, he refused to return home to serve the new regime. He told his son: "Some people are eels. They slither to where the power is. But it is the people who stick to their principles who can look themselves in the mirror." For all his contentiousness, Koh's colleagues at the State Department — and Hillary Clinton — admired his moral conviction. "He's an American hero," said one.

Koh could also be his own worst enemy, alienating potential allies and undercutting his credibility with over-the-top arguments. Early in the administration, Koh took on Elena Kagan, the highly respected solicitor general and former dean of Harvard Law School. As law school deans, the two had been intense rivals, fighting over star faculty and coveted students. At the outset of the administration they had both been touted as potential Supreme Court picks, though as a liberal lightning rod Koh was never a serious contender. Now Koh feared that Kagan was preparing to assert in court briefs that due process should not apply to aliens picked up outside the United States. Koh called David Ogden, the deputy attorney general, and urged him to take the decision away from Kagan. "She reports to you," Koh pleaded. "You can do this." Attempting an end run around the solicitor general in a major litigation decision was an audacious and, perhaps, foolhardy move. But it was vintage Koh, a disdain for process that many found maddening but others found refreshing. Ogden politely declined and Koh blithely moved on to the next battle.

Koh's persistence might also be traced to his childhood battle with polio. At age ten he underwent rehabilitative surgery on his left leg, after which his efforts to walk brought excruciating pain. "On the day after the surgery they told me to walk down the hall putting weight on the foot," he recalled. "I was crying and asked to stop. Later on I overheard the nurse say, 'I never expected him to give up so fast.' I decided I did not want to ever hear that again." He walked through the pain.

Now, walking into the Roosevelt Room, Koh was surprised to see all of the White House brass there, including Vice President Biden, Emanuel, and Axelrod. A few minutes later Obama arrived. He shook Koh's hand and told him it was good to see him again, although they'd never actually met. Craig started the meeting, telling the president, "Harold's going to talk. He's thought about these issues for a long time." Before Koh had a chance to say anything, the president jumped in: "Some people are urging me to consider a scheme of long-term detention," he said. "But to give that kind of power to the president is like giving him a loaded weapon." It wasn't just a casual colloquialism. Obama, the former constitutional law professor, was alluding to Justice Robert H. Jackson's dissent in the Supreme Court's notorious *Korematsu* decision, which upheld FDR's internment of Japanese Americans during World War II. Jackson had written that precedent "lies around like a loaded weapon ready for the hands of any authority that can bring forward a plausible claim."

"You never know who is going to be president four years from now," Obama said. "I have to think about how Mitt Romney would use that power."

Obama raised the issue of the forty-eight Guantánamo detainees who couldn't be charged or released. "Harold, I'm being told that there's a set of dangerous people we kind of have to hold. What shall we do with them, just release them?" Koh didn't go that far. But he warned the president that if he had to resort to prolonged detention for the Guantánamo cases, he should not do it by executive order. "If your name is on it," he told Obama, "you'll own it." Instead, he advised the president to use Department of Defense regulations to set up a system of preventive detention. It would be a lower-level action and that would be easier to reverse. But Koh remained worried that instituting preventive detention even in such a limited way would lead to a broader policy. Koh looked directly at the president and said: "In the history of the United States there have been three large-scale internments: the Palmer Raids, the Japanese internments, and the Bush administration's post-9/11 detentions." Koh was on a roll — which was exactly when he indulged his tendency to go overboard. "Mr. President, if you end up embracing a regime of indefinite preventive detention, it will be your legacy — and it will be worse than what the Bush administration did."

People in the room winced. Koh continued: The more people are held indefinitely, the harder it will be to close Guantánamo. The longer they are held, the more likely they will be mistreated. Finally, Koh implored the president not to allow himself to be trapped by Bush's mistakes. "Mr. President, you need to make a clean break between the past and the future. This was on Bush's watch. But going forward it's going to be on your watch. Don't let the past control the future."

When the meeting ended, Obama thanked Koh and told him, "You've given us a lot to think about." Koh felt as if he'd gotten through to the president, though he was struck by how exhausted the chief executive looked. After Obama left the room, Biden approached Koh, grinning broadly. "You fucking did it," the vice president said, jabbing Koh in the chest. "You fucking connected with him and that's not easy." When Koh returned to his office late that afternoon, he addressed his entire staff, who had been waiting to hear about the meeting. "You should know that you are working for the man you voted for," he said, fairly beaming.

6

HOW NOT TO TRY A TERRORIST

AFTER OSAMA BIN LADEN, no one better personified al-Qaeda's murderous intent toward America than Khalid Sheikh Mohammed, who had been captured in Pakistan on March 1, 2003. Shortly thereafter, the CIA transferred him to a secret prison in eastern Europe, where he was subjected to harsh interrogation for a month, including the infamous 183 waterboarding sessions. When Obama took office, KSM was languishing at Gitmo. Admittedly responsible for the murder of some three thousand Americans on September 11, 2001, his lack of remorse was chilling. Mohammed had gleefully admitted to the beheading, in 2002, of *Wall Street Journal* reporter Daniel Pearl. "I decapitated with blessed right hand the head of the American Jew . . . in the city of Karachi, Pakistan," he declared in an administrative hearing conducted by the military at Guantánamo. "For those of you who would like to confirm, there are pictures of me holding his head on the Internet."

But where should he be put on trial? That question carved a deep fault line through the politics of terrorism. The Bush administration had rejected civilian trials for KSM and his coconspirators. The United States was at war, the logic went, and in an age of stateless terrorism and loose nukes, the traditional law-enforcement model was insufficient. KSM and his coconspirators were "unprivileged enemy belligerents" who had brazenly violated the laws of war by intentionally slaughtering thousands of civilians; they were not entitled to the gold-plated legal protections available in federal court. For liberals, on the other hand, KSM represented a chance to return to first principles, to punish America's enemies without abandoning its laws or institutions. The government's willingness to try Mohammed in a civilian court would send a resounding message to the rest of the world that America was rededicating itself to the rule of law.

To a small group of federal prosecutors in New York, trying KSM in civilian court was the right thing to do for both idealistic and pragmatic reasons. They were also driven by more parochial concerns. KSM would be the ultimate trophy for any prosecutor — the trial of the century.

Ever since 9/11, federal prosecutors in New York and other districts around the country had sat on the sidelines, frozen out of the deadliest conspiracy case in US history. They watched in frustration as the evidence grew stale or was tainted by torture. But they were certain they had the experience and skills to conduct successful prosecutions. New York prosecutors had even secretly indicted KSM for his involvement in a previous plot, hoping to one day deliver justice in an American courtroom. No one was more eager to get his hands on the case than David Raskin, an irrepressible, voluble attorney who headed the Southern District of New York's terrorism unit. Raskin had been a member of the prosecution team that convicted Zacarias Moussaoui, the only 9/11 conspirator to face a jury for his crimes. Raskin had traveled around the world collecting evidence and interviewing witnesses, giving him a vast knowledge of the plot and the evidence. He was hungry to put KSM in the dock.

In late March 2009 Matt Olsen had invited the military prosecutors on the KSM case to brief the Guantánamo Review Task Force in Washington. In a large conference room packed with close to fifty people, including prosecutors from Justice, law-enforcement agents, and representatives of the intelligence community, the military prosecutors laid out their case. Much of it had been built on "custodial" statements — admissions of guilt while KSM was held in a CIA black site and subjected to enhanced interrogation techniques. Such "fruit of the poisonous tree" evidence would likely be suppressed in *both* civilian and military courts. The military prosecutors said they would rely on so-called clean-team statements — interviews conducted by FBI interrogators who had no involvement with the CIA's enhanced interrogation program. But federal judges had thrown out clean-team evidence as well, arguing that once a defendant had been tortured, any future testimony he might give to American authorities would be tainted. Once subjected to such cruel and degrading treatment, the theory went, the stain cannot be removed. There were other problems with the military's case. Many routine investigative leads had not been run down; key witnesses hadn't been interviewed; basic computer forensics were never conducted on computers that had been recovered after the arrests of KSM and the other suspects. Documents seized as evidence had not even been dusted for fingerprints.

In the weeks after the military's presentation, a young prosecutor under Raskin, Adam Hickey, stepped up the Southern District's examination of the evidence. It was while poring over thousands of secret documents pertaining to the Guantánamo detainees that Hickey made a stunning find: for years, it turned out, the military had been secretly recording the conversations of the 9/11 conspirators, including those of Khalid Sheikh Mohammed. Every day, KSM was allowed to spend time in the prison yard mingling with other detainees. His conversations were intercepted by military spies and mined for intelligence. There were hundreds of hours of such recordings, including musings by KSM and other high-value detainees, uttered freely, during unguarded moments. The recordings were highly classified, so Hickey couldn't tell Raskin about them over an open telephone line. Instead, he sent his boss a cryptic message about "new information" he had uncovered, and requested that they meet in person. A few days later, Hickey traveled to New York from the Olsen task force offices in Virginia, and, in a secure room, told Raskin about the intercepts. Raskin immediately understood the importance of the discovery. If KSM had talked openly about his role in 9/11, those statements would be among the most powerful evidence prosecutors could bring before a jury. They would be entirely voluntary statements, making them almost certainly admissible in court. Significantly, Raskin realized, prosecutors would be able to avoid a legal fight over the use of clean-team statements; KSM's lawyers would not be able to, in effect, put the CIA on trial for torture.

The existence of secret recordings was surprising enough. But what Hickey told Raskin next was mind-boggling. Despite the potential gold mine the recordings represented, military prosecutors had decided not to use the evidence. Not only that, they refused to even listen to the recordings. They worried that the intrusive means by which the evidence was obtained might not pass muster with their judges. The tribunals were barely four years old and largely untested. With practically no case law built up to guide lawyers, they were reluctant to take any chances. In short, despite their reputation as less restricted, in this case military tribunals were more difficult venues for prosecutors. The military system had come under such harsh scrutiny — derided by many as victor's justice — that prosecutors and judges tended to lean over backwards to appear fair. For Raskin, the military lawyers' refusal to listen to the tapes bordered on legal malpractice.

Within the department, Holder was initially noncommittal about the prospect of trying KSM in civilian court. In May, when aides Matt Olsen and Amy Jeffress sought a private meeting with him to plant the seed with the attorney general, he was characteristically taciturn — "judge-like," in Olsen's words. He asked questions about the pros and cons of each approach, but did not reveal any preference. Later, at the end of a meeting of his senior staff, he polled the room on the question. There was unanimity in favor of civilian court. Again, however, Holder declined to express a personal view. Yet the attorney general had indicated which way he was leaning to the person who mattered most. On the Fourth of July, Obama and Holder stood together on the White House roof terrace watching fireworks explode over the National Mall, the Lincoln and Washington monuments aglow at either end. Holder was flush with pride. He was the country's first black attorney general, standing with its first African American president, both guardians of the Constitution, presiding over a White House celebration of Independence Day. But he wasn't going to waste a rare moment alone with the president. He had come with an agenda, and told the president that he was thinking about prosecuting KSM in federal court. Obama had simply acknowledged that he would defer to Holder on the matter: "It's your call, you're the attorney general."

By late July, Holder had appointed a team of prosecutors from the Southern District of New York and the Eastern District of Virginia to dig into the KSM case. (By law, the 9/11 defendants could be tried only in jurisdictions where the crimes had been committed.) They had less than two months to produce a "prosecution memo" marshaling the best evidence against the September 11 mastermind — and in favor of civilian courts. Raskin rented a soulless apartment in Tysons Corner, but effectively moved into Olsen's task force offices.

An enduring irony of the counterterrorism debate was the wide acceptance that military commissions were tougher than civilian trials. Indeed, the system as conceived, and unilaterally imposed, by the Bush administration was, in some ways, tougher. But the original commissions were also an international embarrassment, so lacking in basic due process protections that the Supreme Court would later rule them illegal, in violation of both the Geneva Conventions and the military's own code of justice. Still, in some ways, Article III courts did impose more onerous legal standards. Statements made by detainees before they were read their Miranda warning could be excluded in federal court. Critics also asserted that civilian courts, with their tradition of transparency, did not have the means to adequately protect classified information, including the sources and methods used to obtain important evidence. Moreover, trying a mega-terrorist in the heart of New York City could invite al-Qaeda to launch another attack, they argued.

The reality was more complicated. The chances that KSM or any of the other 9/11 defendants would be acquitted in them was infinitesimal. By 2010, more than two hundred terrorists had been convicted in civilian courts after 9/11. Even hardened al-Qaeda terrorists, like Moussaoui and would-be shoe bomber Richard Reid, were prosecuted by the Bush administration — with little opposition from conservatives. Unlike military commissions, the federal courts offered a tested system, built on a strong foundation of case law developed over decades. Furthermore, prosecutors had enormous flexibility in going after terrorists. They could go beyond pure antiterrorism statutes and charge suspects with conspiracy or material support, offenses that appeals courts might have thrown out if military prosecutors tried to bring them. US attorneys' offices, especially in New York and Virginia, boasted an elite cadre of lawyers with deep experience handling complex national security cases. (A typical case for a pre-9/11 military lawyer, by contrast, was an assault in the barracks, or a minor drug offense.) Federal judges were equally practiced in trying terrorism cases, and they ran their trials with iron hands, so the chances that KSM would be able to commandeer the courtroom to make propaganda speeches were slim.

Still, these were nuanced arguments that lacked the bumper-sticker appeal of "military justice." That political reality was not lost on Rahm Emanuel, who believed that most Americans listened to their guts rather than wonky legal arguments when it came to terrorism. Others, like Greg Craig, argued to the president that maintaining the military tribunals would undercut the administration's argument for civilian trials. Once you accepted the premise that commissions were acceptable, it would make it harder to argue that the 9/11 conspirators should be prosecuted in Article III courts. But Emanuel, who as chief of staff was responsible for guiding the broader White House agenda, was thinking on multiple levels. You had to give things up to get things in return. Retaining military commissions would thrill Republicans, and might win back some of the political capital Obama had been hemorrhaging on national security and detainee issues. And Emanuel knew that no one would be more pleased by this action than Lindsey Graham, the courtly and mercurial senator from South Carolina whom he saw as the linchpin to closing Guantánamo.

No politician in Washington was more steeped in the vexing politics of terrorism than Graham. At Eric Holder's Senate confirmation hearing, Graham wasted no time getting to the foundational question. "Is it fair to say that we're at war?" he asked Holder right out of the box. Holder responded unhesitatingly: "I don't think there's any question but that we are at war," he said. "I'm almost ready to

vote for you right now," the senator gushed. Graham was an icono-
clast within the Republican conference. Adopted by John McCain as
a kind of maverick protégé, he delighted in tweaking his own party
and basked in the attention his across-the-aisle forays generated in
the mainstream media. Like McCain, Graham had broken with the
GOP on immigration, climate change, and energy legislation. On
terrorism policy he had been an early Republican critic of the Bush-
Cheney excesses and a proponent of closing down Guantánamo. But
as unorthodox as he could be, Graham clung stubbornly to a single
guiding principle in the war on terror: the 9/11 attacks were an act
of war on the United States. To treat them like conventional crimes
would be to perilously misunderstand the existential nature of the
threat.

Graham believed America needed a whole new legal architecture
for dealing with detained terror suspects. He envisioned a hybrid approach that provided more of the due process protections available
in civilian courts, but that acknowledged limitations imposed by national security risks. Some terror suspects would have to be held indefinitely, removed from the battlefield for the duration of hostilities
under the laws of war. Others would be tried by military commissions. Still others, including some lower-level members of al-Qaeda,
could be tried in Article III courts. How the Obama administration
approached the KSM case, he believed, would reveal whether or not
it was returning to a pre-9/11 mindset that saw terrorism as a law-enforcement matter. "There's a difference between a common criminal
and a committed warrior," he told Holder at his confirmation hearing, referring to Khalid Sheikh Mohammed. Holder did not respond.
For Graham it wasn't just a philosophical difference; it was a matter of personal experience and pride. He had served in the military's
Judge Advocate General's Corps for nearly two decades, both as an
active-duty officer in the air force and as a member of the reserves.

The idea that the military could not handle prosecutions against suspected terrorists was offensive to Graham. He was willing to go along with the administration on many subjects, but not this one: KSM should not be tried in civilian court.

Emanuel had intensively courted Graham during the transition. They were an odd couple — Graham, the genial southerner, and Emanuel, the rough, unabashedly crude big-city pol. But they both saw themselves as pragmatic problem-solvers who professed a disdain for the ideological extremes of their parties. Emanuel's minuet with Graham began in December at a meeting he had arranged with the president-elect at Obama headquarters in Chicago. There, Emanuel took Graham aside and buttered him up, praising him for staying by McCain's side even during the darkest moments of the Arizona senator's ill-fated presidential campaign. Later, Obama poured it on, remarking that he had a "good friend in Lindsey Graham, the judge advocate." Graham told the president he wanted to help him untangle the Guantánamo mess. "These issues are like flypaper, they stick to you if you're not careful," he said. Graham was already beginning to contemplate the contours of a comprehensive deal he hoped to negotiate with the new administration. He'd provide key Republican support for the closing of Guantánamo and for Article III trials for lower-level members of al-Qaeda. In exchange, the administration would have to embrace revamped military commissions for the 9/11 cases — including KSM — as well as indefinite detention for those detainees who could not be charged or released.

For the first two years of Obama's presidency Graham would be treated almost as an adjunct of the administration. He visited the White House some twenty times in 2009 and early 2010. Few Democratic senators could claim that much access. The prospect of being able to deliver a "grand bargain" gave Graham enormous influence within the White House. For Emanuel, playing footsie with Graham had obvious advantages. Not only could the Republican help Obama fulfill his promise to close Guantánamo, he could provide critical bipartisan support for the president's domestic agenda, including health care and energy reform. Others, like Greg Craig and Holder, were less sanguine about Graham's role. They would come to believe that Emanuel had effectively subcontracted out vital national security policy to a member of the opposition who ultimately didn't have the ability to deliver any votes within his own party.

Arriving at the Justice Department on the morning of June 9, Holder walked into a congressional ambush. Overnight, US marshals had secretly transported Ahmed Khalfan Ghailani from Guantánamo to the Metropolitan Correctional Center in Manhattan. Ghailani, an al-Qaeda member, was accused of participating in the 1998 attacks on the US embassies in East Africa. He was also the first Guantánamo detainee to be transferred to the United States for prosecution in the federal courts. The move was a fulfillment of President Obama's pledge in his Archives speech to try Guantánamo detainees in federal civilian courts "whenever feasible" — but detainee politics had moved harshly against the administration. Congress was on the verge of passing legislation that would place onerous restrictions on the transfer of prisoners from Guantánamo to the homeland. Now it looked like the predawn Ghailani operation was an effort to circumvent the will of Congress. Phone messages from angry members had piled up on Holder's desk. One of them was from Alan Mollohan, the West Virginia Democrat who chaired the committee that controlled the Justice Department's $28 billion budget. "Why wasn't I notified?" he demanded to know. Holder attempted to mollify the committee chairman. That day, Holder called seventeen members of Congress in an effort to tamp down the firestorm. If a single low-level al-Qaeda operative whom few Americans had ever even heard of could provoke that kind of storm, what would happen if they tried to bring KSM into a civilian courtroom?

The following week, Justice Department officials had arranged for Holder to meet with families of the 9/11 victims. The meetings, held over two days, were billed as an opportunity for the families to be briefed on the ongoing efforts to close Guantánamo — and to provide their own input. On the first morning, mingling over a breakfast spread, the Justice officials tried to foster an atmosphere of bonhomie. But once the meeting began, things quickly turned tense and confrontational. In the aftermath of the Ghailani operation, many of the family members were fixated on one question: was the administration going to try the murderers of their relatives in civilian courts? Having waited eight years for justice, they were angry that Obama had frozen the military commissions after taking office. Now, they feared, prosecutions would have to start all over again. Even worse, with new legal rights, the terrorists might be able to delay the proceedings even further, and maybe even escape justice altogether. Primed by the military prosecutors, with whom they had met extensively, they pummeled their hosts with questions.

Matt Olsen told them, accurately, that no decisions had been made about trial venues for the 9/11 conspirators. The families then asked about whether more detainees would be moved to the homeland, and whether some might even be released. One 9/11 widow waved a copy of the *New York Post* showing the four Uighur detainees who had been resettled in Bermuda, frolicking in azure Caribbean waters. Her son had vomited when he saw the picture, she said. Holder was jarred by the confrontational tone. As a longtime prosecutor and judge, he had rarely found himself working *against* crime victims. Nevertheless, he gently but firmly pushed back. "Now you need to understand that these people had nothing to do with what happened to your relatives," he said of the Uighurs, on whose behalf Holder had lobbied. But the families were unrelenting. Mark Martins, an army colonel leading an administration task force charged with reforming detention policy, apologized for having to leave early to attend his daughter's high school graduation. "I think I have a pretty good excuse," he said lightheartedly. But a 9/11 relative, whose husband was incinerated in the Twin Towers conflagration, was not so understanding. Taking the microphone, tears running down her cheeks, she told Martins, "No, it's not OK. My son, who is sixteen years old, will never see his father at his graduation."

Holder and the other Justice officials were drained by the searing emotion that suffused virtually every exchange. They told themselves that this was a self-selected group, lashing out as a way of coping with unspeakable tragedy. And yet it was also the case that as lawyers they lived in a more abstract world of constitutional analysis and intellectual reasoning, insulated from the raw immediacy of terrorism and its political fallout.

Congress was far more attuned to the beating heart of the country on the issue, and far more willing to exploit citizens' fears. By May, Republicans sensed Obama's vulnerability on Guantánamo and detainee issues, and they introduced the Keep Terrorists Out of America Act. Democrats ducked their heads and supported it. Even those who had been willing to back the administration were showing signs of panic. All through the spring and summer of 2009, rebellion raged and Hill Democrats clamored for a plan from the administration on how to deal with Guantánamo. Their biggest concern was where to house detainees who would be transferred to the homeland. Jim Moran, a Virginia Democrat who had supported the transfer of the Uighurs, called Deputy Attorney General David Ogden to warn him that the administration was running out of time. "You're fucking this up, and you don't get too many chances to fuck things up," he said. In late June, before Holder was scheduled to testify on the Hill again, the White House asked to see the attorney general's opening statement and the talking points that his aides had prepared for the hearing. Explicit instructions came back that he was to "avoid talking about GTMO" and that he shouldn't "make news." The White House suggested that his staff come up with "flags," safe-harbor subjects where Holder could go to avoid stumbling into controversy.

At a White House meeting in early August, Craig glumly told Holder what by now was evident. The "political people" were in charge of Guantánamo now. Rahm Emanuel, at Obama's urging, had assigned Pete Rouse, the deputy chief of staff and a skilled legislative tactician, to take over management of the Gitmo closing. Emanuel effectively stripped Craig of all meaningful authority on terrorism policy. Under Rouse's supervision, the legislative and communications team finally began developing an initiative known as "the Plan," to respond to congressional demands for a comprehensive strategy that could be explained to nervous constituents. It centered on identifying a secure prison facility in the United States where Guantánamo detainees could be transferred. It made no difference that there were already half a dozen convicted terrorists as dangerous as anybody at Guantánamo locked up for life in supermax prisons like the ones in Marion, Illinois, and Florence, Colorado. With Congress and Dick Cheney stirring up fear, there were not a lot of communities offering themselves up as Gitmo North.

Yet there was a prison in Michigan, Standish Maximum Correctional Facility, that looked promising. It was a state institution on the verge of being closed. Rouse and the administration came up with a plan to federalize the facility and turn it over to the Defense Department. Bart Stupak, the House Democrat in whose district Standish was located, agreed to support the plan. Axelrod took on handholding duties, in an effort to shore up support from other key Michigan politicians. He reached out to Governor Jennifer Granholm and the state's congressional delegation. Granholm wanted assurances that detainees housed in Michigan wouldn't be magnets for al-Qaeda attacks. For Senator Carl Levin, the powerful chairman of the Senate Armed Services Committee, the concerns were more parochial. He wanted a promise from Axelrod that the locally hired prison guards working at Standish would be rehired when the Defense Department took over the facility. (Unemployment in Michigan at the time was hovering around 17 percent.) In the end, however, the plan was thwarted by Pete Hoekstra, the ranking Republican on the House Intelligence Committee, who was planning a gubernatorial run against Granholm. All six members of the Standish City Council voted to withdraw their welcome mat once the prospect of national publicity reared its head.

For the White House, the political environment went from dismal to toxic in August of '09. Populist rage over "Obamacare" and the government bailouts of major banks was exploding across the country, fueling the rise of the Tea Party movement. During their summer recess, members of Congress came under assault at raucous town hall meetings. White House and DNC pollsters were beginning to see signs of serious disaffection among independent voters who had supported Obama's election. A Rasmussen poll found that 75 percent of voters were concerned that shutting down Guantánamo would result in the freeing of dangerous terrorists. Not surprisingly, the percentage of voters who supported the closure of the camp had dropped precipitously since Obama had taken office.

Nevertheless, officials gamely devised an elaborate rollout of the Plan as a way of drumming up public support. Among other ideas, the White House wanted to have a battery of generals lead the charge on Capitol Hill. Who better than the military brass to make the case that closing Guantánamo was vital to America's national security?

The White House approached David Petraeus, the country's most famous general since Colin Powell. But Petraeus, a wily politician in his own right, declined to accept the mission. The White House, not wanting to be accused of politicizing the military, didn't push it. The Plan remained a several-page memorandum filed away in the office of Dave Rapallo, a former Hill staffer who had been recruited to supervise the congressional initiative. It would never see the light of day.

In the late summer, far removed from the politics of the issue, David Raskin, Adam Hickey, and the other prosecutors were in a frenzied sprint to complete their prosecution memo. On most days they worked until as late as two in the morning, including on weekends. Ordering in plain sandwiches from the Harris Teeter grocery store, they worked out of a series of connected cubicles, poring over thousands of exhibits and sharpening their legal arguments. By September they had taken a big step further than their military counterparts: they had listened to the secret recordings from Guantánamo.

They were astounded by what they heard. On the tapes, Khalid Sheikh Mohammed boasted about the 9/11 attacks. He mentioned specific pieces of evidence, documents and computer files, that could now be tied directly to him through his voluntary statements. "We had him dead to rights," recalled one official. When Holder received a report on the intercepted conversations, his first reaction was skepticism. How could it be that the military was refusing to use this evidence? "What am I missing here?" he asked.

On September 9, Najibullah Zazi, a twenty-four-year-old Afghan American, began the long drive from his Colorado home to New York City. Zazi, who had been working as an airport bus driver in Aurora, outside Denver, would sometimes startle passengers with loud rants about America's senseless slaughter of Muslims around the world. He had become obsessed with the US drone war, which he claimed was indiscriminately targeting civilians in Afghanistan and Pakistan. In 2008 Zazi had traveled to Pakistan and trained at an al-Qaeda camp. Now, with explosive materials and bomb components packed in his car, he set off for New York, seeking revenge in the form of a "martyrdom operation," as he would later call it. Along with two friends from Flushing, Queens, he plotted backpack suicide bombings at two of New York's busiest rail stations, Grand Central and Penn Station. Had they succeeded, they would have likely been the deadliest attacks on the homeland since 9/11.

Thankfully, Zazi's plans were thwarted by good old-fashioned police work, including surveillance and information from informants. Agents from the Joint Terrorism Task Force took him to a deluxe hotel in New Jersey, where they plied him with good food and allowed him to watch TV, in an effort to win his trust. Zazi cracked almost immediately, spilling his guts to investigators. He talked about his explosives training at the al-Qaeda camp and about his long path to radicalization. He named names and revealed details about al-Qaeda's operational tradecraft. CIA operatives, in the hotel room next door, analyzed the intelligence in real time in case Zazi revealed anything "actionable," like an ongoing or imminent terrorist plot. Ultimately, Zazi pleaded guilty and cooperated even further.

The episode underscored Holder's faith in the criminal justice system's ability to handle terrorism cases. Critics had always argued that the government's first priority after the arrest of a terror suspect was to quickly gather intelligence. If terrorists could hire lawyers and invoke their constitutional right not to talk, critical information that could prevent future attacks might be lost. But the Zazi case showed that the criminal law provided incentives and levers that encouraged suspects to cooperate, including plea bargains and other forms of pressure. Zazi agreed to plead guilty after the FBI threatened to arrest and deport his mother.

By late October, Holder's team of prosecutors had finished their work. They produced a four-hundred-page document that became known as "the pros memo on steroids," the argument in favor of trying terrorist suspects in Article III courts.

Holder stayed up past one in the morning at his kitchen table reading the memo. The large round table was the same place at which Holder would make wrenching federal death-penalty decisions, staying up late into the night long after his wife and children had gone to bed. He marked up the KSM memo with red and yellow Sharpies, turning down the corners of pages where he had questions or concerns. Not long afterward, prosecutors piled into the seventh-floor Command Center at the Department of Justice and made their case to their bosses. Holder pulled out his dog-eared copy of the memo and scribbled more notes. The former prosecutor and judge was in his element, peppering Bharara and Neil MacBride, the US attorney in the Eastern District of Virginia, with questions, probing for holes in the case. For the first time, Holder showed his hand, literally. He placed it a couple of inches above the conference table. "When we began this process," he told the prosecutors, "I was here." Then he raised his hand high up above the table. "Now I am here," he said. When he walked out of the Command Center, he told Kevin Ohlson, his chief of staff, that he had made up his mind: KSM was headed to Manhattan.

Lindsey Graham had heard rumors that Holder was going to strip the case away from the military and give it to the feds. Anticipating Holder's announcement, he introduced legislation that would have barred KSM and the other 9/11 defendants from being tried in civilian court. "These people are not criminals, they're warriors — KSM, the mastermind of 9/11, did not rob a liquor store," Graham said in a Senate speech. In a rare show of force on counterterrorism policy, the White House legislative office snapped into action, successfully beating back the Graham provision by a vote of 54 to 45.

Late in the day on Wednesday, November 11, Emanuel walked into Craig's office.

"So what's it going to be?" the chief of staff said in a slightly threatening tone. "What's Eric going to do on KSM?"

Craig looked up at Emanuel and said: "It looks like he's decided to do it in an Article III court."

"What about Lindsey?" Emanuel asked. "Didn't he talk to him?"

Not wanting to lobby Holder directly, Emanuel had turned to Graham as his proxy, orchestrating a series of conversations between the South Carolina Republican and the attorney general. It didn't seem to have made a difference, Craig told him. Emanuel stood at the door without saying anything for a few moments. But he couldn't suppress his coiled rage.

"Well someone's going to have to fucking tell the president," he said, slamming the door on the way out.

A series of Emanuel eruptions ensued throughout the White House over the next forty-eight hours. "Eric's trying to be a fucking hero at the expense of the president," he said during one of them, pounding on his desk over and over again. Emanuel believed the KSM decision could have huge negative implications for the president's agenda, from preventing the closing of Guantánamo to potentially imperiling health care reform.

Lindsey Graham was walking through the Chapel of the Ascension on Jerusalem's Mount of Olives when he heard the chimes of his cell phone. Emanuel was on the line. He had tracked Graham down on a congressional trip to Israel.

"I think Holder's going to put KSM in federal court," he said, with near panic in his voice.

"Rahm, I can't live with this," Graham shot back.

"I know, you need to tell him that," Emanuel said. "You need to be firm with Eric."

"How much firmer can I be?" Graham pleaded, referring to the bill he had sponsored that would have prohibited civilian trials for KSM and the other 9/11 conspirators. Still, he said he would try to talk Holder out of it. He put away his phone. Down below Graham saw the Old City, copper-colored light glinting off the Jerusalem stone, minarets, and church steeples poking up between the ancient buildings. The chapel was the traditional site of Jesus's ascension to heaven. It had also been a battleground in the clash between Islam and Christendom — Saladin had wrested away control of the holy place from the Crusaders in 1187, turning it into a mosque. Now, Graham was distracted by thoughts of a much more modern holy warrior.

Holder himself had just returned from a trip to the Middle East, stopping off in London on the way back to Washington. While there he visited with Jack Straw, the British justice secretary, whom Holder had known when he was deputy attorney general during the Clinton administration. With his public announcement on KSM looming, he asked his old friend what he thought. "If you do these cases in military commissions, you will lose Europe, you will lose India, you will lose Africa," Straw said. "We all hold out your [justice system] as being the best in the world and it's true."

Holder liked to think that his decision on the 9/11 cases reflected the beliefs of a hard-nosed prosecutor. And there was no doubt that he was driven in part by pragmatic, tactical considerations. But the KSM decision also amounted to a test of his principles. It was an opportunity to show that the speeches he'd given criticizing the Bush administration — "We owe the American people a reckoning," he'd said in a June 2008 address — amounted to more than just political rhetoric.

As Graham continued to tour the ancient church, his phone rang again. This time it was Holder. Emanuel had kept pushing the attorney general to talk to Graham, to "calm him down." But Holder knew what the chief of staff's true agenda was. He told Graham he had made up his mind to prosecute KSM in federal court.

"This is a bridge too far," Graham told Holder. "I have to fight back on this one. It's just bad policy and it's going to blow up in your face." Holder, who liked the senator and had gotten along well with him, told him he understood where Graham was coming from and acknowledged that it had been a tough decision. But he had made up his mind and it was final.

The next morning, November 12, Obama was ornery. One aide described him as moving through the White House with "storm clouds" hovering over his head. The president's moodiness stood out because of his normally unruffled demeanor, even under unimaginable stress. There were plenty of reasons for him to be irritable. For one thing, he was leaving later in the day on an eight-day trip to Asia and he never liked being away from his family for that long. And the evening before, he had had another in a long series of grueling meetings with his national security team to settle on a new strategy for Afghanistan and Pakistan. He was not satisfied with the advice he was getting. But Holder's decision was also weighing on him. Once, the president had peevishly asked an aide whose idea it was to prosecute the 9/11 defendants in civilian courts in the first place. The adviser sheepishly told him it was his, reminding Obama that in his Archives speech he'd insisted that the presumption would be in favor of Article III courts unless military commissions were the only viable option. I didn't know that meant KSM, Obama answered.

Early that morning, Obama had summoned Greg Craig to the

Oval Office. They were alone with the president, but Emanuel did all the talking.

"Does the AG know that if he tries these cases in Article III courts, we're never going to be able to close Guantánamo?" he asked, directing his ire at Craig. "Does Eric know the consequences of this? Hasn't he talked to Lindsey?"

Holder and Graham had had multiple conversations, Craig responded; he knew full well Graham's position. Craig was seething, stunned that Emanuel would humiliate him like this in front of the president. Meanwhile, Obama said nothing. Even at this late hour, Craig realized, the chief of staff was trying to get the president to persuade Holder to reverse his decision. "He was trying to use me as a missile against Holder," Craig later recalled. "It was obscene." And Craig couldn't believe that a single senator from the opposing party seemed to hold so much sway in Obama's White House. "This was Lindsey reaching into the heart of the Oval Office," he said. And Graham wouldn't have disagreed. "Generally speaking, I don't want to make executive branch decisions, but this was such a big deal that I couldn't be silent," he said many months later in an interview. What was most perplexing was that Obama now seemed to be going wobbly on Article III prosecutions. He had spoken out passionately in favor of civilian trials during the campaign and later defended them at White House meetings. And yet now it looked as if he had unleashed Emanuel as his personal attack dog on Craig. What did it mean?

For Craig it was the lowest moment in a season of downers. It came the day before his long-rumored resignation was to take place. Carefully orchestrated, the White House was preparing to release mutually respectful statements from both Craig and Obama so the proud lawyer could maintain a modicum of dignity. It wasn't to be.

That evening the *Washington Post* reported that Craig was being pushed out. The story was attributed to anonymous "people familiar with the situation." It was a drive-by shooting.

After the meeting, Obama walked across the narrow corridor from the Oval Office and entered the Roosevelt Room. Aides were scurrying around, lining up their travel suitcases against the wall, getting ready for the president's Asia trip. Obama looked annoyed and the room quickly filled with tension. He was moving from one terrorism headache to the next. On the agenda was whether — and how — to announce the White House's latest plan to transfer prisoners from Guantánamo to the homeland. This was the last remnant of the Plan, which Emanuel had kept under wraps to protect health care reform. After the Standish facility in Michigan had collapsed as an option, the White House settled on an empty state penitentiary in northwest Illinois, Thomson Correctional Center. Obama officials knew how easily — and fiercely — local opposition could erupt against such prison transfers. To avoid leaks, they had sent administration officials on a secret mission to investigate the facility under the cover of darkness.

The concern about how to announce Thomson, with a bang or little fanfare, was emblematic of the White House's constant dilemma on Guantánamo-related decisions. Would Obama stand firmly behind his policies? Or would he try to slip it through quietly without stirring up passions on Capitol Hill? As usual, his advisers were divided. Phil Schiliro, the White House's top congressional lobbyist, favored a more public approach; it was time to engage the Congress confidently, or the White House would continue to get rolled. Dan Pfeiffer, the deputy director of communications and an Emanuel ally, argued against a public rollout. It was only days after the House had finally passed health care reform over lockstep Republican opposition and mixed opinion polls. Why roil the waters again by announcing that a large number of Guantánamo detainees were going to be transferred to an American prison? Finally, Obama asked Emanuel what he thought.

"I'll have to think about that," Emanuel said flatly. The Plan would be put off once again.

Holder's team had put together an elaborate PR strategy to build support for the Khalid Sheikh Mohammed decision. They had written an op-ed piece for the *New York Times* explaining the legal and political rationale for trying the 9/11 cases in New York, and they were planning to line up interviews for Holder on the Sunday news programs and with other print and broadcast outlets. But when the White House got word of the media blitz, Emanuel nixed it. Holder was told he could give a single television interview: to PBS's *NewsHour,* with its measly one million viewers, most of whom were likely already in Holder's camp. Emanuel was handcuffing Holder again — and the attorney general was enraged.

That evening Holder called Air Force One to formally notify the president of his decision. Obama didn't take the call, so Holder gave the news to one of his aides. Holder and his team worked into the night, fine-tuning their public statement and preparing for the next day's press conference. Fatally, they did not prepare the ground with any of the key politicians or law enforcement officials in New York. Obsessed with leaks, they wanted to make sure they framed the story themselves. The last thing they needed was a populist backlash sparked by the New York tabloids, which were sure to slap KSM's mug on their covers. "Never lose control of the narrative," was the mantra of Holder's media-savvy communications director, Matt Miller.

They decided to alert New York authorities at the last possible minute. At 7 A.M. on Friday the thirteenth, Preet Bharara, the US attorney for the Southern District of New York, reached Police Commissioner Raymond Kelly at home to tell him the news. Kelly, a two-time police commissioner and crafty politician, was surprised by the abrupt notification. "I guess this is a done deal," he thought to himself. Still, he indicated to Bharara that the police would be able to handle security for the trial. Later that morning, Holder personally informed Mayor Michael Bloomberg, who raised no objections. At 10 A.M., Holder stepped up to the podium in the Justice Department's briefing room to announce his decision. For such a consequential and politically fraught announcement, he appeared as a strikingly lonely figure. None of his fellow cabinet members stood with him, not even Bob Gates, whose presence the Justice Department had requested. Holder told reporters it was the "hardest" call he had made since becoming attorney general. He was grilled by reporters, who zeroed in on all of the vulnerabilities of the decision. What would happen if KSM were acquitted, they asked. Would he walk? Holder stubbornly stayed on message, saying over and over again that their case was strong and he was confident the Justice Department would win convictions. Then he obliquely alluded to the secret evidence that he believed was his trump card: "I will say that I have access to information that has not been publicly released that gives me great confidence that we will be successful in the prosecution of these cases in federal court." No one followed up on Holder's intriguing assertion. When a reporter asked about the inevitable political fallout from the controversial decision, Holder said he was prepared to "take my lumps."

The reaction to the decision was exactly as Emanuel knew it would be. Holder was hammered by Republicans on the Hill. "The possibility that Khalid Sheikh Mohammed and his coconspirators could be found 'not guilty,' due to some legal technicality, just blocks away from Ground Zero, should give every American pause," minority leader John Boehner said after the announcement. Still, at first, all of the key New York pols lined up behind Holder. "It is fitting that the 9/11 suspects face justice near the World Trade Center site where so many New Yorkers were murdered," Bloomberg said.

Oddly, Lindsey Graham declined to publicly criticize the decision. Instead he put out a brief statement noting that the White House had asked him to refrain from commenting until he had a chance to discuss the issue with the president after he returned from his trip to Asia. For his part, Obama did his best to portray it as tough justice, telling reporters in Japan: "I am absolutely convinced that Khalid Sheikh Mohammed will be subjected to the most exacting demands of justice. The American people insist on it and my administration will insist on it."

The next week, Holder stumbled under hostile questioning from Republicans on the Senate Judiciary Committee. What would the Justice Department do if KSM were acquitted? they asked repeatedly. Holder got tangled up in the internal logic of his own decision. "Failure is not an option," he said, suggesting a predetermined outcome to the trial. Worse, he indicated that, if acquitted, KSM could be held preventively under the laws of war, an argument that undercut the reasons for using Article III courts in the first place. White House lawyers and legislative aides were watching the drubbing on TV, cringing with each misstep. They tried to get Holder's aides to slip him a note to clarify his statements. White House lobbyists started calling Senate staffers before the hearing had even ended. "Damage control in real time," as an Obama aide put it.

On December 6 Holder traveled to New York to talk with police and court officials about security and other logistical matters. Holder and Kelly, along with the chief judge and US marshal for the Southern District, walked through the underground tunnel that ran between the federal courthouse and the Metropolitan Correctional Center, where KSM and other 9/11 defendants would be held during the trial. It was a dark, grim passageway between court and jail. Ray Kelly pointed out the small, dirty cell that had been designated as KSM's. "This is worse than Guantánamo," Holder said without irony.

Later that day, Kelly unveiled his security plan to Holder. As the commissioner unfurled his charts and maps, Holder began to realize what an elaborate production Kelly had in mind. He said he would need to create two "perimeters," with police checkpoints at dozens of intersections. Holder looked at the map and saw that Kelly was effectively lopping off the lower third of the island. Meanwhile, hundreds of police would be assigned to the case around the clock and dozens of cameras installed within a several-mile radius of the courthouse. It briefly occurred to Holder that Kelly might be trying to kill the trial by jacking up the security costs beyond what Congress would be willing to pay. But if that were the case, Holder was ahead of Kelly. He had already identified $100 million in Justice Department asset-forfeiture funds that he could spend without congressional approval. The total cost of the trial, including security, surely wouldn't exceed that.

A few days after Obama returned from Asia, he met with Graham in the Oval Office. It was Emanuel who had pleaded with Graham not to publicly criticize the KSM decision until he'd had a chance to sit down with the president. Maybe he would be able to persuade Obama to reverse Holder. Or maybe the president would be able to bring Graham over to his side, though that seemed unlikely. Obama was hoping for a thoughtful conversation on the merits of the decision. He respected Graham for his reasoned, principled approach to national security policy, a rarity in Washington.

Obama began by acknowledging that there were strong arguments on both sides. Honorable people could disagree without trashing each other's positions, he seemed to be saying. He told Graham he believed there was a place for military commissions — that it was the proper venue to prosecute combatants who had violated the laws of war. But he also believed 9/11 was an attack on all Americans, which made civilian courts an appropriate venue for KSM. "It was a very close call," he told Graham. "But I'm with Eric on this one, he's got the better side of the argument." But Graham would not budge. He had made his position abundantly clear: he would not support civilian trials for the 9/11 defendants.

Throughout the winter, Obama tacked back and forth on KSM. In part that reflected his own ambivalence toward the decision. He hated the politics surrounding the issue and did not want to stake his domestic agenda on something that most Americans cared little about. At the same time, *he* cared about the issue, as did many of his closest friends. Obama liked to talk about staying "true to who we are." The pressures and complexities of the office make it difficult for any president to stay attached to his basic touchstones and values. Obama was surrounded by a chorus of political advisers, led by his chief of staff, who were able to make powerful arguments in favor of the pragmatic, politically expedient path. And for Obama that was sometimes the path of least resistance. But time and again, he would pivot back to his more high-minded, idealistic instincts. Sometimes it was because Valerie Jarrett or Michelle Obama or his own inner voice guided him back to first principles.

The contradictory moves could be maddening to the "front office," where Obama's political advisers worked. Just when they thought he'd signed off on the pragmatic choice, he would reverse course. One eternally frustrated White House participant described the dynamic this way: "You're an adviser to the president and the question is: should you speak up in a meeting and say, 'This is crazy, Congress isn't going to let you do this'? So why aren't you going to say that to the president? Because it's going to leak and you're going to get pilloried by the liberal blogosphere. There's just no incentive system for being right about the unpleasant things. And meanwhile, there's always somebody next to the president saying, 'Mr. President, if you just say to the country, "This is consistent with our values and it's in the greatest traditions of the country," you'll be able to persuade the American people.' So you're the one who's going to say, 'No, Mr. President, you can't.' The internal balance of debates weighed more toward optimism."

Obama seemed content to let different advisers believe different things about his position. Holder had made the decision to try KSM in federal court with the confidence that it was his decision, as attorney general, to make. But he'd also had no doubt that Obama agreed with his judgment. Emanuel had every reason to believe that Obama was with him on KSM; why else would he have authorized the Lindsey Graham backchannel? By early 2010, after one year in office, the great question about President Obama had become: what did he truly believe and how much political capital was he prepared to expend? It was one thing to have a "team of rivals," another to let them fight without any resolution or action.

7

THE CHRISTMAS GIFT

ALITTLE AFTER 8 A.M. on Christmas Day 2009, Umar Farouk Abdulmutallab, a twenty-three-year-old Nigerian Muslim, boarded Northwest Airlines Flight 253 in Amsterdam, bound for Detroit. He'd paid for his $2,831 round-trip ticket in cash. He had no luggage. Sewn into his underwear were eighty grams of the explosive chemical PETN.

As the plane made its initial approach to Detroit, Abdulmutallab went into the plane's bathroom, staying there for about twenty minutes. He returned to seat 19A, near the plane's fuel tank, and covered himself with a blanket, complaining of a stomachache. Then, as the plane began its final descent into Detroit's Metropolitan Airport, Abdulmutallab attempted to ignite the PETN with a syringe by injecting liquid acid into the concealed package. Passengers heard a pop and smelled something burning. Some of them noticed Abdulmutallab's pant leg on fire. A Dutch passenger tackled him to the ground, and other passengers helped subdue him. The plane landed safely and no one other than Abdulmutallab was injured.

It was the biggest headline in the war on terror since Obama had taken office — a terrifying reminder that it is all but impossible to prevent individual attackers from slipping past all defenses. Yet Obama waited three days before responding publicly. When he did come forward, he mistakenly called the suspect "an isolated extremist." In fact, Abdulmutallab was a trained operative of al-Qaeda in the Arabian Peninsula, the Yemen-based al-Qaeda affiliate that was of increasing concern to US counterterrorism officials. The more John Brennan learned about the plot, the more officials realized how narrowly they had avoided a catastrophe.

Abdulmutallab, a lonely and sullen young man, had fallen under the sway of Anwar al-Awlaki, an American-born Yemeni cleric who was a rising star within AQAP. Awlaki's charismatic Internet sermons, idiomatic English, and intuitive grasp of American culture made him a uniquely dangerous terrorist. But he was more than just an inspirational figure. By the time of the Christmas Day plot he had risen to become AQAP's chief of external operations. The rise of AQAP was ironic evidence of American *successes* in the war on terror. The unrelenting drone campaign was decimating al-Qaeda's core leadership in Pakistan and disrupting its ability to pull off new "spectaculars." AQAP was fast becoming a more important enemy of the United States. "The branch has become stronger than the trunk," as one senior counterterrorism official put it at the time.

The Christmas plot was an eerie flashback to a time when the country was perpetually on edge in the aftermath of 9/11. Obama would no longer be judged by how eloquently he criticized his predecessor or invoked American values. Now what mattered was his own ability to thwart new attacks as well as project strength in the face of a persistent and ever-evolving threat. The war on terror was finally all his.

But the president's response was flatfooted and detached. Was he too much the law professor and not enough of a warrior? For all of George W. Bush's bravado and gunslinging rhetoric, he had reacted viscerally to 9/11, giving voice to Americans' grief and rage. In the days following Christmas Day, Obama seemed incapable of having his own "bullhorn moment." Behind the scenes, he stayed in touch with his national security team by phone, but he stuck to his vacation schedule in Hawaii. He got up for early basketball games at a nearby marine base, played golf with his buddies from Chicago, and took strolls on the tropical beaches with his family.

Obama's slow reflexes were a gift to Republicans. They had figured out that attacking the president on terrorism was a win-win. It played well with the conservative base, and Democrats, for the most part, were unwilling to stick their necks out to defend the president. Peter King, a GOP congressman from Long Island, cruised the cable news stations lambasting Obama for his lack of "leadership" in what could have been "one of the greatest tragedies in the history of our country." Later, two of Obama's closest aides, David Axelrod and Dan Pfeiffer, apologized for counseling him not to come out sooner. Axelrod, ever protective of his friend and boss, believed Obama deserved time to decompress after such a taxing first year. Only Press Secretary Robert Gibbs seemed to grasp the president's symbolic role in calming a fearful public — not to mention the poor optics of remaining secluded at his Hawaiian villa while the country fretted about terrorism.

Yet it is likely that Obama's own deliberative, intellectualized approach kept him from rushing to the microphones. He did not believe that the country needed to come to a grinding halt every time there was a failed terrorism attempt. That would only play into the hands of terrorists. The president consciously wanted to move away from the anxiety-inducing playbook of the Bush administration. Obama officials remembered all too well Attorney General John Ashcroft bizarrely breaking in on daytime television from a Russian TV studio in 2002 to announce the arrest of José Padilla at Chicago's O'Hare airport. Ashcroft, it would later turn out, inaccurately reported that Padilla was en route to detonate a radiological "dirty bomb" in an American city. By contrast, Obama wanted to encourage American resilience — a word that had gained much currency among counterterrorism officials — in the face of threats.

A few weeks before Christmas the president had participated in a top-secret "tabletop" exercise at the White House. In the exercise, a terrorist plot was unfolding in the United States and the president's national security team had to coordinate a "whole of government" response. The focus of the exercise was on how to communicate the threat to the American people. Should Homeland Security's color-coded alert be raised? How should the White House approach public messaging? And, critically, when should the president come forward to address the country? At the end of the drill, the president fired a series of prepared questions at his advisers. There was some light-hearted ribbing of FBI Director Robert Mueller, whose agency was cast in the role of the gang that couldn't shoot straight. Then Obama moved away from the table, assumed a serious tone, and addressed the entire group. "One of the things for which I am proudest of this administration is that we haven't demagogued these issues," he told the group, according to one of the participants. "We haven't been playing to people's fears and we haven't been playing politics with terrorism. We've been careful about how we talk to the American people about these risks." One participant, a little misty-eyed recalling the episode, called it a "*West Wing* moment," after the NBC series starring Martin Sheen as every liberal's fantasy of a principled, idealistic president.

Yet there were no uplifting Hollywood moments on Christmas Day or the days immediately following. And when the president did come forward, on December 28, his problems went well beyond botched public relations. There had in fact been multiple warning signals within the government about Abdulmutallab. His father, a prominent banker in Nigeria, had walked into the embassy in Abuja and told officials that his son had vanished and that he was worried he was consorting with extremists from Yemen. The father's information had led to Abdulmutallab being placed in a government database of five hundred thousand people with terrorist links, though he was never placed on the much smaller "No Fly" list. Worse still, the National Security Agency had intercepted phone messages that mentioned Abdulmutallab by name and that indicated he might be involved in planning attacks against the United States. But that information was never shared with other agencies. "The system should have been lighting up like a Christmas tree," Ali Soufan, a former senior counterterrorism official at the FBI, told *Newsweek* at the time. Obama was furious when he learned about the multiple intelligence failures. "A systemic failure has occurred and I consider that totally unacceptable," he told reporters at the Kaneohe marine base. It did not help matters that Janet Napolitano, Obama's Homeland Security adviser, had gone on the Sunday news shows proclaiming that the "system had worked." Later, she said she was referring to the increased security measures imposed after the attack — but the damage had been done.

Criticism over the poor communications and dysfunctional intelligence-sharing was fierce, but relatively short-lived. It was a different line of Republican attack that did the most lasting damage: nine hours after he was taken into custody, federal agents gave Abdulmutallab his Miranda warning, affirming his right to remain silent and to be represented by a lawyer. Earlier in the day FBI agents had interrogated the suspected terrorist for nearly an hour prior to the warning. Abdulmutallab provided valuable intelligence about his connections to al-Qaeda operatives in Yemen, the provenance of the bomb that had been sewed into his underwear, and the training he had received. But Justice Department lawyers worried that if too much time elapsed before he was given his legal rights, their prosecution could be jeopardized. (Non-Mirandized statements are not admissible as evidence unless they are elicited under the "public safety" exception, which allows law enforcement officers to engage in a limited, focused interrogation before the warning is given.) During a 5 P.M. secure videoconference chaired by John Brennan after the thwarted attack, a Justice Department lawyer said that Abdulmutallab would be read his rights and charged in federal court the next day. On the call were senior representatives from the White House, Homeland Security, US Customs and Border Protection, the FBI, DNI, and an assortment of other security agencies. No one raised any objections. At about 9 P.M., shortly after Abdulmutallab emerged from surgery, FBI agents attempted to engage him again. As they went through boilerplate information — booking details and the like — they determined that he was hostile and was through cooperating. They Mirandized him at 9:16 P.M., after which he clammed up and asked for a lawyer.

The agents were acting according to long-established protocols, but it opened up the Obama presidency, once again, to charges of governance by lawyer. In the following days and weeks the criticism from the right mounted: the administration's response to the Christmas Day bomber was more confirmation that Obama possessed a "pre-9/11 mentality" and that he was intent on treating terrorists as common criminals. Abdulmutallab should have been designated an enemy combatant and shipped straight to Guantánamo, critics argued. Intelligence was the priority, the ability to quickly obtain information from captured terrorists that could prevent impending attacks.

These arguments, of course, overlooked the fact that every suspected terrorist detained in the United States during the Bush administration had been treated as a criminal defendant. Even José Padilla, who was at first placed in a military brig and held as an enemy combatant, was eventually transferred to the criminal justice system. But any chance to attack, in Washington, is a chance to be seized: often the most effective political offensives are those that reinforce existing perceptions. It was true that Obama, as *Newsweek* put it, was "steeped in a tradition that privileges the Bill of Rights over the crude or arbitrary exercise of power." It was true that he was brainy and nuanced compared to his predecessor, whose instincts were Manichaean and from the gut. It hardly mattered that Obama was killing terrorists at a faster rate than any American president ever had. The CIA drone program was covert and Obama wasn't about to rush out to the White House lawn to claim credit. Worst of all, Obama's reluctance to engage the public allowed his most vociferous critics to set the terms of the debate. The Republican barrage was broad-based. As usual, Dick Cheney was the tip of the partisan spear.

"As I've watched the events of the last few days it is clear once again that President Obama is trying to pretend that we are not at war," the former vice president declared in a statement on December 29. "He seems to think that if we have a low-key response to an attempt to blow up an airliner and kill hundreds of people, we won't be at war. He seems to think that if we give terrorists the rights of Americans, let them lawyer up, and read them their Miranda rights, we won't be at war . . . He seems to think that if he closes Guantánamo and releases the hard-core al-Qaeda-trained terrorists still there, we won't be at war . . . But we are at war and when President Obama pretends we aren't, it makes us less safe."

Some Obama officials struck an air of indifference to Cheney's broadsides. Ben Rhodes, the deputy national security adviser, even suggested that there were political benefits to be gained when Cheney, rising out of the shadows like Darth Vader, went on the attack. "I thought the contrast was helpful," Rhodes said. "In a set of issues in which there are no good options, having the worst option on display helps your arguments." Such is the wishful thinking that infects nearly every administration. In fact, for the White House, the psychic toll of Christmas Day was profound. Obama realized that if a failed terror attempt could suck up so much political oxygen, a successful attack would absolutely devastate his presidency. And much as he liked to talk about returning to first principles, Obama also had a powerful instinct for self-correction — as well as self-preservation.

When the president returned to Washington, he summoned his national security principals to a "come to Jesus" meeting, as one participant called it. The woodshedding was swift and unsparing. "This was a screwup that could have been disastrous," Obama chided his team. "We dodged a bullet, but just barely. It was averted by brave individuals, not because the system worked. And that is unacceptable." He went around the room, closely questioning his team about the cascade of mistakes that led up to the near miss. Several participants in the meeting would later remark that he reserved his most penetrating cross-examination for his friend the attorney general. Obama asked Holder about the conversations that led to the Miranda decision. He wanted to know how the process worked from the ground up. Who had made the call? Why not question Abdulmutallab longer? Who else in the government was consulted? Holder explained that the FBI had followed "standard practice," and walked him through the steps. He also told the president that he had not been involved in the decision and didn't learn about it until after the fact. Obama may have been stoked by a conversation he'd had with Janet Napolitano just before the cabinet session. She'd requested the meeting with the president, in part to defend her agency's role in the burgeoning controversy. Napolitano's "the system worked" gaffe notwithstanding, she was one of the more politically adept members of Obama's cabinet, and was so well regarded by the president that he gave serious thought to putting her on the Supreme Court. But she was also a skilled bureaucratic infighter who knew how to advance her own interests within the cabinet. In the pre-meeting with Obama, Napolitano distanced herself from the Miranda decision, suggesting that the FBI could have taken more time before reading Abdulmutallab his legal rights.

Obama was getting hammered by the Republicans on Miranda and was looking for a way to relieve the pressure. He ordered a top-to-bottom review of the guidelines governing the arrest procedure. His lawyers went even further. They began looking into whether Congress could pass a law allowing the government to detain terrorism suspects longer before presenting them to a judge of magistrate. Both Miranda and speedy "presentment" were bedrock principles of the rights of criminal defendants. Tinkering with them, let alone scaling them back, would be anathema to the civil liberties groups. It would also, no doubt, feed the persistent narrative among liberals that Obama, despite his campaign rhetoric, had embraced the hardline policies of the Bush administration.

But perhaps even more worrisome to liberals was that the president's motives may not have been entirely political. He prided himself on having a less doctrinaire, ideologically rigid approach to the law. Instead of getting caught up in legal technicalities, he would step back and ask whether a law was fundamentally just or practical. He had no problem with military commissions, for example, once he'd satisfied himself that they operated under rules of evidence and procedures that were fair. On Miranda, Obama wanted to make sure the government wasn't simply on "autopilot." He recognized the tension between the need to inform a suspect of his legal rights and the security imperatives in quickly collecting all of the available intelligence that could prevent a planned attack. At the same time, he believed that laws needed to be carefully reevaluated in light of evolving threats. In an age of mass casualty attacks by nonstate actors, wouldn't it make sense to expand the public-safety exception and give law enforcement more time to question a suspected terrorist who may have knowledge of other impending plots? But how far was he willing to go?

Holder believed that the arrest had been handled appropriately, balancing the needs of intelligence, law enforcement, and the rights of suspects. But he also had a pragmatic streak. He recognized that, post-Abdulmutallab, he was operating in a transformed political landscape. After the January 5 Situation Room drubbing, he gathered his ExCom and told them that the Justice Department would have to learn from the event. "The world has changed," he said.

Nothing reflected the change in climate after the Abdulmutallab arrest more than the quick unraveling of Holder's plan to try Khalid Sheikh Mohammed and the 9/11 defendants in Manhattan. The first blow was a letter that Mayor Michael Bloomberg sent in early January to the White House budget office seeking more than $216 million to pay for security for the first year of the trial—and an additional $200 million for every year after that. The letter quickly leaked to Congress. With estimates that the trial could last up to five years, critics seized on the $1 billion total price tag.

By the end of January, local opposition had grown into a full-blown rebellion, led by community groups and business associations in lower Manhattan. On January 27, Bloomberg struck a grievous blow to Holder's plan, telling reporters that a trial for KSM would be too costly and too disruptive for the city to handle. "It would be great if the federal government could find a site that didn't cost a billion dollars, which using downtown will," he said. Other powerful New York politicians, including Democrats Chuck Schumer and Jerrold Nadler, quickly followed the mayor's lead.

Buckling under the pressure, White House aides began leaking to the press that Holder was considering other venues. Around the same time, word reached the attorney general that Lindsey Graham was planning to reintroduce his amendment barring the use of congressional funds to try KSM in federal court. In October, the White House had managed to defeat the measure, but now it would be much harder. And this time, Holder suspected that the White House was working *with* Graham rather than against him. Though he couldn't prove it, Holder suspected that Emanuel was secretly encouraging conservative blue-dog Democrats to vote for the Graham amendment.

On January 29 Obama gathered the principals to assess the fallout from Holder's KSM decision. Holder was noticeably subdued in his defense of what he had called the "defining event" of his tenure as attorney general. He undermined his position with an embarrassing breach of protocol. In White House parlance, the session was known as a "plus one." Cabinet members were permitted to bring a single senior aide, who had the expertise to back them up when complicated questions arose. For national security meetings with the president, Holder would typically bring David Kris, the head of Justice's National Security Division, a heavyweight lawyer and policy maven, or David Barron from the elite Office of Legal Counsel. But on this occasion he brought along Matt Miller, his press secretary. Miller was politically savvy, but he wasn't a lawyer.

One issue that quickly came up was Senator Graham's amendment to bar funding for civilian trials. When Holder was asked whether Congress had the constitutional authority to determine where a criminal prosecution should take place — normally an executive-branch function — Holder was at a loss and had no one to turn to. The gaffe left some with the impression that he was more concerned with his own public relations than the substance of a weighty national security problem. For once, the administration needed *more* lawyers. (A few days later, Holder and Obama had a one-on-one meeting in the Oval Office to clear the air. The attorney general griped that he was being undermined by Emanuel. Obama chastised Holder for bringing his flack to a serious policy discussion. "Really?" he said somewhat incredulously. "You brought your press secretary?" Holder, in a retort that only someone as secure as he was with the president could have made, pointed out that Obama had brought his own press secretary, Robert Gibbs, to the meeting. Obama did not dispute the point.)

Holder left the Situation Room meeting relieved that the KSM plan was still alive, if barely. He had reason to believe that Obama was still in his corner. The president had, after all, ended the meeting with a dramatic flourish, reading the statement that US District Judge William Young had delivered in the 2003 sentencing of Richard Reid, the shoe bomber. Holder knew the odds of success were long, but he was determined to keep fighting. Whatever the outcome, he believed his legacy was at stake. He thought of a line from one of his favorite movies, *Raging Bull*, about the rise and fall of the boxer Jake LaMotta, played by Robert De Niro: "If you win, you win. If you lose, you still win," LaMotta's brother and manager, Joey, tells the aging prizefighter as he prepares him for a bout.

Yet Emanuel also must have left the meeting encouraged. Obama may have spoken stirringly about the rule of law and his faith in American courts, but he had also left himself a pragmatic path forward. He had authorized Emanuel to continue his backchannel negotiations with Lindsey Graham in pursuit of a grand bargain. Obama knew that any deal with Graham would foreclose the possibility of civilian trials for the 9/11 defendants, an absolute red line for the South Carolina senator. Still, if that was what it would take to close Guantánamo, it seemed like a reasonable tradeoff. It was classic Obama — preserving his options, playing key advisers off of each other, and hoping to turn intransigence into consensus.

Emanuel directed Robert Bauer, who had been named White House counsel after Greg Craig's resignation earlier that month, to take over the Graham talks. Soft-spoken and bearded, with a shock of gray, curly hair, Bauer came across more like a university professor than a sharp-tongued Washington lawyer. But he was cunning. He and Craig were a study in contrasts. Where Craig believed passionately in the rule of law and pushed for bold action, Bauer proudly described himself as "policy neutral" and advocated quiet, pragmatic incrementalism. Most importantly, Bauer had the confidence of the president's chief of staff.

In February, Tom Malinowski, the director of the Washington office of Human Rights Watch, went to the White House to lobby Bauer on KSM. He did not argue the substance of the KSM decision; he figured that on the merits there was no disagreement. Instead, he made a political argument. "The more you show you're willing to compromise, the more the Republicans sense weakness and insecurity," he told Bauer. Malinowski's pitch was by now a familiar refrain with respect to the White House. Obama, the argument went, was a weak negotiator who was not willing to stand up to congressional Republicans. It was a paradox of his presidency. He had been elected in part because he promised to change the culture of partisan intransigence in Washington. And yet a significant portion of his supporters viewed his willingness to compromise as fatally naive.

Bauer politely listened and took notes. Like Emanuel, Bauer believed that the only shot at closing Guantánamo was to craft a bipartisan deal with Lindsey Graham that would provide political cover for both Democrats and Republicans. But he had another concern.

"My fear," he told Malinowski, "is that there will be an all-out assault from the right in Congress on a whole range of executive prerogatives in the national security arena that would be much worse than anything we've seen so far."

Already Congress had imposed a forty-five-day notification requirement whenever the administration wanted to transfer a detainee from Guantánamo to the United States. He painted a dire picture of further congressional encroachment — the barring of funding for transfers, or worse still, a requirement that all future terrorist suspects would have to be prosecuted in military commissions. Bauer's implication was that if liberals stubbornly held out for everything on their wish list, they'd end up in a far worse position than if they compromised. Instead of restoring the rule of law, they'd be enshrining a national security state.

Malinowski was appalled by the White House's timidity, which he thought was self-fulfilling. He argued with Bauer, insisting that there was more support for these issues in Congress than the White House was acknowledging. He said the Democrats would get behind them so long as the White House showed some backbone. Bauer had heard this line before and it drove him around the bend. Vote counting is an art, not a science. Some of those same Democrats who were egging on the liberal interest groups were begging the White House to keep Guantánamo and detainee issues off the agenda.

By now, Bauer was deep into negotiations with Senator Graham. Graham had long supported shutting down Guantánamo. His larger goal, though, was for Congress to establish a broad legal framework for dealing with detention in national security cases. He argued, correctly, that there were no clear standards setting out who could be detained, how long they could be held, and under what rules they could challenge their detention. The Bush administration had built a system of detention that was essentially extralegal. But as the federal courts asserted jurisdiction over Guantánamo detainees, they had left behind a mishmash of rulings that provided no clear rules for judges to follow. They disagreed on who was an enemy combatant, what it would take for a member of al-Qaeda to prove he had severed his ties with the terrorist organization, and the extent to which confessions would be tainted by coerced testimony. Bauer agreed that the ad hoc arrangement was bad policy and ultimately unsustainable.

The problem was that Graham's proposed solutions were anathema to the left, since he was insisting on military tribunals and a congressionally sanctioned regime of preventive detention for new battlefield captures. And because he viewed the battlefield as unbounded in the war on terror, that meant that even American citizens could be detained and held indefinitely without a trial. Bauer, with Emanuel's blessing, had to test the limits of the president's flexibility.

In February 2010 Bauer summoned lawyers from the Pentagon, Justice, and the NSC to his office. When the meeting started he passed around a document his lawyers had just produced. Under the title "Determination of Guantánamo Cases Referred for Prosecution," it laid out new protocols for determining which cases would end up in military commissions and which would be tried in the federal courts.

It was essentially a rewrite of the original protocols memo that had divvied up the major Guantánamo prosecutions, sending KSM and four other 9/11 defendants to civilian court. But now there was a line crossing out the key sentence: "There is a presumption that, where feasible, referred cases will be prosecuted in Article III courts." Under the new rules, KSM would be headed for a military trial. It was a lawyerly way of trying to kill the Holder plan.

It was still not clear where Obama stood on the evolving thinking within the administration over civilian versus military trials. The president's restless mind continued to question how best to balance security and liberty, and continued to look for ways to break free from the conventional arguments. But what if there was no transcendent third way?

In March, the president quietly turned to an old mentor for fresh thinking. In a series of secret Oval Office meetings, Obama consulted Laurence Tribe, his professor at Harvard Law School. Tribe had hired Obama as his research assistant at Harvard, and the two spent dozens of hours together talking about the law and the Constitution. Years later they would discuss the legal excesses of the Bush administration, including Guantánamo, torture, and warrantless wiretapping. When Obama was elected, he beckoned Tribe to join his administration. An ambiguous conversation led Tribe to believe that he would have a job in the White House advising the president on the legal challenges arising out of the war on terror — a kind of rule-of-law czar. The prospect of Tribe, undoubtedly one of the most brilliant legal minds in the country but with an ego to match, rambling through the White House and offering up his counsel, touched off a small rebellion in the White House and at Justice. Ultimately Greg Craig deftly arranged for Tribe to get a job at the Justice Department, helping improve legal services for the poor. But Obama had always been grateful to Tribe and recognized his brilliance.

In the spring of 2010 they met three times, and talked about Guantánamo, terrorism trials, and detention issues. Obama insisted that the conversations be "offline and off the record." Obama apparently even hid the meetings from his most senior advisers. But word of the short-lived backchannel eventually leaked to Emanuel, who ripped into Tribe when the two bumped into each other in the West Wing of the White House in April.

On the evening of May 1, much of official Washington was attending the White House Correspondents' Association annual dinner, the ritual schmoozefest between politicos and the media elite. At about 9 P.M., some reporters noticed attendees Ray Kelly and Mayor Michael Bloomberg rise from their seats and slip out of the Hilton ballroom. Earlier that evening, in New York City, an alert T-shirt vendor noticed smoke rising up from a blue Toyota Pathfinder parked near Times Square. He also heard a popping noise that sounded like firecrackers going off. After he alerted a mounted policeman, authorities discovered that the car was packed with gasoline, propane canisters, and elaborate triggering devices. It was only the would-be bomber's selection of the wrong type of fertilizer that had prevented death and mayhem in the center of Manhattan.

The bomber was named Faisal Shahzad, an American citizen of Pakistani origin. Assimilated, well educated, with a good job as a financial analyst, he did not fit the expected profile of an Islamic terrorist. He had undertaken the operation for the TTP, the Pakistani Taliban, which had also been implicated in the assassination of former Pakistani prime minister Benazir Bhutto. The attempted attack put a spotlight on the hundreds of thousands of Pakistanis who travel back and forth between the United States and Pakistan every year; Shahzad had made such trips in order to train with militants. Fifty-three hours after the incident, federal agents arrested Shahzad on the tarmac at JFK Airport minutes before his flight was scheduled to take off for Dubai. It was stellar detective work; but once again a deadly disaster had been averted.

Obama made his first public statement less than eighteen hours after the incident. "We're going to do what's necessary to protect the American people, to determine who was behind this potentially deadly act, and to see that justice is done," he said. Meanwhile, Holder's ExCom saw the Shahzad attack as an opportunity to rehabilitate the attorney general's battered image. In carefully crafted press appearances, Holder was made to look tough on terrorism. Striking a pugilistic tone, Holder vowed to reporters "that the people responsible" would be brought to justice. He finished with a quote from his favorite boxer, Joe Louis: "You can run but you can't hide." As mindful as they were of the public optics, it was the legal decisions behind the scenes that were the most fraught. After Shahzad was arrested near midnight on May 3, Holder rushed down to the Justice Department. Soon he was on the phone with Preet Bharara, the US attorney in New York's Southern District. After a quick briefing on the takedown, Bharara raised the issue that was on everybody's minds: "Do we read the prisoner his Miranda rights?" Holder and Bharara both agreed that the answer was a resounding no. Shahzad was questioned under the public-safety exception until agents could determine there was no imminent terrorist threat. He soon waived his right to an attorney and a speedy court hearing. A committed jihadi who seemed intent on legal martyrdom, he held forth for almost two weeks, providing details of his own involvement in the crime and massive amounts of intelligence on his terrorist handlers back in Pakistan.

For weeks the White House had been crafting legislation to loosen the government's Miranda and presentment requirements. The arrest of Shahzad seemed like the perfect opportunity to roll out the proposals. It would insulate them against the persistent charge that Obama was criminalizing the war on terror, and it might even be a useful bargaining chip in the negotiations with Graham. The White House chose Holder to float the initiative on the Sunday news shows. On May 8, Holder told *Meet the Press* moderator David Gregory, "I think we have to think about perhaps modifying the rules that interrogators have and somehow coming up with something that is flexible and more consistent with the threat we now face." Conservative columnist Charles Krauthammer, who had been regularly lambasting Holder, lavished him with praise in the *Washington Post*.

Floating vague proposals to reform American arrest procedures was the easy part. Once the draft plan began circulating on Capitol Hill and within the administration, however, it quickly bogged down. The Miranda proposal would have codified the public-safety exception, turning it effectively into a "national security exception" for certain terrorism cases — and liberals didn't like it. Far more controversial was the White House's plan to delay the amount of time before a suspect had to be given a court hearing. The courts had held that suspects generally had to be brought before a magistrate within twenty-four to forty-eight hours to ensure there was probable cause that a crime had been committed. The White House initially proposed extending the amount of time to seven days. That was scaled back after Harold Koh pointed out in a sharply worded memo to the White House that no Western nation permitted their police to hold a suspect involuntarily, and without a hearing, for more than four days.

In Congress, meanwhile, Republicans threatened to ram through far more draconian measures. Already there were proposals gaining traction that had police-state overtones. One would have required that all terror suspects, even those caught on US soil, be automatically placed in military custody after arrest. Another mandated that terror suspects be stripped of their US citizenship. The White House, afraid of losing control of its legislative initiatives, backed down. Republicans just kept moving the goalpost to the right, and the White House just kept backing away from the kick.

At one point, sharp-eyed lawyers working for Bauer found a legislative trick that might have allowed the administration to slip through its Miranda plan without Republicans getting their hands on it. An intelligence authorization bill was being hammered out in a conference between the Senate and the House. Democrats could quietly attach the measure as an amendment. The bill was subject to an up or down vote, with no changes permitted, no debates, no hearings. But Obama rejected the idea. He was uncomfortable "just sneaking through something that had significant civil liberties implications," recalled one adviser who was involved in the plan. Ultimately, the White House shelved its proposals. On Miranda, the Justice Department reissued guidance to federal agents, encouraging them to interpret the public-safety exception somewhat more aggressively in terrorism cases.

It was ironic that Obama, who had castigated George W. Bush for bypassing Congress on terrorism, was now doing the same thing. But the Miranda episode confirmed what many had already come to believe: that an institution increasingly defined by demagoguery was not the best place to develop sensible counterterrorism policies.

While the White House was searching for ways to deal with the Miranda problem, the FBI was deploying its most time-honored criminal-justice tactics to great effect. In early January, agents traveled to Nigeria to enlist the support of Abdulmutallab's family in persuading their wayward relative to cooperate with the investigation. It worked. Over the next several weeks Abdulmutallab would provide a trove of valuable information about the plot itself as well as critical new intelligence about AQAP and its dangerous leader. Among other things, he told agents that Awlaki had personally directed him to attack America by blowing up a commercial airliner, and he revealed new information about AQAP's diabolically clever master bomb-maker, Ibrahim Hassan Tali al-Asiri.

By late May, the White House's negotiations with Graham were petering out. Bauer was one of the few who still had any hope for them. At one Roosevelt Room meeting, a marathon session that went deep into the evening, he and Graham believed they had reached the contours of an agreement. Even Senator Dick Durbin, the Illinois liberal and close ally of Obama's, seemed to be onboard. Hours into the White House session, Durbin got up to postpone his flight back home: it looked like a deal was within their grasp. It was an elevating meeting, a rare instance in which serious-minded people from across the political divide could still come together on the toughest issues — even counterterrorism. Graham called it "one of the best" meetings he'd ever attended. In the end, however, consensus between a few insiders did not translate into a viable alternative. Later, when Bauer floated the proposal on the Hill, where it was subject to the competing claims of members and their constituents, the initiative was quashed.

In early August, Holder escaped Washington for a family vacation on Martha's Vineyard. It couldn't have come sooner. Weary from months of warfare with the White House, he now faced editorials questioning his competence and a growing chorus of calls for his resignation. In an interview on Fox News, former House Speaker Newt Gingrich had even suggested that Holder was more preoccupied with the legal rights of terrorists than the safety of his own family. Holder tried to brush off the persistent and increasingly mean-spirited criticism. At

the time, the attorney general was facing a far more personal challenge. His mother, Miriam, who had been ailing badly after a stroke,
was staying with the family on the Vineyard. When he wasn't by her
side, Holder took long walks. He was soothed by the island's wild
beaches, dramatic cliffs, and stunning sunsets. But a few days after
the start of his vacation, Holder was summoned back to Washington.

National Security Adviser Jim Jones had convened a Principals
Committee meeting to once again try to find a path forward on
Guantánamo. Driving the agenda was the Pentagon's desire to revive
military commissions. Even as KSM and a number of the other 9/11
defendants were referred to the civilian system for prosecution, the
military cases remained frozen. In August, Defense officials started
agitating to lift the hold. Jones turned to Bob Gates, who was sitting directly to his left. Gates told the principals that it was "time to
move forward," whether KSM and the other civilian trials got off the
ground or not. Military prosecutors, who'd spent years assembling
the 9/11 cases, would soon start to retire; the evidence was growing
stale. "The system was atrophying," Gates said, according to one participant. Jones then turned to Hillary Clinton. The secretary of state
had largely stayed out of the messy KSM fight, but in the days before
the meeting, Harold Koh had lobbied her to take a strong stance in
favor of Article III trials and the administration's broader rule-of-law
agenda. "We need to stick to our guns," he told her. Clinton had kept
her counsel, refusing even to commit to attending the meeting. But
the night before, she'd told her staff she would go. Clinton's words
carried enormous influence inside the White House, and the room
filled with anticipation as she prepared to speak.

At first the secretary of state stuck to the talking points her staff
had prepared for her. But she soon strayed from her notes and began
to speak with conviction. She argued that the administration needed
to honor the commitments the president had laid out in his National

Archives speech in May, which included a presumption in favor of civilian trials, military commissions only where necessary, and shutting down Guantánamo. Reviving military trials without Article III prosecutions would be a twisting of the framework the president had laid out. "We would be throwing the president's commitment to close Guantánamo into the trash bin," she said. "We are doing him [the president] a disservice by not working harder on this."

Holder followed Clinton, echoing her argument that resuming military commissions on their own could undermine the administration's plan to pursue civilian trials. But then, buoyed by the secretary of state's forceful presentation, Holder launched into his own passionate speech. "Who are we as an administration?" he asked, surprised by the emotion that was welling up inside him. "Why did we take these jobs if not to do what we think is right?"

But it was Clinton who had changed the dynamic in the room. Gate's hard line softened. Military commissions and federal trials ought to operate in tandem, "like two wheels of a bicycle," he told the group. The defense secretary suggested putting off the resumption of commissions for another ninety days, a delay that, coincidentally or not, would take the administration past the midterm elections.

The morning after the principals meeting, his mood brightened by the turnaround on KSM, Holder returned to Martha's Vineyard. But a few days later, his mother died while he was sitting next to her hospital bed, holding her hand. Holder's security detail drove him back to the house where the family was staying. His wife, Sharon Malone, greeted him with a hug. Holder cried. Then he took his bicycle and rode alone to a nearby lighthouse. He sat on a bench and stared out at the Atlantic for nearly two hours. For a black kid growing up in the 1950s in a lower-middle-class home in New York City, Holder knew how much he owed his success to his mother. Her love for "little

Ricky" was unconditional, and yet her firm hand nudged him along. She built up his confidence; she taught him to be a proud black man without allowing himself to be defined by his race.

Two days later, the Holders had dinner with Barack and Michelle Obama, who were also vacationing on the Vineyard. They met at Blue Heron Farm, where the Obamas were staying. The president enveloped Holder in a hug. "You're going to be all right," he told him. For all the talk of his cool, Spock-like demeanor, Obama had a warm, visceral side to him. Later in the evening the president turned on the stereo and ran through his greatest hits of early '80s R & B. As they grooved and danced to the music, he and Malone competed to name the artists, many of whom topped the soul charts while they were in college. Sharon gently teased Eric, who was ten years older than the president. "He's still stuck on the Temptations," she said.

It was a warm and unpretentious evening that lifted Holder's spirits. But when he returned to work later that month he sank into a depression. The loss of his mother, the continuing criticism over KSM, the lashings in the press, and Holder's sense of isolation within the administration had turned his job into a grind. He woke up on many mornings with a knot in his stomach, not sure if he'd be able to make it through the day. The ceremonial aspects of his job, giving speeches and handing out awards, became almost unbearable. He told Sharon he didn't know if he had the emotional strength to go on as attorney general. He thought seriously about returning to his Washington law firm. At the office, he was so disengaged, the ExCom began talking about staging an intervention.

Ultimately, Kevin Ohlson, his chief of staff, confronted him. "You don't have to stay in this job," he told the AG. "You've served the president well, and if your heart's not in it, do what you think is best." Ohlson was being sincere, but he also hoped his advice would relieve the pressure, making it easier for Holder to choose to stay. When Valerie Jarrett heard that Holder was thinking about resigning his post, she took a different tack. Few people could talk to Holder as directly as Jarrett could. She started by gently telling him, "You're my friend and I care about you." Then the former veteran of the Richie Daley machine in Chicago lowered the boom.

"This will not be good for you and it will not be good for your friend, the president," she said, not mincing her words.

Jarrett didn't elaborate, but she didn't have to. Holder understood that if he quit barely two years into Obama's first term, it would be widely assumed that he was either driven out by Tammany Hall or that he'd quit because he was disillusioned with the administration's refusal to back him up. His exit would have become a rallying cry for the liberal base of the party and it would damage Obama politically just as the midterm elections were looming.

He had to stay.

8

FROM WARFARE TO LAWFARE

DECEMBER 16, 2009: Objectives Akron, Toledo, Cleveland. Even the code names sanitized the deadly business at hand. Harold Koh had been the State Department's legal adviser for less than six months when he was asked to consider the legality of a series of targeted killings. The primary target, Akron, was Mohammed Saleh Mohammed Ali al-Kazemi, an AQAP deputy in the southern Yemen province of Abyan. Elite commandos under the Defense Department's Joint Special Operations Command had been hunting him for months. Now they had tracked him to a training camp near the village of al-Majalah. Through high-tech surveillance, the military had discovered a chilling piece of intelligence. Akron was in the late stages of planning a terrorist attack on the US embassy in Sana'a. A team of AQAP suicide bombers would soon be strapping on their explosives-laden vests and heading for the Yemeni capital. There was no time to lose. Cleveland and Toledo had also been located in the area, and JSOC hoped to eliminate them as well.

Events unfolded in a crisis atmosphere. Late that afternoon, Koh was given a set of highly classified PowerPoint slides detailing Akron's terrorist history and laying out the proposed concepts of operations for his elimination. The military dryly called the slides "baseball cards." They displayed a color picture of the target and physical characteristics, including his estimated height and weight. Below the photo was a kind of terrorist curriculum vitae, listing his rank in the organization, professional expertise, and links to individual attacks. Akron was an operational planner and was believed to have been responsible for a July 2007 suicide bombing that killed nine people, including seven Spanish tourists. Farther down, in small print, was the specific intelligence backing up the military's claims — humint if it came from a spy, or sigint if it was based on electronic surveillance. In between a packed schedule of meetings, Koh frantically read through the slides. He had forty-five minutes to absorb the intelligence and assess the legality of what was, in effect, a preplanned, presidentially authorized hit job.

At the end of the day, Koh joined a secure meeting by video link from the State Department's Operations Center. As many as seventy-five officials from across the counterterrorism bureaucracy and the White House took part in the SVTS, government-speak for a secure video teleconference. It was killing by committee.

Kill or capture operations in "denied areas" like Yemen or Somalia are among the most sensitive missions carried out by the military. Far from the "hot battlefields" of Iraq and Afghanistan, they raise complicated legal, diplomatic, and moral questions about who could be targeted and whether the United States could wage its war without geographic constraints. Every operation goes through an elaborate interagency vetting before being signed off on by the president.

Appearing on a large video screen, Admiral William McRaven, the JSOC commander, ran through the concept of operations

(CONOPs) for Objectives Akron, Toledo, and Cleveland, part of "Copper Dune," the military's counterterrorism operation in Yemen. The former Navy SEAL spoke with the authority and precision of someone who had given such briefings dozens of times. There were various forms of missile strikes available — sea-based, a close-in helicopter raid, or an attack from a fixed-wing aircraft. Capture on the ground in Yemen was not an option.

Koh took in the videoconference with morbid fascination. He had had little exposure to military culture or the macho world of special operations forces. During the 1990s he had been the Clinton administration's top human rights official, working to avert humanitarian crises and genocide in places like East Timor and Kosovo. Now he was witnessing the planning of a killing by his own government.

He was awed by McRaven's crisp efficiency. What a contrast, he thought, to the meandering academic meetings at Yale Law School, where he and his colleagues could spend six hours debating a single faculty appointment. But there was also an inexorable quality to the meeting, a machinelike pace that left him feeling more like an observer than a participant. He was unsettled by the bloodless euphemisms the military used to talk about violent death. A targeted killing became a "direct action" or a "kinetic strike." Code names for the hunted militants were bland and impersonal, drawn from the names of provincial American cities. At the time, JSOC was working its way through Ohio. Koh understood the need to "objectify" the enemy. The "operators" had to separate themselves from the brutality of their actions. But as a human rights lawyer, he was trained to do the opposite. "I kept slipping back and forth between the view of the predator and the view of the prey," he later told a friend.

Koh's baptism by fire had come only weeks after he'd joined the Obama administration. It was the Nabhan operation in Somalia in September 2009. Again, Koh had participated in a secure videoconference with little time to prepare for the high-stakes meeting. He'd had questions about the legality of the operation but did not get a chance to raise them, having to leave the meeting early for a business dinner.

Koh was rattled when he left the State Department's Operations Center. To get in and out of the secure bunker, you had to pass through three heavy, pressurized steel doors. As he pushed through the last door, using his shoulder for leverage, a huge burst of compressed air whooshed out of the room. Finally, passing the guards stationed outside the "Ops Center," he exhaled.

That night, Koh had slept fitfully. He had lingering doubts about the quality of the intelligence that had been presented, and he was disturbed by his own passivity during the SVTS meeting. The military was a juggernaut. They had overwhelmed the session with their sheer numbers, their impenetrable jargon, and their ability to create an atmosphere of do-or-die urgency. How could anybody, let alone a humanitarian law professor, resist such powerful momentum? Koh was no wallflower when it came to expressing his views; normally he relished battling it out with his bureaucratic rivals. But on this occasion he'd felt powerless. Trying to stop a targeted killing "would be like pulling a lever to stop a massive freight train barreling down the tracks," he confided to a friend.

The next morning he'd arrived at the office at 7:30, an hour earlier than usual. He went straight to the State Department's SCIF so that he could read the full intelligence file on Nabhan. He wanted to be sure he had not blessed an illegal killing. As Koh went through the classified reports he could feel his body contract and then begin to relax. There seemed to be enough to justify the operation. If there hadn't been, it wouldn't have mattered anyway; word had already come through from the Pentagon: Nabhan was dead.

Koh accepted the legality of targeted killings. He even believed that they had a potential humanitarian upside: precision weaponry and the operators' ability to watch a target for hours or even days before a strike could greatly diminish the risk of civilian deaths. "I would have preferred targeted killings to Hiroshima," he'd often say when debating his friends in the human rights community. As a legal matter, targeted killings were acts of war — not assassinations — permitted under the authority Congress had given the president after 9/11 to "use all necessary force" against al-Qaeda, the Taliban, and associated groups. And it was a well-established principle of international law that nations could use lethal force when acting in self-defense to prevent imminent threats. But Koh also knew that as the fighting moved from established theaters of conflict to places like Yemen and Somalia, the administration's legal authorities grew more tenuous. Could the United States hunt down and kill suspected terrorists anywhere in the world? Were all members of al-Qaeda-linked organizations, even the lowliest foot soldiers, targetable for death? And how could the United States justify violating the sovereignty of foreign countries in pursuit of terrorists and their networks? Barack Obama had vowed to fight an aggressive war against al-Qaeda, but one within a clear legal framework. Koh believed that if that promise meant anything, his administration needed to carefully and consistently police the line between lawful and unlawful killings. As the State Department's top lawyer, Koh played a unique role in ensuring that the administration's military actions conformed with the laws of war.

The next time a set of baseball cards arrived on his desk, Koh knew, he would have to react quickly and confidently. With so little margin for error, he needed to be better prepared. After the Nabhan operation, he began scouring the military's kill or capture lists. He learned as much as he could about al-Qaeda's affiliate organizations, AQAP in Yemen and the Shabab in Somalia. He studied their structures, organizational charts, and strategic goals. He sought in-depth briefings from the State Department's Bureau of Intelligence and Research, whose assessments often differed from the military's. And he boned up on military weaponry and ordnance so he could make informed judgments about which operations were likely to cause the fewest civilian deaths. It was an unlikely turn for one of the most respected human rights lawyers of his generation. At Yale Law he had memorized the names and faces of his students, bright-eyed idealists who wanted to use the law to improve the world. Now he was studying government hit lists, memorizing the profiles of young, vacant-eyed militants, and helping determine which ones could be put to death. "How did I go from being a law professor to someone involved in killing?" he wondered.

On December 16, whatever moral or legal discomfort Koh might have been feeling about targeted killings collided with the cold, utilitarian calculations of war. Joining the conference call from Sana'a that evening were the American ambassador to Yemen as well as the CIA station chief. Koh's own colleagues were in the line of fire.

Established in 1980 in the aftermath of Operation Eagle Claw, the botched effort to rescue the American captives in Iran, JSOC got its start as a hostage-rescue team. JSOC ran the military's elite and secretive special-mission units, including the Navy's SEAL Team Six, formally known as the United States Special Warfare Development Group (DEVGRU); the Army's Delta Force; and the Air Force's Twenty-Fourth Special Tactics Squadron. After 9/11, JSOC operated under a series of classified executive orders first executed under the Bush administration. Obama revised and expanded the classified orders after taking office. He also dramatically expanded JSOC's budget and operating authorities. So intimate was Obama's involvement with JSOC that he personally signed off on each kill or capture operation conducted in Yemen and Somalia.

Obama was drawn to JSOC for many of the same reasons he found the CIA an attractive option. It was relatively small, nimble, and, while not covert in the legal sense, operated in a culture of near-total secrecy. Until recently, the Defense Department did not even officially acknowledge its existence. Some of its missions were so compartmentalized that they took place without the relevant combatant commander's knowledge. Moreover, unlike the CIA, JSOC was not required by law to brief Congress on its clandestine operations. Law and politics so constrained Obama's ability to influence counterterrorism policy, it's easy to appreciate the lure of JSOC, which was sometimes referred to as the president's "secret army."

JSOC's ability to go after terrorist networks with stealth, precision, and lethal force meant that the job could be done without putting boots on the ground. It was a capability that was firmly in line with Obama's approach to the war on terror: surgical and discrete. Obama was a realist who defined American interests carefully and was wary of getting embroiled in other countries' insurgencies. He was also a lawyer, and he understood that in the shadow wars, far from conventional battlefields, the United States was operating further out on the margins of the law. Ten years after 9/11, the military was taking the fight to terrorist groups that didn't exist when Congress granted George Bush authority to go to war against al-Qaeda and the Taliban. Complicated questions about which groups and individuals were covered under the Authorization for Use of Military Force (AUMF) were left to the lawyers. Their finely grained distinctions and hairsplitting legal arguments could mean the difference between who would be killed and who would be spared. Where the Bush administration had consciously marginalized the role of lawyers in counterterrorism operations, Obama had given them a far more overt role. His administration seemed to view the involvement of lawyers in the formulation of national security as a badge of honor — evidence of its commitment to the rule of law.

It had become fashionable to blame lawyers for micromanaging wars. They stood accused of engaging in "lawfare," throwing up a smokescreen of process questions that got in the way of military action — requiring highly restrictive rules of engagement, for example. Lawyers were partly blamed for the intelligence failures that led to the 9/11 attacks — they had created a culture of risk aversion in the military and intelligence services, or so the theory went.

By the time Obama took office, the number of lawyers in the national security establishment had been growing steadily for four decades. Where soldiers and spies had been weakened after the backlash from Vietnam and Watergate, lawyers were emboldened. Take, for example, the case of longtime CIA lawyer John Rizzo. Rizzo joined the CIA straight out of George Washington Law School in 1976. It was right after the congressional Church and Pike Committees had exposed domestic espionage, government assassination, and other abuses. The CIA was "back on its heels and in a defensive crouch," recalled Rizzo. When he joined the agency, there was only one lawyer assigned to work in the Directorate of Operations. By 2010 there were more than sixty, with ten lawyers assigned to the Counterterrorism Center alone.

After 9/11, Bush and Cheney shackled the lawyers and unleashed the military and intelligence agencies. But by Bush's second term, the pendulum had begun to swing back, a reaction to the administration's interrogation practices, warrantless wiretapping, and other excesses. By that time, Rizzo had risen to be the CIA's deputy general counsel. He had hoped to become the agency's top lawyer but was blocked by Senate Democrats when it was revealed that he had been involved in authorizing the Bush administration's enhanced interrogation program. One of the infamous torture memos written by John Yoo had been addressed to Rizzo.

If any two attorneys typified the reassertion of law in the terror wars, it was Harold Koh and Jeh C. Johnson. As the top lawyers at the State Department and the Pentagon, respectively, they exercised considerable influence over counterterrorism operations. But their ideological differences — Koh a liberal idealist and Johnson a pragmatic centrist — colored their legal interpretations. The two were, in many ways, like oil and water. Koh could be brusque and tactless with his colleagues, though he would just as easily break into boyish giggles when something amused him. Johnson, a former prosecutor and partner in a white-shoe Manhattan law firm, was restrained in manner and a deft inside operator. He was as tall and athletic as Koh was rumpled and professorial.

Their rivalry was institutional but it was also personal. Koh regarded Johnson as a careerist who'd gone native at the Pentagon. Johnson thought Koh was an ideologue who dressed up his liberal policy preferences in academic legal arguments. But they had more in common than perhaps they cared to admit. They had both the attributes and the flaws of men who rose to high positions of authority. They were supremely self-assured, but they could also be vainglorious. Koh was thin-skinned about press criticism. Johnson meticulously tended to his scrapbook of professional mementos that included press mentions and even phone messages he had received from Obama during the campaign. Still, the bottom line was that they were serious, intelligent men who genuinely struggled with excruciatingly difficult questions of security, morality, and law. In many ways, their rivalry reflected a healthy government dialectic that led to smarter and better-justified policies.

Koh and Johnson were on a collision course from almost the moment they began working together. For most of Obama's first term they fought a pitched battle over legal authorities in the war on al-Qaeda. Like Johnson, Koh had no problem going after al-Qaeda's most senior members. But things got murkier when the military wanted to kill or capture members of other terrorist groups whose connections to AQ were unclear. Johnson took a more hawkish position, arguing that the United States was in a state of armed conflict with al-Qaeda and as such could pursue its members or "cobelligerents" more expansively. The two men battled each other openly in meetings and by circulating rival secret memos pushing their respective positions with the policymakers.

In September 2009 the Justice Department sought to referee the growing dispute. David Barron, the acting head of the Office of Legal Counsel, staged a debate between Koh and Johnson. Lawyers from around the government crowded into the OLC conference room. The argument had come to a head some weeks before in the case of Belkacem Bensayah, an Algerian man who was arrested in Bosnia and accused of facilitating the transport of new recruits who wanted to join al-Qaeda in Afghanistan. Johnson contended that Bensayah's activities amounted to "substantial support" of al-Qaeda and that he could be detained indefinitely under the laws of war. Koh argued that Bensayah was no more detainable than a little old lady who had unwittingly donated money to al-Qaeda. Everyone in the room knew that there was much more at stake: the same legal arguments that applied to the question of who could be detained without trial directly implicated who could be targeted for death. The White House was loath to have such disagreements between administration lawyers aired publicly. But the Koh/Johnson confrontation landed on the front page of the *New York Times* some months later.

Johnson was simmering after the meeting. He thought Koh had been condescending in making his case, and it got under Johnson's skin. Koh did have a tendency to browbeat his rivals with his intelligence. When challenged, he'd sometimes resort to ad hominem attacks. "I wrote a book on this topic," he'd say imperiously, or, "This has been my life's work," implying that his counterpart had only skated along the surface of the issue. Still, Koh was self-aware enough to understand that his reputation for arrogance could be counterproductive. He would have to work with Johnson on vital national security policy, including issues of life and death. They'd have to try to get along. He organized a dinner with Johnson and their wives at Café Milano, a swanky Italian restaurant. But the conversation was stilted. The charm offensive failed.

For much of Obama's first year in office, Koh and Johnson's disagreement remained largely theoretical; the administration was not capturing any new detainees in Yemen or Somalia, nor was it engaged in many targeted killings outside Pakistan. That changed toward the latter part of 2009. The targeted killing of Nabhan in Somalia was a seminal event in the Obama administration's war on terror, presaging a far more aggressive campaign against al-Qaeda's affiliates.

On December 16, 2009, Jeh Johnson was in his Pentagon office when a military aide brought him a set of baseball cards. Although he had served as general counsel to the air force during the Clinton administration, he had never had to weigh in on a lethal operation until he joined the Obama team. Now he had forty-five minutes to prepare for a meeting to approve the cards. The targets were Akron, Toledo, and Cleveland. He sat down with the deck and started cramming.

Soon thereafter, Johnson was sitting at a table for a secure conference call when Tom Donilon, the deputy national security adviser and a lawyer himself, piped in. "Is Jeh Johnson on the line?" Johnson said he was. Well what's it going to be? Yes or no, can we take the shots?

Johnson felt like there was a giant spotlight shining down on him. It was moments like these when he wished he could be just a policy adviser who could fudge his answers. Instead, his choice was binary: green light or red light, you take the shot or you can't. Johnson gave a split verdict: two of the three were targetable. Akron was involved in an unfolding suicide plot; Toledo was a lawful target as well. But Johnson was uneasy about the other "objective," Cleveland. The intelligence indicated that the terrorist suspect was likely surrounded by women and children. Johnson advised against the strike. There were no objections. When the meeting ended, Johnson returned to his office and processed the enormity of the advice he had just given. Like Harold Koh, he thought about how hard it would be to resist the momentum toward kinetic force — the heavy pressure exerted by the military to kill. It was easier to say yes than to say no, he realized. In his mind he used the same metaphor as Koh — it was like a one-hundred-car freight train hurtling down the tracks at eighty miles an hour. You would have to throw yourself on the tracks to try to stop it. He wasn't entirely comfortable with his decision; he'd felt rushed and unprepared. Later that evening he watched the aerial imagery on a monitor from a command center in the Pentagon's E-ring. Digital images of the attacks were being fed back in real time. Johnson could see the shadowy images of the militants running drills in a training camp. They looked like toy soldiers scurrying around a grainy landscape. Then suddenly there was a bright flash. The figures that had been moving across the screen just moments before were gone. Johnson arrived at his Georgetown home around midnight that evening, drained and exhausted. Later he would confide to others, "If I were Catholic, I'd have to go to confession." There were reports from human rights groups that dozens of civilians had been killed in the attack, a claim that was not confirmed by the US government, although a military source involved in the operation said that the reports were "persuasive."

Johnson ran one of the largest law firms in the world; twelve thousand lawyers worked for the Department of Defense. His decisions had real impact: lives were at stake, as well as foreign policy consequences. Johnson was one of Obama's earliest supporters, moved that a black man like himself could become president. He held fundraisers for him and trudged through the snows of Iowa and West Philadelphia knocking on doors. He saw himself as the "president's man" at the Pentagon, and he felt a responsibility to protect the president's political interests. He wanted to make sure that the military, with his blessing, did not exceed its authorities.

He began a careful examination of the law. Who could be legally targeted? How far did the battlefield extend? Which groups were "part of" al-Qaeda, which meant that they were directly covered by the congressional AUMF, and which groups were "associated" or cobelligerents with AQ? What about making individual determinations? Was a facilitator or a financier targetable? What about a "cutout," a foot soldier who carried a terrorist leader's cell phone to confuse the enemy? He studied the March 13 brief that laid out the administration's positions on many of these questions, but it was insufficient. He began reaching out to experts on international law, detention, and the use of force, reading law review articles and probing other sources that had guided the Justice Department's conclusions.

One expert whose opinion Johnson solicited was Jack Goldsmith, a professor of international law at Harvard, who had written extensively on the government's detention and targeting authorities in the war on terror. Goldsmith was a brilliant legal scholar with impeccable conservative credentials. But he was not a political ideologue.

He was probably best known for sparking the legal rebellion against the Bush administration's enhanced interrogation and warrantless-wiretapping programs. Goldsmith may have had more influence on the legal underpinnings of Obama's war on terror than any other lawyer — inside or outside the government. His legal insights were all over the March 13 brief, including, crucially, the proposition that detention (and, by extension, targeting) could apply to nonstate actors outside Iraq and Afghanistan. Johnson studied Goldsmith's scholarly writing, including a particularly influential article he coauthored in the *Harvard Law Review,* and even sat down with him over breakfasts and dinners to seek out his advice.

One day, Goldsmith was walking outside the Metropolitan Club in Washington when his cell phone rang. Johnson was on the line, and he wanted Goldsmith to take part in a conference call at that very moment. The question was whether an al-Qaeda financier could be detained under the AUMF. Johnson made clear that they were discussing a hypothetical case, not a real one. But Goldsmith knew that actual scenarios like this were now coming up regularly. "It depends," Goldsmith told Johnson. "The bigger the financier and the more you could tie him to a plot, the more you could go after him." Goldsmith's bottom line was that it was a "murky" area and that each judgment had to be carefully analyzed in light of the law and the facts on a case-by-case basis. There was no one-size-fits-all solution. In January, Johnson wrote a twenty-page legal opinion to lay out his own views.

On February 4, 2010, Johnson was called upon to participate in another SVTS. Another operation was being planned, this time targeting several members of the Shabab. Johnson watched as the ritual played out in its usual fashion. Obama's advisers went through the CONOPs and assessed the appropriate levels of ordnance. It was the first opportunity for Johnson to apply his refined legal analysis to a real-world scenario. Before the meeting, he had conveyed some of his concerns to the White House. Well into the meeting, John Brennan called on Johnson, noting that he had wanted to raise an important legal issue. Softly but deliberately, Johnson said he would no longer approve the targeted killings of Shabab members. There would be exceptions for the most senior operatives, those who had "dual-hatted" status as sworn members of al-Qaeda, but it was no longer his view that the Shabab was broadly covered under the AUMF. The room swelled with an awkward silence. Johnson had largely acquiesced to major targeting requests in the past. Yet now he was effectively putting an entire al-Qaeda-affiliated terrorist organization off-limits. It was a stunning reversal, just as JSOC was amping up its operations in Somalia. The Nabhan operation in September had been one of their biggest successes to date, helping exorcise the ghosts of Black Hawk Down. The military had wanted to build on that momentum. The ability to go after militants lower down the chain was considered crucial for JSOC, whose leaders believed that attacking their networks and support infrastructure was as important as targeting individual leaders. Johnson's uniformed colleagues left the meeting without saying a word to him. It was a lonely moment for an ambitious lawyer who was used to getting along with his Pentagon colleagues.

A few days later Johnson went to see Koh at the State Department. He wanted to personally deliver a copy of his secret legal memo. Koh, who had taken part in the SVTS on the Shabab targets, greeted him with a big smile. He told Johnson it was his "finest moment" and that he should be proud of himself. Johnson was pleased, but he admitted he wasn't very popular back at the Pentagon.

A government lawyer does not have a license to advance his or her personal policy objectives. The job is to interpret the law in light of executive branch precedents and traditions. That means sometimes standing in the way of policies you favor. Other times it means vig-orously defending government actions you may find distasteful, as long as you can plausibly argue that they are legal. Ironically, Koh the idealist and Johnson the pragmatist had now switched sides. While the Pentagon's top lawyer was restraining the war fighters, Koh, the administration's most forceful advocate of human rights law, was preparing to defend a covert government killing program. His clients were the secretary of state and the president. But among his most important constituents were America's foreign allies. As he traveled around the world attending legal conferences and meeting with his counterparts, Koh got an earful from tut-tutting European officials about Obama's "extrajudicial" killing spree. Koh forthrightly stood up for the legality of the program.

But in private, he started to question whether its opaqueness was doing more harm than good. Covert programs were widely perceived to be illegal, or at least subject to abuse. And Koh was also worried that his own silent acquiescence would damage his reputation within the human rights community. Already academics and bloggers were asking whether Koh was AWOL on one of the administration's most controversial national security policies.

Koh began lobbying Secretary Clinton and the White House to let him make a speech in defense of targeted killing. It was time to bring the program, or at least the legal reasoning behind it, out from the shadows. Despite Koh's reputation as a renegade, the White House saw an upside in making him the unlikely public face of the CIA's drone program. It was a Nixon-goes-to-China play: it would give the president cover with both the human rights community and America's allies. The military and CIA, too, loved the idea. They called the State Department lawyer "Killer Koh" behind his back. Some of the operators even talked about printing up T-shirts that said: "Drones: If they're good enough for Harold Koh, they're good enough for me."

The White House had another motive. In early 2010 word leaked to the press that Obama had approved the placement of Anwar al-Awlaki on the CIA's kill list. Awlaki's ties to the attempted Christmas Day bombing and other planned attacks, as well as new evidence that indicated he had become AQAP's chief of external operations, had compelled Obama's response. But it was a fateful step, one that the White House knew would require careful messaging.

Koh was troubled by the decision and worried that the White House might be trying to use him. Awlaki had been born in Las Cruces, New Mexico, in 1971, while his father was a Fulbright scholar studying for a master's degree in agricultural economics at New Mexico State University. Awlaki had lived in the United States until he was eleven, when his family moved back to Yemen, where his father held prominent positions as a university dean, government minister, and top adviser to the president. Young Anwar had gone from one of the most permissive societies on earth to one of the most traditional. It was this dual identity that would make him so dangerous, according to counterterrorism officials. Pious and intellectually ambitious, Awlaki returned to the States in 1991 to attend college in Colorado. It was only after 9/11 that he set out on a trajectory toward radicalization and violence.

Targeting an American citizen for death without his being allowed to contest the evidence in a court of law presented serious constitutional issues. The Fifth Amendment guarantees that a citizen's life or liberty cannot be deprived without due process of law. There was little doubt that Awlaki wanted to strike at his birth nation, yet could a group of anonymous security officials secretly reviewing highly classified evidence claim to be judge, jury, and executioner? Koh also worried about reciprocity. Would the Russian or Chinese governments track down dissidents whom they viewed as terrorists and take them out on the streets of Washington, DC, or Paris with their own drones? And Koh was skeptical of some of the counterterrorism community's conclusions about Awlaki. He had seen how quickly intelligence analysts would elevate a propagandist to an operator. Or how they used fudged terms like "facilitator" to imply that suspected militants represented grave threats to the United States. What was a facilitator? A driver? A chef? Koh wanted to see the intelligence that was being relied on to justify Awlaki's execution. If Awlaki wasn't going to be able to defend himself in a court of law, then perhaps Koh could at least ensure that the government's case against him was legitimate.

One day in late March, Koh went up to the State Department SCIF, a "crappy little room," as he put it, and began reading through stacks of intelligence. He stayed in the room for almost five hours, mesmerized by the detailed reporting on Awlaki's plots. Every half hour or so he would emerge from the secure room to cancel another meeting he had scheduled. He had set his own legal standard to justify the targeted killing of a US citizen: evil, with iron-clad intelligence to prove it. It was not exactly a technical legal standard but it was a threshold he was comfortable with. Now, he was reading about multiple plots to kill Americans and Europeans, all of which Awlaki had been deeply involved in at an operational level. There were plans to poison Western water and food supplies with botulinum toxin, as well as attack Americans with ricin and cyanide. Awlaki's ingenuity at coming up with newer, deadlier plots was chilling. Koh was shaken when he left the room. Awlaki was not just evil, he was satanic.

Still, before giving the speech Koh insisted on getting a briefing from the CIA's lawyers and drone operators. He wasn't about to put his reputation on the line without having a detailed understanding of the program and its protocols. At first the agency balked. Why should they share their operational secrets with a squishy human rights lawyer? But they relented after Koh threatened to cancel the speech. So Koh spent hours at Langley cross-examining agency lawyers and operators. He wanted to understand what kind of analysis the lawyers did before signing off on a killing. Were they trained in the laws of war? How well did they understand the concepts of distinction and proportionality? Not surprisingly, the operators were suspicious of Koh. And Koh didn't help matters with his bull-in-a-china-shop approach. "I hear you guys have a PlayStation mentality," he blundered in. The operators of unmanned aerial vehicles were civilians, but most of them were former air force pilots; they took pride in their technical skills and resented the suggestion that they were "cubicle warriors," morally detached from killing. The lead operator lit into Koh. "I used to fly my own air missions," he started, defensively. "I dropped bombs, hit my target load, but had no idea who I hit. Here I can look at their faces. I watch them for hours, see these guys playing with their kids and wives. When I get them alone, I have no compunction about blowing them to bits, but I wouldn't touch them with civilians around. After the strike, I see the bodies being carried out of the house. I see the women weeping and in positions of mourning. That's not PlayStation; that's real. My job is to watch after the strike too. I count the bodies and watch the funerals. I don't let others clean up the mess."

On March 25 Koh gave a dry and largely technical speech to an association of international lawyers in downtown Washington. About three-fourths of the way through his talk, he delicately raised the issue of targeted killing. Koh laid it all on the line: "It is the considered view of this administration — and it has certainly been my experience during my time as legal adviser — that US targeting practices, including legal operations conducted with the use of unmanned aerial vehicles, comply with all applicable law, including the laws of war."

Koh carefully laid out the core legal arguments, including asserting that the program adhered to fundamental principles of the laws of war. Drone strikes were limited to military objectives. Civilian targets were off-limits. The damage caused by attacks had to be proportional to the anticipated military objective. He rebutted the suggestion that the laws of war prohibit the targeting of enemy leaders, pointing out that during World War II the United States had intentionally shot down the airplane carrying the architect of the Japanese attack on Pearl Harbor. Koh obliquely addressed the issue of targeting people outside traditional battlefields, arguing that it is lawful to use lethal force under international principles of self-defense. One issue he did not address, however, was the legality of targeting an American citizen.

In the aftermath of Johnson's decision to declare the Shabab off-limits, the military mounted a fierce campaign to persuade him to reverse course. Officers from the Joint Staff and Special Operations community brought him intelligence and threat streams pointing to the al-Qaeda affiliate's terrorist activities. They told him "bad things" would happen in their AOR, or areas of responsibility. The implication was that Johnson's decision could lead to future attacks against Americans. Johnson understood the political risks. There would be an uproar if the Shabab launched a successful attack against the United States and it later turned out that Obama administration lawyers had declared the group off-limits.

For months, officers from JSOC and J2, the Joint Chiefs intelligence staff, pounded him with new threat information about the organization, and about its al-Qaeda ties. They told Johnson that Somalia was becoming another Afghanistan and that bin Laden was using the Shabab to establish a "caliphate" there. Johnson was at first skeptical of the intel, but he began to have second thoughts. Was he being intransigent for the sake of being intransigent? he wondered. He decided to take a fresh look at his assessment in light of the new intelligence.

Harold Koh, meanwhile, was digging in. While Koh believed that the United States could kill suspected terrorists away from the battlefield in highly defined circumstances of self-defense, he developed elaborate legal tests for who was targetable. Some had argued that a low-level Shabab foot soldier could be analogized to a private in the Japanese Army during World War II. If American forces could reach him, he could be taken out. But Koh rejected the comparison. Unlike the war against Japan, military operations against the Shabab were not taking place on a recognized battlefield. Koh established his own elaborate four-part test: First, the prospective target would have to be clearly "part of al-Qaeda." Second, he would have to be a "senior" member of the organization. For that Koh developed a theory of "uniqueness versus fungibility." A low-level member, like a driver or a cook, was easily replaced and therefore posed no unique threat to the United States or its interests. Third, to justify a killing, the target would also have to be "externally focused." Groups like AQAP and al-Shabab were insurgencies preoccupied with local political struggles. Koh's view was that only those militants who were predisposed to attacking America could be killed. Finally, there had to be evidence that the suspected terrorist was plotting to strike. Under international law, states could kill in self-defense when they were faced with a "continuing and imminent threat." But in an age of terror and asymmetric warfare, it was too late if you waited for a specific plot to unfold. Koh developed a theory of "elongated imminence," which he likened to "battered spouse syndrome." If a husband demonstrated a consistent pattern of activity before beating his wife, it wasn't necessary to wait until the husband's hand was raised before the wife could act in self-defense. Similarly, terrorists wouldn't have to be boarding the plane with bombs before American commandos could take them out. It would be enough if they were designing the suicide vests.

This was just the kind of legal nitpicking that drove the operators crazy. It was hard to imagine knife-in-the-teeth commandos asking themselves whether they'd passed the four-part Koh test on uniqueness versus fungibility before blowing a bad guy to kingdom come.

On July 11, 2010, bombs ripped through a soccer stadium in Kampala, Uganda, killing seventy-four people and leaving hundreds more injured. It was the first attack staged by the Shabab outside Somalia, raising concerns that the group was ready to take its jihad global. US counterterrorism officials had been increasingly nervous about the Shabab, in part because of the large number of young Somali Americans who seemed to be disappearing off the streets of Minneapolis, where their immigrant families had settled. Over time officials would learn that dozens of them had returned to Somalia and joined the organization. For the most part, they were motivated by nationalist fervor and a desire to fight the US-backed Ethiopian army, which had entered Somalia in 2006 to defend the Transitional Federal Government against incursions by the Islamic Courts Union. But what they learned in the training camps of Somalia could be used to spread terror in the streets of America. And it wasn't just Somali Americans who were joining the ranks of the Shabab from the United States. One day before the Kampala bombing, Zachary Adam Chesser, a middle-class twenty-one-year-old from suburban Virginia, was arrested by the FBI as he was attempting to board a flight to Uganda with his infant son. Chesser, who had been radicalized in part by watching YouTube videos of Anwar al-Awlaki, was on his way to Somalia to join the Shabab. In October 2010 Chesser pleaded guilty to attempting to provide material support to a foreign terrorist organization and was sentenced to twenty-five years in federal prison. During that same year, US intelligence officials saw increasing signs that the links between the Shabab and AQAP were growing stronger. US drones with infrared cameras and spy planes detected a steady traffic of guns, money, and militants across the Gulf of Aden between Yemen and Somalia. In the wake of the Johnson edict back in February, the number of targeted killings in Somalia had dropped precipitously. Now the military was itching to step up its operations.

By the end of 2010, Johnson had come around to the view of the operators. He reviewed sensitive intelligence that showed increasing communications between Shabab commanders and the al-Qaeda leadership in Pakistan. And there were more signs that even lower-level members of the Shabab had effectively "gone over" to al-Qaeda.

The Koh-Johnson rivalry was reignited during a secure conference call in the fall of 2010. The call was convened by Mary DeRosa, the top lawyer for the National Security Council. The purpose was to nail down final approval for the military to target the top leadership of the Shabab. On the list were the three top members of the organization. DeRosa went through the list to make sure there was consensus. She mentioned the leader of the organization, Sheikh Mohamed Mukhtar Abdirahman, widely known simply as Abdi. He had sworn an oath of allegiance to al-Qaeda, and the intelligence indicated he favored striking out against the West. Both Johnson and Koh agreed he was targetable.

Next DeRosa asked about the second in command. Same story. Neither Johnson nor Koh was opposed to killing him. Finally, she mentioned Sheikh Mukhtar Robow. He held the number three position but had previously led the organization. Johnson believed

Robow could be killed. Koh, however, disagreed, and he did so vigorously. He had studied the intelligence. There were credible indications that Robow represented a moderate faction of the Shabab that was opposed to attacking America or other Western interests. There had been a split in the organization, and Robow was among those arguing that the Shabab should limit its aims to overthrowing the Transitional Federal Government in Mogadishu. Koh asked what kind of message it would send "if we killed the leader of the faction who was advocating *against* targeting Americans."

DeRosa brushed Koh off, telling him she understood his policy concerns and would represent them within the White House. She was touching a raw nerve with Koh. Within the administration, critics argued that Koh was a true believer and would tailor his legal arguments to fit his policy agenda. But DeRosa may have had another motive for characterizing the disagreement as a policy dispute. Policy positions could easily be overruled in the White House. Legal conflicts, by contrast, were more difficult to overcome.

Koh pushed back hard. His objection to targeting Robow was a matter of policy *and* law, he said. If Robow was not focused on attacking Americans, then the United States could not use self-defense as a justification for killing him. "The State Department legal adviser, for the record, believes this killing would be unlawful," he said slowly and emphatically. DeRosa did not conceal her irritation. She hung up the phone without resolving the fate of Robow. But Koh had jammed her. The implicit message was clear: they would have to authorize the targeting of Robow over the unambiguous legal objections of the top lawyer at the State Department. The White House hated dissent among the lawyers. If word leaked that Robow was killed against the explicit advice of the State Department, it could cause a scandal. Additionally, some in the administration had feared that Koh might resign on principle, or out of overweening self-righteousness, as they would have it. He had never threatened resignation in a meeting (he'd heeded the advice of Moshe Dayan, the famous Israeli general and politician, who'd said that "one never threatens resignation, one simply resigns"). But he believed it was always an option.

Robow was removed from the targeting list.

====

9

"THE PRESIDENT IS ANGUISHED"

S ITTING IN HIS DARK, wood-paneled office at the Justice
Department, Eric Holder sometimes drew inspiration from a
picture hanging on his wall. It showed Holder, clad in a black
windbreaker and dark pants, walking amid the graves at the American Cemetery in Normandy, a forest of matching white crosses in
seemingly endless rows and columns. During a routine ministerial
trip to France in May 2010, Holder had taken an extra day to visit the
site of the Allied landings on D-day. The photograph was a reminder
that the most important battles were only won through extreme sacrifice and perseverance.

By mid-2010, Holder was the most embattled member of the
Obama cabinet. For months he had been under assault from congressional Republicans and shrill editorialists for his handling of terrorism cases. Even more stinging was the sneering criticism, always
sotto voce, emanating from within the administration itself. He knew
that the brickbats went with the territory. As attorney general, he

made tough calls at the combustible intersection of law, security, and politics. He also knew that some of his wounds were self-inflicted. He dismissed them as superficial gaffes — stumbling at a congressional hearing or botching message coordination with the White House. But they had reinforced a narrative of political bumbling that had been hard to shake.

Still, Holder had impressive regenerative powers. Maybe it was his ability to compartmentalize. Or the generally sunny outlook on life that he had inherited from his mother. Whatever it was, by the fall of 2010 he had begun to come out of his funk. Earlier in the year he had told the *New Yorker* magazine that the trial of Khalid Sheikh Mohammed would be "the defining event of my time as attorney general." Now, even as the decision was looking more like an albatross, weakening Holder politically and isolating him further within the administration, he clung to the belief that if he stuck to his principles he could turn around his fortunes. It was time for one final attempt — however quixotic — to revive the KSM prosecution.

It was time to set in motion "Project Juno." After the Bloomberg-led insurrection, trying the case in downtown Manhattan was no longer a viable option. But Holder had remembered hearing about a small town in upstate New York that was a possible alternative site for the trial. Nestled in the foothills of the Catskill Mountains, the tiny hamlet of Otisville, population 1,068, was an unlikely spot for the biggest mass murder trial in American history. Yet it had a few things going for it, including a federal penitentiary where KSM could be securely held and tried. And crucially, Otisville was situated within the borders of New York's Southern District.

There was another obstacle that Holder would have to overcome. By the fall of 2010, Republicans in Congress were again threatening to bar the use of appropriated funds to try KSM in a civilian court. With Democrats ducking and covering, there was little question

Republicans would have the necessary votes if they carried out the threat. But Holder still had a backup plan for financing the trial: the Justice Department's nearly $100 million asset-forfeiture fund. Congress had no say in how that money could be used.

In October Holder sent Kevin Ohlson, his chief of staff, on a secret mission to scope out Otisville. Only Holder and his ExCom knew about the plan. The White House was kept in the dark for fear that Tammany Hall would sabotage the initiative with leaks to the media.

On the pretext of a visit to relatives, Ohlson traveled to Otisville, having made arrangements with the Bureau of Prisons for a tour of the penitentiary. The prison turned out to be ideal. Down a long rural road away from the town and isolated at the top of a small mountain, it was so secluded that the only intruders were wild turkeys and the occasional bear. One of its newer buildings housed inmates in the witness protection program. It was secure, and bore a close resemblance to some of the facilities at Guantánamo. There was even a nearby watering hole called the Bada Bing for thirsty reporters who might be assigned to cover the trial.

Holder began working to build support for the Otisville plan within the cabinet. He started with Hillary Clinton, who was a supporter of civilian trials and had forcefully backed Holder at the White House in August. Clinton was a rock star even among her fellow cabinet members. Both principals were carefully briefed by their staffs prior to a stage-managed get-together. When they finally sat down, much of the conversation had a stilted and formal quality to it. Holder laid out the plan in detail. The secretary of state listened attentively, subdued and noncommittal. She gave him some tactical advice. "You need to get Bob onboard," she said, referring to Robert Gates, the influential defense secretary. When Kevin Ohlson mentioned the proposed site for the trial, Clinton perked up for a moment. As a tireless campaigner in New York, she knew all of the upstate hamlets and townships, including Otisville. But when Holder finished his pitch, she said little. Harold Koh, who also attended the meeting, told Holder he needed facts on the ground. The best way to establish the legitimacy of Article III trials, he argued, was to just start bringing damn cases.

It was an appealing battle cry, but it wasn't realistic. The administration was still required to give Congress forty-five days' notification before moving any detainees out of Guantánamo for trial. As soon as notice was given, everyone knew, a political firestorm would erupt. As the meeting ended, Secretary Clinton had only weak words of encouragement. "Forget about the criticism," she told Holder, lightly touching his arm. "If you do the right thing you'll be proven right."

In truth, Clinton questioned whether Holder had the requisite fire in his belly. He talked about going into the crucible one last time, but she wasn't convinced he was prepared to do it. After the meeting broke up, she turned to Koh and said plaintively, "It's sad." As they filed out of the State Department, under a stormy late-October sky, Holder and his aides were deflated by Clinton's tepid reception. She clearly knew it was a hopeless cause.

The political horizon continued to darken. On November 2, riding a massive wave of voter discontent over the stalled economy and Obama's big-government agenda, Republicans swept back into power in the midterm elections. They recaptured the House and significantly narrowed the Democrats' majority in the Senate. The results had been so widely predicted that the political impact, initially, was somewhat discounted by Holder and his inner council. In the months leading up to the election, Ohlson had fretted that his boss might be forced out — a sacrificial offering to the ascendant Republicans. But for all of Obama's reputation as a bloodless realist, he was loyal to his advisers, especially those he was personally close to. Besides, he was not going to toss Holder overboard for fighting on behalf of a policy he fundamentally believed in. So Holder had survived and believed his position was secure.

In the wake of the election, the attorney general and his team even convinced themselves to keep their hopes up for the KSM prosecution. Basking in victory, the GOP focused on big-ticket items like repealing health care reform and Democratic spending initiatives. Maybe they would have less of an incentive to block the administration on detainees and civilian trials? Holder and his deputies pressed on. They conducted cost estimates for enhancing security at the Otisville prison and worked on the logistics of building a makeshift courtroom that could accommodate government and defense lawyers as well as a large contingent of reporters.

Two weeks later, a federal jury in New York City returned a stunning verdict in the terrorism trial of Ahmed Ghailani. Accused of participating in the deadly 1998 East Africa embassy bombings, Ghailani was the first and only Guantánamo detainee who had been transferred to the United States for trial in an Article III court. As such, the Justice Department considered the trial a crucial test. But the case also exposed some of the weaknesses inherent in prosecuting terrorists in federal court. Judge Lewis Kaplan had barred the testimony of one of the government's key witnesses because agents had learned of his identity from Ghailani while he was being held at a CIA prison overseas where enhanced interrogation techniques were used on detainees. "I'm acutely aware of the perilous nature of the world in which we live," Judge Kaplan said when he announced his ruling. "But the Constitution is the rock upon which our nation rests. We must follow it not only when it is convenient, but when fear and danger beckon in a different direction." It had been a serious blow to the case, but Holder's prosecutors believed there was still enough evidence to tie Ghailani to the conspiracy.

On the afternoon of November 17, the cable stations broke in with the news: Ghailani had been acquitted of all but one of 284 counts of murder and conspiracy. He was convicted of a single charge of conspiracy to destroy property and government buildings. Holder's deputies crowded into his small office to watch the coverage. At first the reports offered only a neutral recitation of the facts. Holder told Matt Miller, his press adviser, to put out the word that even this single-count conviction was likely to lead to a life sentence. But soon the news reports gave way to a parade of talking heads crowing about the Justice Department's humiliating defeat. Holder and his team were grimly quiet, but they were all thinking the same thing: it was a death-knell for their plans to revive the KSM prosecution.

In December, Congress formalized what Holder and the White House already knew. The 2011 National Defense Authorization Act stripped away any remaining legal authority the administration had to try KSM or the other 9/11 defendants in civilian courts. It barred the transfer of any Guantánamo detainees into the United States, and imposed onerous new restrictions on the transfer of detainees to foreign countries. If signed into law by Obama, the NDAA would have stopped any movement toward closing Guantánamo dead in its tracks.

The attorney general, alone among cabinet members, refused to give up the fight. There was much at stake for him personally but also for the "building," as cabinet secretaries often referred to their departments. Justice Department prosecutors were elated that he refused to capitulate without a fight. But for Holder there was a much deeper principle to uphold: deciding how and where to prosecute accused terrorists was a core function of the executive branch. Congress did not have the right to dictate terms to the administration on this issue.

Holder began by lobbying Obama to veto the bill outright, though that was a political nonstarter, since the measure was part of a legislative package that contained funding for the troops in Afghanistan and Iraq. Yet there was another option, legally questionable, with heavy political risks: Obama could sign the legislation but assert that he was not bound by certain provisions he deemed unconstitutional. George Bush had quietly made use of so-called signing statements to circumvent the will of Congress in his war in terror. But the ploy stirred outrage when it was later exposed by reporter Charlie Savage in the *Boston Globe*. And it was a tactic that Obama himself had criticized during the campaign. "We're not going to use signing statements as a way of doing an end run around Congress," he had promised at one rally.

Still, Holder pushed hard for Obama to ignore the legislation's controversial detainee provisions. Holder's staff even crafted language for a proposed signing statement and sent it over to the White House. But in the end, Holder's own constitutional experts in the Office of Legal Counsel concluded that Congress *was* well within its rights to impose the restrictions on the executive branch. And the White House was loath to open itself up to the inevitable charges of hypocrisy that would follow such a Bush-style maneuver. On January 7, Obama reluctantly signed the legislation. He did issue a statement alongside the bill, but it was strong in indignation and weak in effect. The detainee measures represented "a dangerous and unprecedented challenge to critical executive branch authority to determine when and where to prosecute Guantánamo detainees, based on the facts and circumstances of each case and our national security interests." He fell short of calling them unconstitutional, or of asserting his right to disregard them.

On January 20, 2011, Obama spoke at the Kennedy Center gala in honor of the fiftieth anniversary of JFK's inauguration. At a time of bitter partisan warfare and national gloom, Democrats, however briefly, allowed themselves to look back nostalgically at Camelot. During the campaign, Obama's lithe frame and easy grace had, in the minds of many, recalled Jack Kennedy. And Obama could still give gorgeous speeches. Yet by now his ability to evoke a new spirit of American possibility was severely diminished.

David Axelrod watched the festivities from the Kennedy family box. It was a brief respite from the catcalling Republicans and second-guessing Democrats who were a galling part of his daily routine. The Kennedy children read "The Gift Outright," the poem Robert Frost had recited on that cold, brilliantly sunny day in January 1961. The elegiac strains of cellist Yo-Yo Ma filled the concert hall in an echo of the great Pablo Casals, who'd performed at the Kennedy White House. Axelrod had worshipped Jack and Bobby Kennedy, whom he'd credited with inspiring his own passion for politics and public service. As a five-year-old boy he'd sat on top of a mailbox near his family's apartment on New York's Lower East Side to watch JFK speak at a political rally. Seven years later, he was handing out buttons and bumper stickers for Robert Kennedy's presidential campaign.

When the ceremony ended, a stream of Kennedys and their friends gathered around Axelrod, complimenting him on how well the president was doing under difficult circumstances. He beamed with pride. Sitting nearby, Thomas Wilner watched the scene with disgust. A genteel but passionate liberal, Wilner was a DC lawyer who had represented Guantánamo detainees and won two landmark cases on their behalf in the Supreme Court. He walked up to Axelrod and told Obama's senior adviser that he begged to differ with the rosy assessments of the Kennedy family. "I don't feel that way at all," he remarked. "I've been involved in all of the Guantánamo issues and I've been terribly disappointed in how the administration has done." In Wilner's retelling, Axelrod deflated right in front of him:

"He just kind of caved over." Axelrod walked away, but returned a few minutes later. His usual hangdog expression was even droopier than normal. "I'm just anguished about this, and the president is anguished," he said, according to Wilner. "We talk about this all the time. We want to close Guantánamo. We want to find a way out." Axelrod did not dispute the encounter, nor did he deny that he and the president were disappointed by the outcome of their efforts on Guantánamo and other parts of the terrorism agenda. But he said he had restrained himself from lashing out at Wilner and all of the other dewy-eyed liberals who felt free to judge Obama from the comfort of their cocooned law offices and think tanks. "*You* see what it's like to sit in the president's chair," he'd wanted to tell Wilner. Presidents have to live in the world as it is, not as they want it to be.

For Obama, the late winter of 2010 was a season of compromise — or capitulation, depending on one's point of view. On March 7 the administration released its long-debated executive order on indefinite detention for the forty-eight Guantánamo prisoners who could neither be released, nor tried, nor transferred. This was the same proposal that had been laid out in July 2009 by Greg Craig and Jim Jones, which Obama had refused to back. The order was a tacit acknowledgment that Guantánamo was not going to close, at least not during Obama's first term. Reaction from liberals and civil libertarians was scathing. And the fact that the announcement fell on the same day that military commissions officially resumed after a two-year hiatus did not help. "In a little over two years the Obama administration has done a complete about-face," said the president's liberal nemesis, the ACLU's Anthony Romero. Obama had done exactly what he had expressed misgivings about as far back as the summer of 2009 — institutionalized a system of preventive detention under his own name. He had worried about "owning" the policy, in part because of the precedent it would set. If Barack Obama, a liberal constitutionalist, signed off on a regime of prolonged detention without trial, what would a President Mitt Romney do? But in the end, Obama concluded he had no choice. He was persuaded that he could neither release nor prosecute the "Guantánamo 48" without doing grievous harm to national security. He tried to draw a sharp line between these cases — the legacy of George W. Bush's lawless policies — and those of future captures. It was the pragmatic choice, one that balanced security and American values. But that wasn't the way his liberal supporters saw it: to them, Obama was enshrining into law a system he had once derided as a "legal black hole."

With his term more than halfway complete, there seemed to be no end to the legal and political morass surrounding counterterrorism policy. And yet, ironically, the more Obama was stymied or forced to compromise on policy matters, the more muscular his administration's conduct of the war on terror became. It was as if a president so constrained by politics could only operate freely in the shadows.

Exactly one week after the executive order, Obama held perhaps the most sensitive Principals Committee meeting since becoming president, as CIA Director Leon Panetta and Hoss Cartwright presented him with the kill or capture options for the biggest target of all: Osama bin Laden.

In August 2010 Panetta had informed the White House of a promising lead in the nine-year hunt for bin Laden. His trail had gone stone cold midway through the Bush presidency, but now the CIA had located a man who intelligence officials believed could be the key to finding the al-Qaeda leader. His name was Abu Ahmed al-Kuwaiti, and he was bin Laden's most trusted courier. The agency had been able to track al-Kuwaiti to a fortress-like compound in the town of Abbottabad, Pakistan. Its high walls and elaborate security apparatus raised suspicions that the building had been especially constructed to hide an individual of high value. By February 2011, counterterrorism authorities had determined there was enough sound intelligence indicating the compound was bin Laden's hideout to develop courses of action for a prospective raid.

Two scenarios were under consideration. The first was a B-2 stealth bomber strike. The second was a special-forces-led helicopter assault. Obama grilled Cartwright and Panetta on the pros and cons of both options. Cartwright's main concern was that the terrorists might have constructed a maze of deep tunnels below the compound where they could hide. It was a technique they had encountered before with al-Qaeda. If the United States attempted a helicopter assault with boots on the ground, they might not find anyone there. The best plan, in Cartwright's mind, was to use massive two-thousand-pound bombs that would obliterate anything submerged below the compound. Obama was concerned about collateral damage, but the advantage of the bunker busters, Cartwright told him, was that they exploded deep below the surface. The effect would be more like a minor earthquake than a massive conventional explosion. Still, houses and buildings would collapse and civilians would surely die.

What about the commando operation? Obama asked. It could be done, but there was no question it was the riskier of the two options. Much could go wrong. The compound was likely heavily booby-trapped. If they got to bin Laden, he could set off a suicide vest. The Americans could find themselves in a deadly firefight with Pakistani security forces. Robert Gates was the leading skeptic of the boots-on-the-ground option. He was haunted by two daring special ops raids that had gone disastrously wrong, Operation Eagle Claw, in 1980, and Black Hawk Down, thirteen years later. (One option that was raised but never gained serious traction was a joint US-Pakistani raid. Obama was not comfortable that the Pakistanis would keep the planning under wraps.)

Obama leaned toward the bomber strike. Cartwright asked the air force to start working on a more detailed plan that could be submitted to the president for his approval.

The operational planning surrounding bin Laden was known to only a tiny circle of national security officials, on a need-to-know basis. One person who was not brought into the loop was the attorney general. He was Obama's closest friend on the cabinet and the proposed raid raised important legal questions. But Obama determined that the mission would be a "Title 50 operation," conducted under the auspices of the CIA. As a covert action, there had already been a legal finding prepared, so additional Justice Department approval was not required.

Besides, Holder was busy trying to publicly walk back his KSM decision. Even his own backers were urging him to stand down. Among them was Preet Bharara, the Manhattan US attorney whose office would have tried the case and who had aggressively pushed for a civilian trial. His prosecutors were increasingly uncomfortable sitting on a secret indictment of KSM for so long knowing there was no chance he was going to be tried in a civilian court.

On the evening of April 3, Holder called Obama and told him he planned to announce the following day that he had reversed his decision to try KSM and the other 9/11 defendants in civilian courts. Instead, the cases would be referred back to the Pentagon for prosecution in military commissions. It was a short, almost perfunctory conversation. Obama told Holder it was the pragmatic thing to do.

Sharon Malone urged her husband to hold his head high. As she had always said, he was "strongest when he left the nice guy behind." But she also told him to be cool. She was concerned that an emotional outburst would play into the hands of his critics. "Say what you need to say, but don't go overboard," she counseled him. As he read his statement at the press conference later that afternoon, Holder at first seemed subdued, even dispirited. But as the press jackals hammered him with their questions, he grew increasingly pugnacious. And he aimed his fire at Congress. "The reality is I know this case in ways that members of Congress do not," he said in response to a reporter's question. "I have looked at the files. I have spoken to the prosecutors. I know the tactical concerns that have to go into this decision. So I do know better than them. Yes."

The *New Yorker* magazine, which had earlier published Holder's statement that the KSM decision would be his "defining event," now tartly observed that it *had* defined him, though not in the way he had hoped.

As Holder made his forlorn announcement, half a world away spy planes and drones with infrared cameras were tracking the movements of a slight, dark-skinned Somali named Ahmed Abdulkadir Warsame. Warsame, the principal liaison between the Shabab and AQAP, had been a "kill or capture" priority for months. Large amounts of guns and money were flowing back and forth between Yemen and Somalia across the Gulf of Aden, and there was evidence that AQAP operatives and other foreign fighters were being trained in Shabab camps.

Admiral McRaven developed several options for targeting Warsame: he could be killed in Yemen, if American drone operators could get a good shot, or he could be captured or killed in Somalia. (A capture operation in Yemen was not feasible because of the political backlash it would cause.) But from the start, JSOC was hopeful it would be able to mount a successful capture. Warsame, the operators believed, would prove exactly what they had been saying all along:

that captures were to the war on terror what compound interest was to finance — the way to transform success into vastly greater success. The intelligence they could extract from a prize like Warsame could help them foil plots and take even more dangerous terrorists off the battlefield.

In mid-April JSOC got a lucky break. Tracking Warsame's cell phone, they learned that he would soon be crossing the Gulf of Aden on his way back to Somalia. A snatch-and-grab operation on an international body of water was a far easier proposition than putting boots on the ground in Yemen or Somalia. And the intelligence indicated that Warsame would be traveling with a single associate. He would not have a contingent of heavily armed bodyguards with him. Using local spies, JSOC had been able to penetrate his network and manipulate the timing and logistics of his movements. This was the moment they'd been waiting for. Ever since the Nabhan operation in September 2009, the Obama administration knew it would eventually be faced with the opportunity to capture a high-value terrorist. After months of arduous debate and legal wrangling, a process led by Tom Donilon and known in bureaucratese as the "detention policy straw man," the principals had settled on a set of protocols to govern such a capture. Warsame presented the first opportunity to use them. The capture plan had at least one false — and somewhat farcical — start. Warsame had been planning to travel to the coast on his way home, but delayed the trip after an apparently painful trip to the dentist.

Finally, at dusk on April 19, a traditional wooden ship sailed toward Warsame's fishing trawler in the Gulf of Aden. It was a screen vessel that US commandos use to retain the element of surprise. Hidden behind it were SEAL Team Six commandos in Navy fast boats. (Snipers were positioned on a nearby vessel in case force was necessary.) The SEALs approached Warsame's boat undetected, stealthily boarded, and subdued him and an associate. Not a shot was fired. The two men were transported to the USS *Boxer,* an amphibious assault ship that had been outfitted as a kind of floating prison, steaming nearby. Ironically, the easy part was the capture. The hard part was about to begin.

10

TEXTBOOK

O N T H E V E R Y D A Y of the Warsame capture, April 19, 2011, Barack Obama was secretly briefed again on the most high-profile potential kill of his presidency: Osama bin Laden.

The bombing strike had been taken off the table after intelligence indicated that the water table in the area surrounding the Abbottabad compound made the existence of tunnels beneath the complex unlikely. Obama had also been worried about collateral damage from such a strike. The president had thus instructed the military and the CIA to start planning a boots-on-the ground raid.

Admiral McRaven presented Obama with a detailed helicopter-assault plan. In the previous weeks he had put together a team drawn from Red Squadron, of SEAL Team Six fame. He'd watched his elite commandos stage dry runs at secret locations in North Carolina and Nevada. Relying on satellite imagery and other intelligence, the Joint Special Operations Command had constructed container boxes scaled to the exact dimensions of the Abbottabad compound.

To McRaven, JSOC's warriors were astonishing specimens. They had conducted hundreds of similar missions before in Iraq, Afghanistan, and even in countries where the United States was not at war, like Syria. He had no doubt they could get the job done. But would the president go for it? Obama had shown a willingness to take calculated risks. And he had always said that he would consider using force unilaterally in Pakistan if he had an opportunity to take out bin Laden. On the other hand, he had often pushed back against counterterrorism operations that involved sending in American troops outside conventional theaters of war. He wasn't going to get "bogged down," he'd say.

Obama listened intently as McRaven presented the plan. When the briefing ended, the president zeroed in on the proposal's main vulnerability. What if something went terribly wrong? What if the building was booby-trapped, or the American troops found themselves in a fight with Pakistani security forces who had detected the presence of foreign invaders? Obama was echoing the anxieties of Bob Gates. As a young CIA officer Gates had been in the White House Situation Room on the day of the disastrous Iran hostage-rescue mission in 1980. Haunted by the memory, Gates continued to be skeptical about a boots-on-the-ground operation to kill bin Laden. Obama wanted to know what contingencies McRaven had put in place in case his forces came under assault. McRaven told the president he'd ordered the prepositioning of a quick reaction force along the Afghanistan-Pakistan border. If the SEALs found themselves pinned down, Admiral Mullen would be ready to call General Ashfaq Parvez Kayani, his Pakistani counterpart, to request Pakistani backup for the Americans. Obama was not impressed. He ordered McRaven back to work, telling him he wouldn't approve the plan unless it had a credible "fight your way out" scenario.

On Thursday, April 28, Obama held his fifth and final national security meeting on the bin Laden operation. Mullen presented McRaven's refined plan. In addition to the two stealth Black Hawk helicopters selected for the operation, McRaven had added two Chinook CH-47s, workhorse copters that could be used for difficult extraction missions. Attack aircraft would also be at the ready if necessary. Still, the military, continually looking for ways to minimize risk, built in one more contingency plan. It would involve a classified weapon that had never been deployed before. Images from the CIA's surveillance drones indicated that the tall figure believed to be bin Laden took regular walks in the compound's courtyard. (Intel and military officials had dubbed him "the pacer.") The Americans would drop a small and very precise laser-guided glide bomb that could take out the al-Qaeda leader during his constitutional. The mission remained risky, but now they would be sending a *lot* of firepower.

Obama brought the meeting to a close, but kept his counsel. He was methodical about assessing risk, and the evidence that bin Laden was at the compound was completely circumstantial — Obama put the chances at 50 percent. He said he wanted one last conversation with McRaven before making his decision. When the president spoke with the JSOC commander later that day, McRaven assured Obama that his men were ready. They had trained all their adult lives for a mission like this.

Early the next morning, as he was preparing to leave for Alabama to survey the damage caused by a recent outbreak of devastating tornadoes, Obama met in the Diplomatic Room with Tom Donilon, John Brennan, Denis McDonough, and Bill Daley, who had succeeded Rahm Emanuel as his chief of staff. The president had made up his mind. Operation Neptune Spear was "a go." Donilon prepared the official papers to execute the order.

The mission, which had been scheduled to take place on Saturday, had to be delayed for a day because of cloud cover. After returning from Alabama, the president called McRaven one final time before the operation. "Godspeed to you and your forces," he told him. "Please pass on to them my personal thanks for their service and the message that I personally will be following this mission very closely."

On Saturday morning, George Little, CIA Director Leon Panetta's press secretary and one of his most trusted advisers, placed a sixty-six-page document into a secure "lock-bag" and drove to the White House from Langley. Mild, discreet, and imperturbable, Little was the only "communicator" brought into the loop from nearly the beginning of the bin Laden operation. He knew that however the raid turned out, the administration would need a comprehensive messaging plan. His office prepared elaborate talking points for two scenarios: success or failure. (The CIA was also prepared to put out a cover story to obscure the true purpose of the operation, should its existence become public.) Little's document contained draft presidential statements for either outcome. At the northwest gate of the White House, a Secret Service officer punched Little's name into the computer. "Sir, you are not in the system," came the reply. Standing in the park across the street as he waited to be cleared for entry, Little had dark visions of being mugged and his bag stolen. He clutched the lock bag tightly against his chest.

The evening before the bin Laden mission, the president spoke at the White House Correspondents' Association annual dinner. In a wryly ironic performance worthy of James Bond, the tuxedoed Obama singled out real estate mogul and television personality Donald Trump, who was in attendance. Trump, positioning himself for a possible presidential run in 2012, was fueling the "birther" rumor that Obama had not been born in the United States. Obama nimbly mocked Trump's leadership credentials, invoking the difficult choices "the Donald" had to make on his reality show *The Celebrity Apprentice*.

"These are the kinds of decisions that would keep me up at night," he told the audience without cracking a smile. "Well handled, sir. Well handled."

On Sunday morning Obama played nine holes of golf at Andrews Air Force Base, outside Washington. Light rain and a chill in the air cut his game short. Immediately after returning to the White House he joined his top national security advisers in the Situation Room. Panetta and his team gathered in the director's conference room at Langley, which had been turned into a high-tech command center. At 1:22 P.M. Panetta communicated the president's final authorization for the raid to McRaven, who was hunkered down in Jalalabad, Afghanistan. "You and your men have our prayers and confidence," he told McRaven.

A little after 2 P.M. Panetta, via video link, reviewed the operation with the group one last time. One contingency discussed was the highly unlikely event of a capture. Everyone involved regarded the undertaking as a kill mission, but international law required a capture option in the event that bin Laden managed to surrender or if he did not die in the attack. (Hoss Cartwright had made arrangements for bin Laden to be taken to Bagram if that should happen. If the Afghan government had refused to have him on Afghan territory—a possibility—bin Laden would have been transported via a V-22 Osprey aircraft to a ship at sea with a temporary brig. In that scenario, Washington still would have had to figure out what to do with their prize.) But as one Pentagon official put it, "The only way bin Laden was going to be taken alive was if he was naked, had his hands in the air, was waving a white flag, and was unambiguously shouting, 'I surrender.'"

By about 3 P.M. Washington time the mission was under way. Panetta narrated from Langley. "They've crossed into Pakistan," he said. Grim-faced and solemn, Obama silently watched the Situation Room screens. Then Panetta announced that the SEALs had "reached the target." Seventy-nine commandos and a military dog named Cairo in four helicopters approached the compound.

Moments later came hair-raising news: one of the stealth helicopters had crash-landed. There were no injuries, but the mission commander had had to quickly improvise, calling in reserve forces and ordering the downed aircraft to be destroyed. Brennan would later remark that the "minutes passed like days." Obama, famous for his sangfroid, was worried. (He'd later say it was the most anxious he'd ever been, with the possible exception of when his daughter Sasha got meningitis at three months old, and he could only wait for the doctor to tell him she wasn't going to die.) The commandos stormed the compound, breaching walls and blowing through barricades with explosives. They methodically made their way up the stairs. One by one, they extinguished "hostiles" in bursts of silenced gunfire, including one of bin Laden's sons and the courier who had led them to the compound in the first place.

Minutes into the operation, the commandos came face to face with bin Laden, unarmed, wearing a prayer cap and the baggy tunic and trousers known as a shalwar kameez. One of the SEALs, whose identity will likely never be known, fired two quick rounds at the world's most wanted terrorist — the "double tap" heard round the world. The first shot hit bin Laden in the chest. The second struck him in the head, above the left eye. Then the SEAL reported back through his radio, "For God and Country — Geronimo, Geronimo, Geronimo," the code word indicating that bin Laden had been found. McRaven, monitoring the operation from Jalalabad, relayed the message back to Langley. Panetta and his team looked around at each other quizzically — no one had informed them of the code word. Moments later the word came: "Geronimo E-KIA" — the target had been killed in action. After nearly an hour of agonizing tension for those waiting in the Situation Room, Obama allowed himself the briefest expression of satisfaction: "We got him. We got him."

The Americans were not out of danger yet. Unable to identify the foreign intruders, the Pakistanis had scrambled fighter jets and were preparing other hostile measures. The assault team still needed to conduct the "sensitive site exploitation," or intelligence-gathering phase of the mission. They hoovered up documents, computer hard drives, CDs, DVDs, and flash drives. It proved to be an intelligence gold mine, the single largest haul since the beginning of the war on terror. Later, analysts sifting through the material would learn that bin Laden was still very much in communication with his far-flung field commanders, and that he aspired to pull off major attacks.

By the thirty-eighth minute of the operation, the SEALs were choppering back to Afghanistan on the remaining stealth Black Hawk. Onboard with them was bin Laden's corpse. After a quick midair refueling along the border, the Americans crossed into Afghanistan. President Obama and the others monitoring the operation could finally breathe easily. A few hours later, on the USS *Carl Vinson,* bin Laden's body was administered Muslim religious rites before being dumped into the Arabian Sea in a weighted body bag. Osama bin Laden, the world's most hunted man, who had skillfully eluded US forces for nearly a decade, was no more.

It was a Hollywood storyline. Not only had Obama eliminated America's Enemy Number One, he had ordered one of the most daring military operations in the country's history. Yet it was a storyline that played out against a toxic political backdrop. Ironically, Obama's political opponents had caricatured him as a feckless Democrat who didn't possess the inner steel to stand up to the terrorists. A significant portion of Americans believed he was a Muslim. Only two days before he authorized the assault, Obama had had to release his long-form birth certificate to convince skeptics that he was an American-born citizen and thus constitutionally eligible to serve as president. "We do not have time for this kind of silliness," he said at a press conference announcing the action. The consequences of failure for the bin Laden mission would have been catastrophic, politically for Obama and psychically for a country battered by a persistently weak economy and a widening sense of national decline. With the news of bin Laden's death, for a brief, exultant moment, Americans danced in the streets in front of the White House and at Ground Zero in New York City. They waved American flags, shouted "USA! USA!" and raised placards exalting Obama. Even congressional Republicans praised the president's gutsiness. The pride in Obama's actions was best captured by Robert Gates, who told *60 Minutes,* "I worked for a lot of these guys and this is one of the most courageous calls . . . that I think I've ever seen a president make."

In another time, the killing of Osama bin Laden might have been a transformative event for a president, a stunning military and moral victory that all Americans would rally around — and not just for a few days. But this was no ordinary time. It was a time of such partisan animus that even bringing bin Laden to justice for the thousands of lives lost on 9/11 failed to stop the bickering. It was only a matter of days before Republicans resumed their attacks against Obama's "criminalized" war on terror. Typical was the case of two Iraqis arrested in Kentucky in May and charged by the Justice Department with plotting to send arms back to insurgents in Iraq. It was hardly an example of a dire domestic threat. But Mitch McConnell, the top Republican in the Senate, ripped the Obama administration for risking "retaliatory attacks" in his home state by prosecuting the suspects in the civilian court system. "Get these men out of Kentucky," he inveighed in June. "Send them to Guantánamo, where they belong."

Meanwhile, Obama and his advisers were still tying themselves in knots over the fate of a midlevel terrorist completely unknown to Americans.

For more than two months after the bin Laden raid, the White House held no less than a dozen secret principals or deputies meetings to resolve the case of Ahmed Warsame, the Somali operative who'd been acting as a conduit between al-Qaeda in the Arabian Peninsula and the Shabab. He was the first significant terrorist captured overseas since Obama had become president. As Warsame languished on a US ship in the middle of the Arabian Sea, he became a kind of test case for Obama, a chance for the administration to thread the needle of law, security, and politics. Obama wanted to prove that he could capture high-value terrorists and lawfully extract the kind of intelligence needed to prevail in the war on terror, even in the face of the polarizing national discussion surrounding the issue.

But there were no easy ways to do this. It was no accident that Warsame was Obama's only major capture and that he was being held in a floating brig on the USS *Boxer*. As the Warsame exception would prove, the rule was true: killing was a lot easier than capturing. As they pondered their options, Obama's advisers knew that they all carried heavy political and legal risks. Warsame could be prosecuted in a civilian court or tried in a military commission. He could be transferred to a third country, like Ethiopia or Saudi Arabia. Or he could be held indefinitely, or released.

From the start Harold Koh and others at the State Department lobbied aggressively for a civilian trial. After the collapse of the Khalid Sheikh Mohammed effort, what could be more redemptive than flying an accused terrorist into New York City, unsealing an indictment, and trying Warsame in the very courtroom where prosecutors had planned to try the 9/11 mastermind? Yet the Justice Department reacted warily. Holder was still licking his wounds from the KSM calamity and was wary of being exposed without administration support. At one White House meeting, James Cole, the deputy attorney general, said Justice would only support an Article III trial for Warsame if it was a "case of necessity" — in other words, if there were no other options. The White House knew that bringing Warsame to New York would provoke a firestorm on Capitol Hill. Congress was once again tightening the screws on detainee policy. One proposed bill would have explicitly barred the government from bringing any accused terrorists into the country for civilian prosecution.

Early in the discussion, Gates, and some in the White House, leaned toward a military commission, mostly for evidentiary reasons. But there were significant downsides with that approach as well. For one thing, it would have signaled to the left and civil libertarians that the administration had given up on its commitment to using civilian courts to enforce the laws against terrorists. Moreover, it was unclear that the military would even have jurisdiction to prosecute Warsame, a member of the Shabab, not explicitly covered by the congressional authorization to use force against al-Qaeda.

Meanwhile, the longer the administration held Warsame while it puzzled through its options, the more risks were incurred. The White House knew that the circumstances surrounding Warsame's abduction and detention would be controversial when they became public knowledge. Maritime detentions during wartime had a long, dark history, evoking the rat- and disease-infested British hulks during the American Revolution and Japanese "hell boats" in World War II. From the outset Brennan was adamant that Warsame be treated "above and beyond" international standards. Members of the High-Value Detainee Interrogation Group, Obama's answer to the Bush enhanced interrogation program, composed of interrogators from the military, CIA, and FBI, were flown in to question him. The detention facilities on the *Boxer* replicated JSOC's supersecret temporary screening facilities in Iraq and Afghanistan. Terror suspects began their detention in small, spare cells that had no more than a bed, chair, table, and prayer rug. But as they cooperated, their conditions were upgraded. Warsame was fed well, taken on walks on the ship's deck, and given other amenities to help win his cooperation. According to one Obama official, the treatment harked back to World War II, when US military police gave Nazi POWs cigarettes "to acknowledge their humanity." At first, Warsame held back. Later, he slowly began opening up, but only by talking in the third person about terrorist plots and tactics. When intelligence analysts probed his statements, they figured out he was talking about his own activities. When the interrogators confronted him with what they had learned, the floodgates opened. It took weeks, but eventually Warsame "sang like a bird," according to a source who had received regular briefings. He told his interrogators how he had met on multiple occasions with the American-born jihadi cleric Anwar al-Awlaki, had arranged major weapons deals between the Shabab and AQAP, and acquired important tactical and logistical skills he planned to bring back with him to the training camps of Somalia. In addition, he provided invaluable intelligence on the structures and operational capabilities of both organizations.

As Warsame talked, the Obama lawyers and policymakers continued to argue over the best path forward. Early on, civilian prosecutors were doubtful they could prove their case without revealing highly sensitive sources and methods. Nevertheless, they impaneled a grand jury in New York's Southern District and began trying to assemble a case. Meanwhile, Pentagon officials were losing confidence that military commissions would be an adequate venue. They continued to worry about jurisdictional challenges, but the concerns were even more fundamental than that. At one deputies meeting, Jeh Johnson had to acknowledge that the military prosecutors were unfamiliar with newer groups like AQAP and the Shabab and how they related to al-Qaeda. "Well that's a pretty basic thing," McDonough, Obama's deputy national security adviser, said. Johnson pointed out that the experience of the military prosecutors was limited to detainees who were captured in the aftermath of the 9/11 attacks — members of al-Qaeda's core organization and the Taliban. Koh scribbled a note on a piece of paper and pushed it toward McDonough. It read: "Well it's a little awkward when the prosecutors are prepared to prosecute the crimes of the past but not the crimes of the present or future."

To preserve the possibility of a civilian prosecution, the administration had to arrange for a separate law-enforcement interrogation. None of what Warsame had told the first group of interrogators would be admissible in court, since he hadn't been given his legal rights. A "clean" FBI team would have to conduct its own interview, complete with a Miranda warning, a risky proposition. Warsame was a sophisticated player. Educated in England, he spoke fluent English. What if he clammed up and demanded a lawyer?

As Obama's security council was devoting hundreds of hours to the fallout from a single capture, the military was pressing for a more scattershot approach to killing in Yemen. Brimming with confidence in the wake of the bin Laden operation, the generals believed they could deliver a "knockout blow" to al-Qaeda and its most dangerous affiliate, AQAP. The core group in Pakistan was already knocked flat on its back. But JSOC began talking about "running the table" in Yemen, while the CIA began pushing to expand its signature strikes beyond Pakistan to Yemen and Somalia. This was the same tactic the generals had backed in the first weeks of the new administration but that Obama had rejected. He wanted to stay "AQ-focused," as he put it, and not unnecessarily widen the conflict. But in the summer of 2011, the military believed the approach would hold greater appeal to the president. In principals meetings, Mullen argued that if they went after large numbers of leadership targets quickly they might be able to extract themselves from Yemen altogether. They could tell President Ali Abdullah Saleh that America had completed its war and they were not going to continue fighting his. It was a clever pitch to a president who they knew was eager to end US entanglements in the Muslim world and who was loath to do the bidding of a dictator.

The issue came to a head in late May when the military proposed killing eleven AQAP operatives at once, by far the largest targeting request since it had stepped up operations in Yemen. The Arab Spring's turmoil had spread to the country, and al-Qaeda was moving quickly to take advantage of the chaos. For the first time, AQAP was threatening to seize control of new territory in the south. By early June a battle was raging between AQAP forces and government soldiers for the strategic port town of Zinjibar on the Gulf of Aden. General James Mattis, the combatant commander of US Central Command, which included Yemen, wanted to hit AQAP hard and stop its momentum. Even among combat-hardened veterans, Mattis was known as an unusually fierce war fighter. A gruff Marine in the Hollywood mold, his nicknames included "Chaos" and "Mad Dog." Mattis had a warrior-scholar side to him. He was known to pack the *Meditations* of the Stoic philosopher and Roman emperor Marcus Aurelius before departing for battle. But occasionally his loose tongue revealed a cruder side. "It's a hell of a lot of fun to shoot . . . people," he'd remarked at a forum about Afghanistan in 2005. "It's a hell of a hoot." Over the years Mattis had learned to exercise more discipline, but the White House remained wary and kept him on a tight leash.

Mattis forcefully made his case for the Yemen strike at a June 10 meeting. If AQAP wasn't stopped in its tracks it would establish a dangerous toehold on the coast. Access to the strategic waters of the Gulf of Aden would allow the group to vastly strengthen its operational ties to al-Shabab in Somalia. This was about preventing a terror hub in the Horn of Africa. The militants would often congregate at a soccer stadium outside of a Yemeni military compound. But there was a problem with the plan: while a small number of the targets were senior members of AQAP already approved for "direct action," most of them came from a wing of the organization that was not "externally focused," not interested in attacking the United States, and therefore, according to some, not targetable. AQAP was a terrorist group but it was also an insurgency with tribal elements, largely preoccupied with a local agenda rather than attacking Western or American interests. Yet Mattis's view was that countries like Yemen and Somalia were the future Afghanistans, terrorist incubators. It was better to extinguish the threat before it could grow.

At the meeting, the generals pushed for a speedy approval so that they could strike before their window of opportunity closed. As was the custom, Joint Chiefs Chairman Mullen went around the table to solicit everyone's view of the proposed operation. There was unanimity from the military side. Finally, toward the end of the meeting, Brennan spoke for the first time. Targeting this many militants at once would represent a dramatic shift in policy, he said. He would not take the recommendation to the president until a higher-level deputies meeting could vet the plan. Though he did not explicitly say so, Brennan was opposed to the broad-based strike. He may have been attempting a deft bureaucratic maneuver to scale back the operation before it reached the president for approval. He and Obama were in agreement on kinetic activity: they both believed their surgical approach was working and that the United States should remain "AQ-focused." How would it look if we started killing large numbers of antigovernment insurgents in Yemen — especially ones who were not clear threats to the United States? The fact that at that very moment US warplanes and drones were operating over Libya in support of the insurgency against the government of Muammar al-Qaddafi would make the optics look even worse.

Obama did not want to get sucked into Yemen's civil war on the side of a dictator bucking the tide of Arab reform. Moreover, he'd been badly burned by President Saleh before. In May 2010 Cartwright told the president that the military had "eyes on" a high-level al-Qaeda target and wanted approval to take him out. Obama had approved the hit. A day or two later the target was incinerated in his car along with several bodyguards. The only problem was, they'd accidentally killed a local deputy governor who was working against AQAP, a "friendly." "How could this have happened?" Obama asked Cartwright. The military had relied entirely on a member of the Yemeni security forces to identify the target. In effect, Saleh had used the Americans to eliminate a political rival. Obama was furious, and he let Cartwright know it. "I got a pretty good chest thumping from the commander in chief, and deservedly so," Cartwright later recalled.

On the morning of Saturday, June 11, Brennan chaired the emergency deputies meeting to go over the proposed AQAP strike. Four of the original eleven targets had been removed from the list for legal reasons, yet the State Department still had reservations about some of the remaining targets. The main objection continued to be what Obama had so often expressed to Brennan and Cartwright in their Oval Office sessions: This set of targets, as Brennan put it, was a "slippery slope" to counterinsurgency. It's not where the president wants to go. The deputies carved the list back further. Finally, Brennan and Cartwright took it to the president later that day. The men scaled the list back even more. By 6 P.M. that evening word went out from the National Security Council to the military and the other national security precincts in the government: "POTUS" (the President of the United States) had agreed to add four individuals to the existing pre-vetted list "for Direct Action," a target set vastly whittled back from the original eleven. A few days later, all of them were eliminated.

As the push for more sweeping signature strikes continued to issue from the Pentagon, Brennan began to get irritated. A few days after the Yemen attack, Brennan decided to roll out the big gun in his arsenal: an unequivocal statement from the commander in chief. Brennan told Obama that he needed to clearly state his position on signature strikes so that it would echo throughout the "interagency," meaning all of the national security stakeholders.

It happened in mid-June, during one of the president's regular "Terror Tuesday" briefings. Brennan, who chaired the sessions, had planned a "deep dive" on Yemen. At one point during the discussion, one of the president's military advisers made a reference to the ongoing "campaign" in Yemen. Obama abruptly cut him off. There's no "campaign" in Yemen, he said sharply. "We're not in Yemen to get involved in some domestic conflict. We're going to continue to stay focused on threats to the homeland — that's where the real priority is."

In the midst of the administration's continued wrangling over the scope of its war on terror, a consensus was beginning to form around Ahmed Warsame. At a June 14 principals meeting, Bob Gates backed the idea of a civilian trial for the Somali detainee after concluding that a military commission was too risky. The Justice Department lawyers were starting to feel more confident that they could successfully prosecute Warsame for providing "material support" to both the Shabab and AQAP. But the FBI still had to conduct its interview. Obama officials had arranged to bring the Red Cross onto the USS *Boxer* to inspect Warsame's conditions of confinement as part of the "clean break" between the military and the law-enforcement interrogations. (It concluded that his detention complied with the Geneva Conventions and other international humanitarian standards.) Agents then advised Warsame of his right to remain silent and to have a lawyer present during questioning, which he waived. During the subsequent interview, Warsame was fully cooperative. The government now had evidence that could be used in a civilian trial.

On June 29 Admiral McRaven testified before the Senate Armed Services Committee as Obama's nominee to lead the US Special Operations Command. It was more a coronation than a confirmation hearing: senators basked in McRaven's reflected glory. "By leading the mission that killed Osama bin Laden, you and your men won an enduring place in military history," gushed Senator John McCain. But toward the end of the hearing Senator Lindsey Graham deftly led McRaven down a line of questioning intended to expose a key weakness in the administration's counterterrorism policies.

"If you caught someone tomorrow in Yemen, Somalia, you name the theater, outside of Afghanistan, where would you detain that person?" asked the South Carolina Republican. Graham was a master of the rhetorical question: he knew that all he needed to do was present the scenario and McRaven would make the point for him. "Sir, right now, as you are well aware, that is always a difficult issue for us," McRaven responded. He told the senator that one option would be to place a captured terrorist on a "naval vessel" until a viable plan could be developed. At the time, Graham had no idea about the drama that was playing out on the high seas with Warsame. "What is the longest we can keep somebody on a ship?" Graham asked. It would depend, McRaven answered, on whether the suspect could be prosecuted in the United States or by a third-party country. Graham skillfully led McRaven to the money moment: And if he couldn't? "Sir, again, if we can't do either of those, then we will release that individual. I mean that becomes the unenviable option, but it is an option."

There it was. The admiral was conceding that the legal and political contortions it had been forced into had led to a policy that could seriously harm the security of Americans. The Obama administration would rather let dangerous terrorists go than send them to Guantánamo. Or so it seemed.

The very next day, the national security principals met at the White House to finally decide the fate of Warsame, who had now been held at sea for close to seventy days. The meeting was chaired by National Security Adviser Tom Donilon. He went around the table asking officials to lay out all of the different scenarios in detail. Then Donilon asked the principals to weigh in. It was unanimous: Warsame would be surreptitiously flown into New York and tried in a federal courtroom in downtown Manhattan. Holder agreed — but after everything he'd been through, he struck a note of wry skepticism. "I'll support it so long as we take a whole-of-government approach." That was government-speak for "I'm not going to be left to twist in the wind again by my own administration." There was a collective sense of satisfaction in the room, a sentiment captured by Brennan. "We've proved we can kill terrorists," he said. "Now we have to prove we can capture them consistent with our values."

As dawn broke on Independence Day, Warsame was transported by military helicopter from the USS *Boxer* to an air force base in the region. As a criminal defendant, he had been placed in the custody of the Justice Department. He boarded an FBI plane and was soon bound for New York City. Back in Washington, Barack and Michelle Obama were hosting their annual Fourth of July party, this one in honor of military heroes and their families. There was a barbecue, a rousing USO show, and a view of the fireworks from the South Lawn. Eric Holder was munching on a burger when the president walked over to him. They chitchatted about their families and basketball. Then Holder brought up the Warsame case. It had been exactly two years before, under a brilliant display of fireworks, that Holder let Obama know he wanted to try Khalid Sheikh Mohammed in Manhattan. Obama had never criticized his friend for how he handled the KSM case. This time, referring to the Warsame decision, the president, in his cool way, showed a bit of pride. It was "textbook," he said. "Textbook."

The handling of the Warsame case was also textbook Obama. Nuanced and lawyerly, it was a classic split-the-difference approach that sought to balance all of the competing interests. After hundreds of hours of careful analysis and debate, his national security advisers found a way to navigate the Scylla and Charybdis of security and law. Warsame was held humanely under the laws of war, long enough for the government to conduct a thorough intelligence interrogation. Obama's national security team arrived at a consensus that a civilian court would be the most effective venue for Warsame's prosecution. It was a perfectly Obamaesque resolution, pragmatic and rational. It vindicated the principle that in the war on terror there were no one-size-fits-all solutions. The Obama Doctrine on counterterrorism was a hybrid approach to an asymmetric war. Sometimes a military model made the most sense. Other times a law-enforcement model was the way to go. And in the case of Warsame, the two approaches worked together in tandem.

But if the handling of the Warsame case was vintage Obama, the political reaction to it was also textbook. Republicans immediately pounced on the president for bringing a terrorist into the country and endangering the security of the American people. Minority Leader Mitch McConnell lambasted Obama on the Senate floor the day after the Justice Department unsealed Warsame's indictment. "The administration has purposefully imported a terrorist into the US and is providing him with all the rights of US citizens in court.

This ideological rigidity being displayed by the administration is harming the national security of the United States of America." Obama's liberal critics also reacted in character, accusing him of mimicking the worst of the Bush policies. He'd created a "floating Guantánamo," charged civil libertarians and human rights activists. According to the *New York Times* editorial page, Obama had "created yet another parallel system of unlimited detention and interrogation without rights outside the constitutional norms that served us well for more than two centuries . . ."

For Obama, the reflexive criticism from both ends of the political spectrum suggested he had gotten Warsame exactly right. Yet as was so often the case in his presidency, he got no credit for slicing a path through the sensible center. For all of its efforts to ensure that the capture complied with the laws of war — secretly whisking Warsame off to international waters, conducting painstakingly by-the-book interrogations, a dozen Situation Room meetings — Obama's team remained mired in the same protracted debates. Privately, even some of the president's closest advisers groused that the resolution of the Warsame case was flawed and reflected a political process that could not tolerate pragmatic decision making: "The administration got it right within the existing constraints," said one Obama confidant. "But the case illustrates that none of the outcomes are good. It's a classic example of the raggedness of these issues, both politically and substantively. None of the tradeoffs are good."

The Warsame case was an anomaly that did not presage a new wave of captures over kills. Most terrorists remained hidden in remote places where American forces could not operate freely. It was unlikely that many more would expose themselves to capture by venturing out onto the open seas. And there seemed to be little prospect that a consensus would emerge in Congress over how to best detain terrorists once they were seized. And yet Warsame underscored the potential value of captures: the Somali militant provided a vast amount of critical information about the tactics, operational capabilities, and personnel of the Shabab and AQAP, as well as important insight into the burgeoning alliance between the two groups. Ironically, his capture (and the intelligence he provided) would also lead to the most controversial kill of Obama's presidency.

US intelligence had been tracking Anwar al-Awlaki for years, but in the wake of the bin Laden operation, Obama had become fixated on taking out the charismatic cleric. FBI Director Robert Mueller, an active participant at the Tuesday counterterrorism briefings, plied the president with chilling intelligence reports on Awlaki. During one briefing, Obama told his counterterrorism advisers that Awlaki was his top priority, even over Ayman al-Zawahiri, who had succeeded bin Laden as the leader of al-Qaeda. The assessment of the intelligence community was that Zawahiri's utter lack of charisma and leadership qualities made him far less of a threat. "Awlaki had things on the stove that were ready to boil over," one of Obama's national security advisers observed. "Zawahari was still looking for ingredients in the cupboard."

The president made sure that Brennan had Awlaki updates at every Terror Tuesday meeting. "I want Awlaki," he said at one. "Don't let up on him." Hoss Cartwright thought Obama's rhetoric was starting to sound like George W. Bush's, whom he had briefed on many occasions. "Do you have everything you need to get this guy?" Obama would ask. Most lethal operations in Yemen had been conducted by the US military. But in the summer of 2011, the Awlaki hit job was turned over to the CIA, for a highly pragmatic reason: the United States had built a new drone base in a strategically located Persian Gulf country. It was a regime with which the CIA had far better ties than the military, allowing it to conduct sensitive operations from certain locations that were off-limits to JSOC. The Defense Department turned over as many as eight of its drones to agency operators so that they could keep a bigger presence focused on Yemen. Meanwhile, the Pentagon put additional drones into nearby Djibouti, finished construction on a base in Ethiopia, and transferred drones there from the Seychelles. What was striking was that JSOC accepted the CIA's primary role in the hunt for Awlaki without complaint. Like the bin Laden mission, it was an example of the near-seamless integration of counterterrorism operations between the military and the CIA, a hallmark of Obama's war.

It was more than just Awlaki's ability to recruit over the Internet or his intuitive grasp of American society that drew Obama's attention. What worried Obama most was Awlaki's relentlessness and ingenuity in developing murderous plots that could get around America's best defenses. There had been the Christmas Day plot, which had come perilously close to succeeding. Then, in October 2010, AQAP had managed to put improvised bombs — ink toner cartridges filled with explosive material placed inside HP printers — on cargo planes headed to the American homeland. (They were intercepted as a result of a tip from Saudi intelligence.) Over the summer of 2011 Obama was regularly updated on a particularly diabolical plan that AQAP's master bomb builder, Ibrahim Hassan Tali al-Asiri, was devising. The intelligence indicated that AQAP was close to being able to surgically implant bombs in people's bodies. The wiring was cleverly designed to circumvent airport security, including metal detectors and full-body scanners. AQAP's terror doctors had successfully experimented with dogs and other animals. Obama and his advisers were in a race against time to kill Awlaki.

Warsame's capture couldn't have come soon enough. The Navy SEALs seized his laptop computer, a hard drive, two USB thumb drives, and a memory card. The hardware was filled with emails and other evidence tying him directly to Awlaki. Warsame had met with the cleric only days before, completing a major weapons deal between the two groups. Warsame's exposure to Awlaki and other high-ranking members of AQAP gave him access to critical "patterns of life" intelligence, which he divulged to US officials when they interrogated him. He told them how Awlaki traveled, including the kinds of vehicles he used and the configuration of his convoys. He provided information about Awlaki's modes of communication as well as the elaborate security measures he and his entourage took. All of this intelligence turned out to be critical in the hunt for Awlaki, who for the previous two years had left precious few traces.

Finally, in the spring and summer of 2011, US and Yemeni intelligence started to draw a bead on him. Days after the bin Laden killing, American drone strikes narrowly missed him as he was traveling across the desert with his entourage.

In the end, Awlaki's demise was the result of several factors: a mosaic of intelligence the Americans were able to assemble with the help of Warsame, a tip from a Yemeni source, and a fatal lapse in operational security by the cleric. In September, US intelligence had tracked Awlaki to Al Jawf province, an al-Qaeda stronghold in northern Yemen. In a departure from his peripatetic ways, Awlaki stayed in the same house for two weeks. But he often surrounded himself with children, and the standing orders from Obama had always been to avoid collateral damage at almost any cost. In many previous instances Hoss Cartwright would not even take a proposed operation up the chain to the president if there was a reasonable chance that civilians would be killed. But as the Americans were closing in on Awlaki, Obama let it be known that he didn't want his options preemptively foreclosed. If there was a clear shot at the terrorist leader, even one that risked civilian deaths, he wanted to be advised of it. "Bring it to me and let me decide in the reality of the moment rather than in the abstract," he said, according to one Obama confidant. "In this one instance," recalled the source, "the president considered relaxing some of his collateral requirements." But in the end Obama was never forced to confront that awful dilemma.

On the morning of September 30, after finishing breakfast, Awlaki and several of his companions left the safe house and walked about seven hundred yards to their parked cars. As they were getting into the vehicles, they were blown apart by two Hellfire missiles. (Also killed was Samir Khan, the Pakistani American propagandist for AQAP and editor of the terrorist organization's Internet organ, *Inspire.* Justice Department lawyers had told the military that they could not approve Khan's killing, but after officials learned he had died in the raid, Khan was deemed "acceptable collateral damage.")

Within less than six months, Obama had taken America's two top terrorist enemies off the battlefield, delivering crippling blows to al-Qaeda's morale and its ability to carry out new attacks. And yet perhaps no other action upset liberals and civil libertarians more than the killing of Anwar al-Awlaki. What Obama considered a necessary and lawful act of war, one that was vital to protecting the lives of Americans, his critics saw as a summary execution carried out on the basis of secret evidence. Even Bush had not gone this far — the deliberate killing of an American citizen without a trial. But for all the handwringing, Obama had "no qualms," recalled one of his top advisers. For months lawyers in the Justice Department's Office of Legal Counsel had carefully debated the legality of targeting an American citizen for death, finally issuing a secret opinion authorizing the action in June 2010. They'd concluded that it was lawful, as long as capture was not feasible. But it was largely an exercise in post hoc justification. Obama had already been given oral approval to take out Awlaki as far back as December 2009, around the time of the Christmas Day bombing attempt. Obama had wrestled endlessly with the consequences of embracing a policy of indefinite detention for terror suspects. During those debates he had invoked Justice Robert Jackson's admonition that a president's actions would "lie around like a loaded weapon." Now he might have been thinking about another quote from Justice Jackson, that the Constitution was not a "suicide pact." Obama had seen the intelligence and had no doubt that Awlaki posed a serious and imminent threat to the security of the American people. That he was an American, Obama believed, was immaterial.

EPILOGUE

HEADING INTO 2012, Obama faced a difficult reelection campaign. Having come into office with a singular confidence in his ability to transform American politics, to bridge the bitter national divide, the president had been forced to confront the limits of his abilities as a change maker. After a dispiriting fight with obstreperous Republicans over raising the debt ceiling in the summer of 2011, his rhetoric and actions began to grow more plainly partisan and populist. The election would once again be dominated by economic issues, as persistent joblessness continued to plague the Obama presidency. When terrorism issues did come up they were increasingly viewed through the prism of politics. Rahm Emanuel was long gone, but Tammany was still in control: David Plouffe, the wiry, intense political strategist who had quarterbacked Obama's election in 2008, was back in the White House, charting the president's political comeback. Plouffe had replaced David Axelrod as the president's senior adviser, allowing Alexrod to devote his full energies to the 2012 campaign. Cool and disciplined, Plouffe was far less volatile than Emanuel. But he wasn't about to let hot-button terrorism issues distract from the reelection effort. Nor, it seemed, was the man he was working for.

When Obama was challenged by the Republicans on national security he now had a devastating rejoinder. Asked at a press conference
in December about GOP charges that he had a weak foreign policy
that amounted to "appeasement," Obama responded with a rare display of bravado. "Ask Osama bin Laden and the twenty-two out of
thirty top al-Qaeda leaders who've been taken off the field whether I
engage in appeasement." In one of the great political turnarounds of
his presidency, Obama's approval ratings on national security hov-
ered around 60 percent heading into the reelection campaign.

But he still needed to rally his base in order to win a second term.
For the Democratic left, could a tally of dead terrorists make up for
the fact that Guantánamo remained open with 171 prisoners, suspected terrorists would not be tried in civilian courts, and Obama
had not been able to prevent Congress from passing ever-more-rigid
legislation restricting the rights of suspects? He knew as well as anyone that prevailing in the fight against violent extremism was not
a numbers game. He had said as much during the 2008 campaign.
"America must be about more than taking out terrorists and locking
up weapons, or else new terrorists will rise up to take the place of
every one we capture or kill," he said in one speech. "My strategy will
be drying up the rising well of support for extremism."

At the time, he had defined one key yardstick of success: how do
desperate people in violence-torn, impoverished places feel when
they look up at American military helicopters? "Do they feel hope,
or do they feel hate?" he asked. "The America I know is the last, best
hope for that child looking up at a helicopter." But three years into
Obama's war on terror, it seemed fair to ask what the children in
Waziristan or Kunar province felt when they heard the buzzing of an
expectant drone lingering high over their villages. They were drawn
to radicalism not only by a religious fervor but by a persistent sense
of futility in their lives. Hellfire missiles materializing suddenly and

devastatingly out of the thin mountain air were unlikely to change that.

Ever since he had taken office, feeling the full weight of his responsibility in preventing the next terrorist attack, Obama had been guided by a different set of metrics: the more terrorists killed or captured, the less likely one of them would slip through and attack the homeland. Without notice or public debate, Obama had gone far beyond what his liberal supporters had ever imagined, appalling them with a steady torrent of targeted killings and other kinetic operations. It had to be said that he had succeeded far beyond all expectations. No one was willing to declare outright victory in the war on terror. After all, for terrorists to succeed by their own measures, all they needed to do was strike fear into the American population with a single successful attack. But by early 2012, al-Qaeda was largely a spent force, its leaders dead or in hiding, its finances drying up, and its seemingly endless pipeline of recruits blocked.

In December 2011 a seventeen-year-old Afghan boy who went by the nom de guerre Hafiz Hanif left Peshawar, Pakistan, and disappeared into the wilds of North Waziristan. He was hoping to rejoin his al-Qaeda cell and was curious to see how they had fared after the death of the man he called "the Sheikh," Osama bin Laden. In 2009 Hanif had run away from home to join the jihad. He had been trained as a suicide bomber. For Hanif there was a romantic allure to the jihadi life: sleeping under the stars with Arab fighters, eating simply by a campfire, and living his idea of a pure, unadulterated form of Islam. In 2010, when Hanif gave an interview to *Newsweek* magazine, he was full of brio and optimism about the holy war. Back then, even though militants were being taken out by drone strikes in large numbers (Hanif had witnessed some of his comrades obliterated in a car by a pair of Hellfire missiles), money was plentiful, morale was still high, and al-Qaeda easily replenished its forces as new recruits, many of them blue-eyed Westerners, arrived across the Iranian border. Eighteen months later, all of that had changed. The Sheikh was dead; only four of fifteen fighters from Hanif's cell remained. They were hunkered down in a mud-brick house, scrounging for food, with no resources and no ability to carry out operations. They told Hanif to go home unless he wanted to be killed by an American drone strike. "Al-Qaeda was once full of great jihadis, but no one is active and planning operations anymore," Hanif told *Newsweek*. "The flower is wilting . . . the once glorious chapter of al-Qaeda is being closed."

Yet at the same time, the war in Washington raged on with no sign of abatement. Congress and the White House were engaged in yet another contentious policy debate over detainees, Guantánamo, and the rights of accused terrorists. Democrats had joined Republicans to support a defense authorization bill that would have renewed restrictions on transferring detainees from Guantánamo, effectively banning civilian trials. But this time they included some of the most draconian measures of Obama's presidency. One provision mandated military detention for terror suspects captured in the United States. Another would have enshrined into law a regime of indefinite detention for terror suspects, even US citizens. These had always been Obama's red lines. He had vowed to veto the bill if the controversial measures were not removed. His supporters hoped that maybe this time it was not an empty threat. A president who had taken out Osama bin Laden and the rest of al-Qaeda's leadership surely had the guts to take on Congress. But Obama was under pressure from the Defense Department to sign the legislation so critical funding would continue to flow to the troops and their families; bucking the generals in an election year would not be helpful. Moreover, he was finally on a roll politically; the GOP primaries had turned into a circular firing squad and the White House was beginning to win the populist argument on jobs and the economy. Why jeopardize that for a set of issues that had been losers since day one?

On New Year's Eve day Obama was in Hawaii for his annual family vacation. He'd escaped Washington with a critical victory under his belt. Republicans had caved on their opposition to an extension to the payroll tax. The president had one last piece of legislative business before he could relax with his family: he had to sign the defense bill. He read through the legislation one more time. He remained outraged by what he considered to be extreme and dangerous provisions. His lawyers had once again resorted to a signing statement to challenge the problematic sections of the bill, but it was not strong enough for Obama. In a conference call that morning he bucked his advisers, asking for a tougher statement. In the end it read: "I have signed this bill despite having serious reservations with certain provisions. My administration will not authorize the indefinite military detention without trial of American citizens. I believe that doing so would break with our most important traditions and values as a nation." By late February, Obama's lawyers had found a way to gut the congressional restrictions — for a time. And there it was again. The president as law professor and would-be protector of America's defining principles.

There was no greater symbol of the intractability of the politics of terrorism than the prison at Guantánamo Bay. He was not responsible for its creation, but as long as it remained open under his watch it was inescapably part of his legacy. One of Obama's fundamental governing instincts had been to take the long view. Never rash or slapdash, he argued that for change to be real and durable it could not simply be willed or dictated. It could only be achieved through sober, persistent persuasion. That was the true source of presidential power, as Richard Neustadt, the great American political scientist, had written.

By late winter 2012, Obama's political prospects had begun to brighten; job growth was coming back and the economy appeared to be shifting from recovery to expansion. Meanwhile, Obama was blessed with a self-immolating Republican primary field. As his approval ratings shot past 50 percent, his advisers began seriously contemplating a second term. If he could have four more years in power, maybe Obama *would* be able to bend the arc of history toward justice. Maybe he'd be able to finally close Guantánamo. But it wasn't something he was talking about on the campaign trail. And his closest advisers believed that, whichever way the election went, Obama would have to stake his legacy elsewhere. As one of them put it, "Guantánamo is going to be like Spandau Prison. Decades from now there may be only one toothless Taliban fighter left, but the prison will still be open for business."

POSTSCRIPT

FOR ALL OF THE ANGST inside the Obama White House over counterterrorism, the issue barely registered during the 2012 campaign. Only *The Daily Show*'s Jon Stewart tried to hold the president's feet to the fire. Throwing his own words back at him, Stewart asked Obama about "trading ideals for security." But Obama nimbly shifted the blame to Congress and went on vaguely about the need to develop a new legal architecture for the war on terror.

In the end, it appeared that Rahm Emanuel and the Tammany faction he led had been right. Tackling terrorism and its knot of Guantánamo-related issues would only hurt Obama politically; conversely, he would not be punished at the polls for keeping them low on the list of presidential priorities.

As in 2008, the 2012 campaign was overwhelmed by concerns about the economy. Obama and his political advisers skillfully — and relentlessly — framed the race around fears of increasing economic inequality. In Mitt Romney, Obama had the good fortune of drawing an opponent who evoked the Monopoly Millionaire. Obama's admen devastatingly portrayed him as an out-of-touch plutocrat.

The race was hard-fought but Obama eventually cruised to victory, becoming the first Democrat since FDR to win back-to-back elections with a majority of the popular vote.

Liberals hoped that Obama, no longer concerned with reelection, would shelve his timidity and take the fight more aggressively to Congress. But as always there would be other priorities competing for his attention. A second term presaged tough battles over entitlement reform, immigration, and gun control, all of which would require significant expenditures of precious political capital.

On terrorism and Guantánamo, the same desultory rituals were playing out just as they had been for years. In late December, Congress pushed through its annual defense authorization bill, and once again it contained onerous measures that would prevent the administration from closing the military prison. Even Lindsey Graham, who Obama had once hoped would be his partner in a "grand bargain" to shutter Gitmo, sounded as if he'd given in to the forces of fear. "Simply stated," Graham said, "the American people don't want to close Guantánamo Bay . . . to bring these crazy bastards that want to kill us all to the United States."

Obama threatened to veto the legislation, but almost no one believed he would go through with it. Sure enough, he signed the bill into law on January 2, while vacationing with his family in Hawaii. He issued another signing statement objecting to Congress's restrictions on detainee policy, but it lacked the sharp, sweeping language of his earlier decrees.

One thing Obama had learned was that he had a lot more autonomy on the battlefield than he did back in Washington. For much of his presidency that had meant waging a brutal and secret war of targeted killings in Pakistan, Yemen, and Somalia. But it also meant that he had the power to restrain the military and the CIA when he thought it was necessary. He had exercised such discretion with his kill lists — personally determining who would be killed and who would be spared. Similarly, he'd barred the military from conducting broad-based "signature" strikes in Yemen, though he relented in early 2012 as AQAP seized more strategic territory in that impoverished and increasingly unstable country. By the fall of 2012, Obama had quietly begun searching for ways to more systematically reform his targeted killing program. He had even obliquely hinted at this in his *Daily Show* appearance, telling Stewart that although "there are bad folks on the other side of the world," he and future presidents needed to be "reined in, in terms of some of the decisions we're making." Once again, Obama fretted about leaving behind too *much* power for his successors.

John Brennan began working on a set of standards and procedures to codify and institutionalize the CIA's drone operations. Brennan called it his "playbook," but it was more than just an effort to enshrine the rules of the road for targeted killings; Obama was seeking to fundamentally reform the way the CIA's killing decisions were made. In the short term, the goal was to subject the drone program to a more vigorous interagency vetting process and to place its targeting decisions under tighter White House supervision. But the ultimate goal was to shift the program over to the military, whose criteria for strikes were more transparent and which operated under clearer legal authorities. The CIA needed to return to its primary focus of collecting and analyzing intelligence — and get out of the killing business. Obama's nomination of Brennan to head the agency in January 2013 sent a clear signal that the administration intended to put its full weight behind these efforts.

Brennan's initiative was playing out against the backdrop of a far more profound and vexing question: How do you end a constantly evolving and mutating war against an enemy that is dispersed, hidden, and driven by an ideology that transcends borders? Obama's drone campaign against al-Qaeda's core organization in Pakistan had placed the terrorist group on the brink of strategic defeat. But al-Qaeda's offshoots still posed a threat. And the danger had metastasized beyond groups like AQAP and the Shabab. The Arab Spring had birthed or strengthened countless splinter groups in places like Libya, Mali, and Syria.

Still, behind the scenes, Obama was questioning whether America should remain engaged in a permanent, ever-expanding state of war, one that had pushed the limits of the law, stretched dwindling budgets, and at times strained relations with key allies. He had no illusion that the war could draw to a close neatly or quickly. But as one of his closest national security advisers asked, "Isn't it time to start winding down the state of emergency?"

In August 2012, Jeh Johnson sat on the porch of his Martha's Vineyard summer home grappling with that same question. It was a conundrum that had gnawed at the Pentagon lawyer even as he'd blessed countless drone strikes and developed the military's legal arguments for expanding the war in places like Yemen and Somalia. Now, on the eve of his retirement, he planned to give a speech broaching the delicate subject. Overlooking Nantucket Sound, he drafted the address in longhand and then let it marinate for several weeks. In December, with Obama's full backing, he became the first senior member of the administration to publicly state that the war on terror must at some point draw to a close. "Now that the efforts by the US military against al-Qaeda are in their twelfth year," Johnson said at the Oxford Union, the British university's fabled debating society, "we must ask ourselves how will this conflict end?"

And yet as 2013 dawned, the American killing machine was once again in high gear. After significant lulls, the pace of drone strikes was rising in the lawless regions of Pakistan and the militant strongholds of Yemen, a reminder of the grinding, inexorable momentum toward more violence. Obama had succeeded in ending the war in Iraq, and the troops would soon be coming home from Afghanistan. As he prepared to take the oath of office for another four years, the question was whether Obama could find a way to move America beyond the forever war.

JANUARY 2013

ACKNOWLEDGMENTS

One thing I learned writing a book is that no matter how lonely it can feel, it is truly a collective enterprise. This book simply never would have happened had it not been for the support, encouragement, faith, prodding, expert editing, wisdom, patience, and love of so many friends, colleagues, and family. There are too many to name here but I would like to acknowledge some of them.

First, I am indebted to the many sources who talked to me for this project. They all had hugely busy schedules and yet generously took the time to give me their perspectives and, in some cases, share their notes, correspondence, and memos. I am especially grateful to those sources who were willing to reveal their innermost feelings—their doubts, frustrations, and fears—as they struggled with difficult questions of security, law, and morality. Some of these people talked to me literally dozens of times, taking pains to convey important nuances and context.

I would also like to thank all of the people at Houghton Mifflin Harcourt, beginning with Bruce Nichols, a wonderful editor and a lovely person. His keen insights and graciously delivered criticisms made this book immeasurably better. His enthusiasm, calmness, and decency kept me going. Thanks also to Lori Glazer, Christina Ma-

mangakis, Ayesha Mirza, Lisa Glover, Ben Hyman, and Loren Isenberg. And a special thank-you to copyeditor Melissa Dobson, whose deft edits and cheerleading helped drag me across the finish line.

There's no chance this book would have seen the light of day without the cheerful persistence of my agent, Gail Ross of the Ross Yoon literary agency. It was never the right time to write a book—whether it was new jobs, new houses, or new babies. Until it was. I thank Gail for sticking with it, and for her faith and friendship. Thanks also to Howard Yoon, who had many good suggestions when I was pitching the book.

I am enormously grateful to the numerous researchers who helped out at different times. Thanks to Sam Register and Michael Cruz at *Newsweek,* Josh Diamonstein at the Aspen Institute, and especially my principal researcher, Johannah Cornblatt, who is any book writer's dream, with her intelligence, efficiency, organization, and extraordinary attention to detail.

Many thanks to my colleagues at *Newsweek,* current and former. Ann McDaniel, a mentor and friend, supported this project from its inception and has been a loyal champion throughout my career in journalism.

Evan Thomas hired me at *Newsweek* and taught me many of the things that made this book possible. Among the most important things Evan taught me is to never lose sight of the human dimensions of the story. Jonathan Alter, whose book *The Promise* is the gold standard for books about Obama, has been an incredible source of advice and encouragement throughout the project.

Nisid Hajari and Jeff Bartholet, great friends and two of the best editors I have ever worked with, were excellent sounding boards. Douglas Baumstein was a good listener and helped me sharpen my ideas.

I've never had more fun or learned more than when working stories with Mark Hosenball and Michael Isikoff, two of the best reporters in the business. And though we've gone our separate ways, we will always be comrades in arms.

Special thanks to Lally Weymouth, who has been a huge supporter and friend, and who has taught me a lot about the art of the interview. And to her brother Don Graham, who has made great journalism possible for a long time, and continues to do so, despite the vicissitudes of the news business.

Also thanks to all of my other ex-*Newsweek* colleagues, including John Barry, Bret Begun, Eleanor Clift, Alexis Gelber, Michael Hirsh, Larry Kaplow, Wes Kosova, Matt McAllester, Jon Meacham, Lisa Miller, Matt Rees, Steve Tuttle, Debra Rosenberg, Mark Whitaker, Pat Wingert, and Fareed Zakaria.

At the new *Newsweek,* I would like to thank Tina Brown for bringing me back to the magazine and for being such an ardent champion of reporting and storytelling. I'd also like to thank Justine Rosenthal, Tom Watson, Tunku Varadarajan, Mark Miller, Lucas Wittmann, David Jefferson, Dan Ephron, Andrew Romano, Christopher Dickey, Sami Yousafzai, Melinda Liu, and Ron Moreau.

There are many journalists whose work informed my reporting and thinking and for whom I owe much gratitude. Among them are Stuart Taylor Jr., Peter Baker, and Charlie Savage of the *New York Times,* Jane Mayer of *The New Yorker,* Massimo Calabresi of *Time* magazine, David Ignatius of the *Washington Post,* and the ABC News team that wrote the excellent e-book *Target: Bin Laden* about the raid on Abbottabad. I would also like to thank all of the people at *Lawfare,* including Benjamin Wittes, Jack Goldsmith, and Robert Chesney. Their blog is indispensable for anyone who values the dispassionate and careful analysis of security law and politics. Peter Bergen's reporting on al-Qaeda has also been invaluable, as has the research he and Katherine Tiedemann have done on drone strikes for the

New America Foundation. I am also grateful to Jennifer Griffin of Fox News for serendipitous meetings on the New York–Washington Acela.

Thanks to all of my friends at Princeton University's Council of the Humanities, Carol Rigolot, Lin DeTitta, Cass Garner, and Susan Coburn.

To my fishing buds, Steve Lewis and Patrick Symmes. Watch out, trout, I'm back!

During the past two years I missed a lot of family functions and forgot to make a few birthday calls. For all of their support and forbearance I want to thank Lisi, Elyakim, Liam, and Itai; Carole and Alan; Gerry and Carol, Michael, Sarah, and Scott; Sherri, David, and Jack; Adam, Mirna, and Hector.

Whatever success I've had I owe to my parents. Steve Klaidman, a great journalist and book writer, taught me to be curious, skeptical, and always honest. My passion and empathy comes from my mother, Kitty Klaidman. Anybody who knows Kitty knows that she's the real reporter in the family. A bonus throughout this project was that while reporting in Washington I got to stay with my parents. Thanks for the home-cooked meals and unconditional love.

Most of all I want to thank my wife, Monica Selter, and my daughters, Bella and Shayna. Monica is the best partner a book writer could have — wise, supportive, and endlessly patient. I appreciate her more than I can ever express here — for this book and for everything else that is good in my life. I love you, and am awed by you. Bella and Shayna, my cutie pies, were a much-needed source of joy and diversion throughout. They also kept the deadline pressure on ("Daddy, are you done with your book yet?"). As Evan Thomas says, the great thing about writing a book is you get to spend a lot of time at home with your family.

INDEX

Abdirahman, Mohamed Mukhtar: as US target, 221
Abdullah (king), 94–95
Abdulmutallab, Umar Farouk, 5
   botched interrogation of, 177–78, 180–82
   Brennan and, 178
   failed terrorist attack by, 173–74
   Holder and, 180–81, 182
   Obama's reaction to, 174–76, 180–81
   provides intelligence, 192–93
   Soufan on, 177
   as US security failure, 177–78, 180–81
Abu Ghraib: prisoner abuse at, 14, 46, 71
Addington, David: views on presidential power, 31
Afghan War, 18, 20, 21, 57–58
al-Qaeda, 34, 49, 59–60, 207–8, 235
   and affiliated terrorist organizations, 122–23, 203
   attack on USS *Cole*, 44, 93–94
   decline of, 268–69
   devastated by CIA's covert drone program, 118, 268–69
   North Waziristan raid on (2005), 18–19
   philosophy of, 15
   Shabab joins with, 220–21, 249
   Yemeni affiliate of, 174, 177, 178, 193, 199, 203, 215, 221, 237, 249, 251–52, 258, 261, 262
American Civil Liberties Union (ACLU), 46, 60, 76, 129, 134–35, 233

American constitutional values: Axelrod and, 38
   Obama and, 5, 18–19, 25, 30, 37–38, 63, 133, 136, 269–70
   Republican Party threatens, 191–92
American Enterprise Institute, 137
AQAP. *See* al-Qaeda: Yemeni affiliate of
Ashcroft, John: reaction to possible attack, 176
Asiri, Ibrahim Hassan Tali al-, 193, 262
Aspen Institute, 3–4
Audacity of Hope, The (Obama), 134
Authorization for Use of Military Force (2001), 205, 250
   Koh and, 140
Awlaki, Anwar al-, 220, 251
   as American citizen, 215, 218, 264–65
   Brennan and, 261
   Cartwright and, 261
   Koh and, 215–16
   Mueller and, 261
   Obama and, 261, 263–65
   rise to power, 174
   strike against, 263–64
   as US target, 215–16, 261–62
Axelrod, David, 48, 52, 79, 84, 91, 112, 142, 175, 266
   and American constitutional values, 38
   attitude toward Craig, 111
   and closure of Guantánamo, 232–33
   confronts Holder, 87–88
   on continuing terrorist threat, 118
   and "media training," 74–76, 85–86

Axelrod, David (*cont.*)
  on Obama's "framing speech," 132, 136
  on terrorist threat to inauguration, 34–35

Bharara, Preet: and Mohammed trial,
    167–68, 236
  and Shahzad's capture, 190
Baker Manning, Susan, 103, 108, 114–15
banks, federal bailout of, 158
Barron, David, 184, 208
Bash, Jeremy: and CIA's covert drone
    program, 121–22
Bates, John: and Guantánamo detainee
    court cases, 58–59
Bauer, Robert: and Graham, 187, 193
  and Miranda rights, 192
  supports military commissions, 187–88
  as White House Counsel, 185–86
Beck, Glenn, 28
Beers, Rand: and war on terror, 17
Bensayah, Belkacem, 208
Bermuda: Uighurs resettled in, 113–16, 155
Bhutto, Benazir: assassination of, 121, 189
Biden, Joe, 84, 106–7, 142, 143
bin Laden, Osama, 27, 132, 218
  death and burial of, 246–48, 257, 263,
    268–69
  escapes, 20
  Pakistan protects, 234–35, 242
  search for, 43–44, 52, 234
  strike against, 234–36, 241–48, 252, 262
Black Hawk Down (1993), 125–26, 213, 235
Blackmon, Douglas A.: *Slavery by Another
    Name,* 71
Blagojevich, Rod, 25
Blair, Dennis, 54, 102
  and release of "torture memos," 61–63
Bloomberg, Michael, 189
  and Mohammed trial, 1, 6, 168–69,
    182–83
Boehner, John: opposes civilian trial for
    detainees, 168
Boren, David, 29
  attacks CIA's use of torture, 31
Boumediene v. Bush (2008), 19–20, 28
Boxer, Barbara, 90
Brennan, John, 34, 40, 90, 102, 213
  and Abdulmutallab, 178
  and Awlaki, 261
  and CIA's covert drone program, 119–20

and civil liberties, 103
  and military commissions, 250
  on Obama's "framing speech," 132
  and proposed "signature strike" in
    Yemen, 254–56
  and release of "torture memos," 61
  and resettlement of Guantánamo
    detainees, 94, 103, 112
  and strike against bin Laden, 243, 246
  and war on terror, 22–23, 51–52
  and Warsame trial, 250
Brown, Ewart: and resettlement of
    Guantánamo detainees, 113–14
Brown, Scott: and war on terror, 5
Burch, David: and resettlement of
    imprisoned Uighurs, 114
Bush, George W., 34
  executive power claims by, 20, 25, 59
  extralegal detention policy, 187
  and military commissions, 27, 28, 44,
    128–29, 150
  Obama compared unfavorably to, 59, 129,
    134–35, 181, 192, 260
  personal style and beliefs, 39, 119, 175, 261
  policies in war on terror, 2, 4, 13, 16–17,
    25, 37–38, 43, 46, 49, 54, 60, 67–68,
    79, 90, 117, 123, 131, 135, 140, 143, 146,
    205–7, 234, 264
  and "state secrets" doctrine, 45, 117
  use of signing statements, 231

Cartwright, James: and Awlaki, 261, 263
  on laws of war, 125
  and long-term detention policy, 127
  and proposed strike against Somalia,
    50–51
  and strike against bin Laden, 234–36, 245
  and war on terror, 51–52, 255
Central Intelligence Agency: black sites and
    secret prisons, 14, 20, 26, 67, 124,
    147, 229
  congressional investigation of, 206
  covert drone program, 21–22, 32, 39–43,
    117–21, 213, 217–22, 243, 261–62,
    268–69
  extraordinary rendition by, 45
  fears release of "torture memos," 60–61
  kills Mehsud, 121–22
  kills Muslim civilians, 40, 120
  missile strikes in Pakistan, 39–40

Obama and role of, 121, 205
Panetta as director of, 32
and possible torture investigation, 69–71, 73
relationship with JSOC, 261–62
"signature strikes" by, 39–43, 49–50, 117–18
and strike against bin Laden, 236, 244
tortures Mohammed, 67, 73–74, 145, 147–48
use of torture, 14, 20, 23, 26, 28–31, 62–63, 66–68, 229
Cheney, Dick, 31, 49
attacks Obama, 44, 60, 129, 133, 137, 179–80
exploits fear of terrorism, 157
on Guantánamo, 26–27, 98
Rhodes on, 180
Chesser, Zachary Adam: convicted as terrorist, 220–21
China: threatens any nation accepting detained Uighurs, 108, 114
Uighur resistance to government of, 95–96
civil liberties: Brennan and, 103
Obama and, 192
Clarke, Richard: advises Obama on terrorism, 13–17
Clinton, Bill, 24
Clinton, Hillary, 6, 214
challenges Obama, 19
and closure of Guantánamo, 54–55
on Obama's "framing speech," 194–95
and resettlement of imprisoned Uighurs, 114, 115
as secretary of state, 24–25, 139
supports civilian trials of detainees, 194–95, 227–28
on terrorist threat to inauguration, 34
Cole, James: and Warsame trial, 250
Collins, Art: and resettlement of imprisoned Uighurs, 114
courts, civilian: detainee trials in, 2, 4–5, 131, 136, 138, 146–47, 149, 150–51, 153, 155–56, 160–68, 187, 188, 194–95
Craig, Gregory: Axelrod's attitude toward, 111
and closure of Guantánamo, 127, 157
Emanuel humiliates, 165
Emanuel's attitude toward, 47–48, 111, 157

leaves White House staff, 112–13, 165–66, 185
and long-term detention policy, 137–38, 139, 142, 233–34
marginalization of, 47–48, 139, 157
on Obama's "framing speech," 132
political background, 23–24
and reform of war on terror, 30, 32–33, 38, 53, 76, 98
and release of "torture memos," 60–61, 63
and resettlement of imprisoned Uighurs, 98–100, 111–16
supports civilian trials of detainees, 151, 162, 165
as White House counsel, 24–27, 44, 47–48, 91

Daley, William M.: and strike against bin Laden, 243
demagoguery: Obama opposes, 176–77
Democratic Party: and national security, 15, 156
DeRosa, Mary, 221–22
detainees, Guantánamo: abuse of, 71
Brennan and resettlement of, 94, 103, 112
Brown and resettlement of, 113–14
Congress prevents resettlement of, 129
DHS opposes resettlement of, 99–100
disposal of, 55–56, 74, 93–95, 98, 99–116, 127–28, 131, 136
Emanuel and resettlement of, 110–11, 112, 114
FBI and resettlement of, 99–100
Holder and resettlement of, 103, 104, 107–8
indefinite detention of, 27, 46, 58, 60, 127, 128, 131–32, 134–38, 142–43
McConnell denounces resettlement of, 109
military commissions and, 128–29, 131, 138, 140, 147, 148–49, 186, 194–95
Mueller and resettlement of, 102–3
Napolitano and resettlement of, 102–3
Obama and prosecution of, 128, 135
Obama and resettlement of, 106–7, 109–10, 111–12, 129
Panetta and resettlement of, 102
Reid denounces resettlement of, 109
Saudi Arabia and, 94–95
Strautmanis and resettlement of, 113

detainees, Guantánamo (*cont.*)
  Tannenbaum interviews, 100–101
  trials in civilian courts, 2, 4–5, 131, 136,
    138, 146–47, 149, 150–51, 153–56,
    160–68, 187, 188, 194–95, 226–31,
    248, 250, 256–57, 259, 267
  Wolf denounces resettlement of, 105–6,
    109
  from Yemen, 93–95
detention, long-term, 2, 76, 208
  Bush's extralegal policy of, 187
  Cartwright and, 127
  Craig and, 137–38, 233
  Donilon and, 127, 137–38
  Graham and, 136, 152, 187
  indefinite for Guantánamo detainees, 27,
    46, 58, 60, 127, 128, 131–32, 134–38,
    142–43, 153
  Johnson and, 126
  Jones and, 137–38, 233
  Koh and, 137–38
  Malinowski and, 135
  Mullen and, 26
  Obama and policy problem of, 125–28,
    131–34, 135, 137–38, 142–43, 233–34
  Roth and, 134
Donilon, Tom, 43, 90, 238
  and CIA's covert drone program, 42
  and long-term detention policy, 127,
    137–38
  and Obama's "framing speech," 136
  and strike against Kazemi, 209–10
  and strike against bin Laden, 243
  and Warsame trial, 258
drone program, covert, 21–22, 32, 39–42,
    243, 261–62
  al-Qaeda devastated by, 118, 268–69
  Bash and, 121–22
  Donilon and, 42
  Emanuel obsessed with, 121–22
  Johnson and, 213, 218–19
  Koh and, 217–18, 219–20
  McDonough and, 119–20
  Obama and, 39–43, 117–21
  Panetta and, 120–21
  popular reaction to in Muslim world, 119
  reactions to, 118–19
  Rizzo and, 32
  strategic shortcomings of, 118
  tactical success of, 118, 120

Dunn, Anita, 85
Durbin, Dick, 193

economic recovery: Obama and, 20
Emanuel, Rahm, 34, 142
  attacks Tribe, 189
  attitude toward Craig, 47–48, 111, 157
  attitude toward Holder, 75, 83–84, 91,
    162
  attitude toward Reno, 78
  and closure of Guantánamo, 89–90, 157,
    166–67
  and control of information, 80
  as enforcer of staff discipline, 74–76,
    78–80, 84, 88
  humiliates Craig, 165
  jealousy of Jarrett, 83–84
  leaves White House staff, 243, 266
  and Mohammed trial, 4–6, 151, 162, 172
  on Obama's "framing speech," 132, 136
  obsessed with CIA's covert drone
    program, 121–22
  opposes civilian trials of detainees, 151,
    162
  personal relationship with Obama, 80
  personality, 2, 63, 72, 75, 78, 79–80, 88,
    162
  relationship with Graham, 153–54,
    162–63, 183, 185
  and release of "torture memos," 61–63
  and resettlement of Guantánamo
    detainees, 110–11, 112, 114
  and search for bin Laden, 43
  and suppression of torture investigation,
    74
  undercuts Holder, 101–2, 167, 170
  as volunteer in Gulf War (1991), 122
  and war on terror, 4–5, 76
enhanced interrogation. *See* torture
Ethiopia: occupies Somalia, 220
extraordinary rendition: by CIA, 45
extremism, political: Islam and causes of, 16,
    22–23, 267–68

Federal Bureau of Investigation:
    and botched Abdulmutallab
      interrogation, 177–78, 180–81
    interrogates Warsame, 252
    and resettlement of Guantánamo
      detainees, 99–100

Feingold, Russ, 74
Feinstein, Diane: and CIA's use of torture,
    30
financial crisis, global: Obama and, 2,
    110–11, 266
Fitzgerald, Patrick, 70
Fried, Daniel: and resettlement of
    imprisoned Uighurs, 107–8, 114,
    116

Garland, James, 84, 85
Gates, Robert, 6, 168
    and closure of Guantánamo, 26–27, 33,
        55
    and military commissions, 194
    and Mohammed trial, 227
    and resettlement of imprisoned Uighurs,
        114
    and strike against bin Laden, 235, 242,
        248
    and terrorist threat to inauguration, 34
    and Warsame trial, 250, 256
Geithner, Timothy, 57
Geneva Conventions, 60, 257
Germany: refuses to accept resettled
    Uighurs, 108
Ghailani, Ahmed Khalfan: civilian trial of,
    154–55, 229–30
Gibbs, Robert, 85, 104–5, 112, 175, 184
Gingrich, Newt: attacks Holder, 193
Goldsmith, Jack: and laws of war, 211–12
Graham, Lindsey, 76
    Bauer and, 187, 193
    and closure of Guantánamo, 152, 153–54,
        187
    on detention of captured terrorist
        suspects, 257
    Emanuel's relationship with, 153–54,
        162–63, 183, 185
    Holder and, 164, 165
    and long-term detention policy, 136, 152,
        153, 187
    and Mohammed trial, 164, 169, 183–185,
        186
    opposes civilian trials of detainees,
        152–53, 161, 162–63, 170–71, 172,
        187
    and war on terror, 151–52
Granholm, Jennifer: and closure of
    Guantánamo, 157–58

Guantánamo Bay: Camp VI, 95
    Cheney on, 26–27, 98
    closure of, 2, 19–20, 26, 32–33, 53–57, 89,
        93, 152, 153–54, 156–59, 162, 166–67,
        185, 187, 194–95, 232–33, 258
    Congress rejects closure of, 89–90, 129,
        230
    court cases of prisoners, 58–59
    disposal of detainees at, 55–56, 74, 93–95,
        98, 99–116, 127–28, 131, 157
    Gates and, 26–27, 33, 55
    Napolitano on, 33
    Obama orders closure of, 37, 100, 124,
        127–28, 131, 154, 270–71
    prisoner abuse at, 71
    prosecution of detainees, 128
    rights of prisoners at, 19–20, 27–28
    Uighurs wrongly imprisoned at, 97–98
    See also detainees, Guantánamo
Guantánamo Review Task Force, 26, 53–54,
    93, 98, 148, 150
    and resettlement of detainees, 99–103
Giuliani, Rudy: and war on terror, 19–20
Gulf War (1991): Emanuel as volunteer in,
    122

Hagel, Chuck, 29
Hanif, Hafiz, 268–69
Hayden, Michael: defends "signature
    strikes," 40–42
    defends use of torture, 28–32, 38–39
    demands authority, 42
    and release of "torture memos," 61
health care reform: Obama and, 2, 110, 154,
    158, 162, 166
    Republicans attack, 229
Hickey, Adam: and Mohammed trial,
    147–48, 159
High-Value Detainee Interrogation Group,
    250–51
Hitchens, Christopher: in waterboarding
    demonstration, 68–69
Hoekstra, Pete: undercuts closure of
    Guantánamo, 158
Holder, Eric: Axelrod confronts, 87–88
    background and personality, 71–73,
        195–96
    and botched Abdulmutallab
        interrogation, 180–81, 182
    and CIA use of torture, 66–69

Holder, Eric (*cont.*)
   and civilian trials of detainees, 154–56,
     160–61, 195
   and closure of Guantánamo, 53–54,
     89–90, 157
   confirmation hearing, 151–52
   considers resignation, 196–97
   considers torture investigation, 69–71,
     73, 79, 80
   declines to prosecute CIA officers, 73
   Emanuel undercuts, 101–2, 167, 170
   Emanuel's attitude toward, 75, 83–84, 162
   friction with White House staff, 2, 8–9
   Gingrich attacks, 193
   and Graham, 164, 165
   on Miranda rights, 191
   and Mohammed trial, 1, 4, 6–7, 149–50,
     159, 161–64, 167–72, 182–84, 188,
     195–96, 226–30, 236–37, 249–50,
     258–59
   and need for political independence,
     77–79, 88–89, 90–91
   on Obama's "framing speech," 132
   Ogden tries to undercut, 85, 86–87
   personal relationship with Obama, 79–83
   portrayed as political bumbler, 225–26
   and release of "torture memos," 61, 73
   and resettlement of Guantánamo
     detainees, 103, 104, 107–8, 155
   and Shahzad's capture, 190
   and war on terror, 77, 150
   and Warsame trial, 258
   and White House "murder board," 85–86,
     88
Homeland Security, Department of:
     Napolitano as secretary of, 177
   opposes resettlement of Guantánamo
     detainees, 99–100
   theoretical reaction to attack, 176
human rights: Koh as specialist in, 6, 139,
     201, 203–4, 214
   Obama and, 117, 132, 134
   in war on terror, 108, 118, 211
Human Rights Watch, 135, 185

Inauguration Day (2009): terrorist threat
     to, 33–35
Iran, hostage-rescue mission in. *See*
     Operation Eagle Claw
Iraq War, 14, 17–18, 20

Islam: and causes of political extremism, 16,
     22–23, 267–68
Islamic Courts Union, 49, 220

Jackson, Lisa, 80
Jackson, Robert H., 265
   and limits on executive power, 142
Jaladin, Jalal, 115
Japanese-Americans: wartime internment
     of, 142–43
Jarrett, Valerie, 87, 112, 171, 196–97
   Emanuel's jealousy of, 83–84
   on Obama's "framing speech," 132
   and reform of war on terror, 76
Jeffress, Amy: and Guantánamo detainee
     court cases, 58–59
   and Mohammed trial, 149
   and possible torture investigation, 69–70
Johnson, Jeh C.: background and
     personality, 207, 210–11
   and CIA's covert drone program, 212–13,
     218–19, 221–22
   declares Shabab off-limits, 213, 218, 221
   JSOC pressures, 218–19
   and laws of war, 211–12, 218
   and long-term detention policy, 126
   and military commissions, 251–52
   relationship with Koh, 207–9, 213, 214,
     221–22
   and strike against Kazemi, 209–11
Johnson, Katie, 46–47
Joint Special Operations Command (JSOC):
     Obama and, 204–5
   pressures Johnson, 218–19
   proposed "signature strike" in Yemen,
     252–56
   relationship with CIA, 261–62
   and strike against bin Laden, 241–43
   targeted killings by, 199–201, 204–5,
     212–13, 237–38, 252–53
Jones, Jim, 46
   and closure of Guantánamo, 194
   and long-term detention policy, 137–38,
     233–34
Jordan, Vernon, 81
Justice Department: need for political
     independence, 77–78, 88–89, 90–91

Kagan, Elena: Koh and, 141
Kaplan, Lewis: on tainted CIA evidence, 229

Kappes, Steve, 30
  on "signature strikes," 41
Kayani, Ashfaq Parvez, 242
Kazemi, Mohammed Saleh Mohammed
      Ali al-: strike against, 199–201, 204,
      209–11
Kelly, Raymond, 189
  and Mohammed trial, 168, 169–70
Kennedy Center anniversary gala (2011),
      231–33
Khan, Samir, 264
"kinetic" operations, 41–42, 43, 49, 52, 118,
      201, 210, 254, 268
King, Martin Luther, Jr., 110
King, Peter: attacks Obama, 175
Koh, Harold Hongju: and Awlaki, 215–16
  and Authorization for Use of Military
      Force (2001), 140
  background and personality, 140–41, 201,
      207, 209
  and CIA's covert drone program, 217–18,
      219–20, 221–22
  conservative attacks on, 140
  and defense of targeted killing, 214–15,
      216–18, 219
  on holding suspects without charge, 191
  as human rights specialist, 6, 139, 201,
      203–4, 214
  and Kagan, 141
  and laws of war, 203, 217–18, 219
  and long-term detention policy, 138–39,
      142–43
  and Mohammed trial, 6–7, 228, 249
  relationship with Johnson, 207–9, 213,
      214, 221–22
  and strike against Kazemi, 199–201, 204,
      210
  and strike against Nabhan, 201–2, 203
  support for international law, 139–40
  supports civilian trials of detainees, 194,
      228, 249
  tests for legal targeted killing, 219–20
  and Warsame trial, 249
Krauthammer, Charles, 191
Kris, David, 183
Kuwaiti, Abu Ahmed al-: and strike against
      bin Laden, 234

LaBolt, Ben, 85
Lake, Anthony, 22

law, international: Koh's support for, 139–40
law, rule of, 146
  Obama and, 2–3, 5–6, 8, 63, 131–32, 185
lawyers: role in war on terror, 205–8, 213–14
Leahy, Patrick, 74
Letter, Douglas: and "state secrets" doctrine,
      45
Levin, Carl: and closure of Guantánamo, 158
Libya: anti-Qaddafi Libyan insurgency in,
      254–55
Limbaugh, Rush, 28
Lippold, Kirk: and attack on USS *Cole*,
      44–45
Little, George: and strike against bin Laden,
      244
Louis, Joe, 190

Malinowski, Tom: and long-term detention
      policy, 135
  and Mohammed trial, 185–86
Malone, Sharon, 195–96, 236
  background and personality, 70–72, 82
Marchant, Ann Walker, 81
Martin, David: and resettlement of
      imprisoned Uighurs, 103–4, 113
Martins, Mark: and long-term detention
      policy, 156
Mattis, James: and proposed "signature
      strike" in Yemen, 253–54
McCain, John, 151, 153, 257
  and war on terror, 19–20
McCarthy, Eugene, 15
McConnell, Mike, 39
  and war on terror, 21–23
McConnell, Mitch: attacks Obama, 248,
      259–60
  denounces resettlement of Guantánamo
      detainees, 109
McDonough, Denis, 25, 34, 112
  and CIA's covert drone program, 119–20
  on Obama's "framing speech," 132
  and release of "torture memos," 63
  and strike against bin Laden, 243
McRaven, William H.: on detention of
      captured terrorist suspects, 257
  and proposed capture of Nabhan, 123–24
  and strike against Kazemi, 200–201
  and strike against bin Laden, 241–44,
      245, 247
Mehsud, Baitullah: CIA kills, 121–22

Meltzer, Daniel: and closure of Guantánamo, 57
Messina, Jim, 75, 80, 84, 86
Mikulski, Barbara, 90
Miliband, David: protests resettlement of imprisoned Uighurs, 115
military commissions: Bauer supports, 187–88
  Brennan and, 250
  Bush and, 27, 28, 44, 128–29, 150
  Gates and, 194, 250
  Guantánamo detainees and, 128–29, 131, 138, 140, 147, 148–49, 186, 194–95, 233, 236, 250
  Johnson and, 251–52
  9/11 victims' families support, 155–56
  Obama and, 128–29, 131, 138, 155, 188, 233
  Supreme Court rules illegal, 150
Miller, Matt, 68, 85, 167, 184, 230
Miranda rights, 150, 177–78, 179, 180–82, 190, 252
  Bauer and, 192
  Holder on, 191
  Obama and, 180–82, 192
Mohammed, Khalid Sheikh: boasts of terrorist attacks, 145, 159
  CIA tortures, 67, 73–74, 145, 147–48
  conversations secretly recorded, 147–48, 159
  trial of, 1–8, 80, 145–50, 152–53, 159, 161–64, 167–71, 182–88, 194, 195–96, 226–30, 236–37, 249, 258–59
Mollohan, Alan, 154
Moran, Jim: and resettlement of imprisoned Uighurs, 156
Moussaoui, Zacarias: convicted in civilian court, 146–47, 150
Mueller, Robert, 176
  and Awlaki, 261
  and resettlement of Guantánamo detainees, 102–3
Mullen, Mike: and long-term detention, 26
  and proposed capture of Nabhan, 123
  and proposed "signature strike" in Yemen, 254
  and proposed strike against Somalia, 49–50
  and strike against bin Laden, 242–43

Musharraf, Pervez, 18, 21
Muslim world: popular reaction to CIA's covert drone program, 119

Nabhan, Saleh Ali Saleh: killed in helicopter raid, 126, 127, 201–2, 203, 209, 238
  proposed capture of, 122–26
Nadler, Jerrold: and Mohammed trial, 183
Napolitano, Janet: and botched Abdulmutallab interrogation, 181
  on Guantánamo, 33
  and resettlement of Guantánamo detainees, 102–3
  as secretary of homeland security, 177
Nashiri, Abd al-Rahim al-: charges against suspended, 44
Nasser, Abdul, 115
National Defense Authorization Act (2011): denies civilian trials to detainees, 230–31
national security: Democratic Party and, 15, 156
  as presidential proving ground, 4
Neustadt, Richard, 272
Nobel Peace Prize, 117
North Waziristan al-Qaeda raid (2005), 18–19

Obama, Barack: and Awlaki, 261, 263–64
  and American constitutional values, 5, 18–19, 25, 30, 37–38, 63, 133, 136, 269–70
  attitude toward use of force, 119–20
  The Audacity of Hope, 134
  bans use of torture, 37–38, 131
  Cheney attacks, 44, 60, 129, 133, 137, 179–80
  and CIA's covert drone program, 39–43, 117–21
  and civil liberties, 192
  and civilian trials of detainees, 131, 136, 164, 165, 188
  Clarke as counterterrorism adviser to, 14–17
  Clinton challenges, 19
  commander-in-chief authority of, 59–60
  compared unfavorably to Bush, 59, 129, 134–35, 181, 192, 260
  consults with Tribe, 188–89
  and continuing terrorist threat, 118

criticized from the left, 59, 129, 134–35,
181, 186
early life, 16, 22
and economic recovery, 20
and foreign policy issues, 14–15
"framing speech" by, 129–33, 136–37,
194–95
friction with Romero, 134–35, 137, 233
and global financial crisis, 2, 110–11, 266
and Guantánamo detainee court cases,
58–59
and health care reform, 2, 110, 154, 158,
162, 166
and human rights, 117, 132, 134
and JSOC, 204–5
King attacks, 175
and limits on executive power, 133, 142
and long-term detention policy, 125–28,
131–34, 135, 137–38, 142–43, 233–34
McConnell attacks, 248, 259–60
meets with USS *Cole* families, 44–45
and military commissions, 128–29, 131,
138, 155, 188, 233
and Miranda rights, 180–82, 192
and Mohammed trial, 1–8, 16, 169, 170–71
national security speech (2007), 17–19
opposes demagoguery, 176–77
orders closure of Guantánamo, 37, 100,
124, 131, 154, 195, 258, 270–71
overall policy in war on terror, 130–37,
205–6, 252, 267
personal relationship with Emanuel, 80
personal relationship with Holder, 79–83
personal style and beliefs, 2–3, 5–6, 8,
11, 15–16, 20–21, 27, 41–43, 76–77,
129–30, 171–72, 179
and photos of prisoner abuse, 129
policy priorities of, 2, 5
as political realist, 2, 5, 7–8, 15, 20, 76, 171,
185, 228, 260
portrayed as weak on terrorism, 119, 122,
129, 175, 178–79, 247, 259–60, 267
and proposed "signature strike" in
Yemen, 252–53, 255
and prosecution of Guantánamo
detainees, 128, 135
reaction to Abdulmutallab attack, 174–76,
180–81
reaction to continuing legal crises, 46–47
receives Nobel Peace Prize, 117

redefines legal position in war on terror,
59–60
reform of war on terror, 2, 4, 14–19, 25,
41–43, 46, 48–49, 58–59, 95, 117
and release of "torture memos," 60–63, 73
and resettlement of Guantánamo
detainees, 106–7, 109–10, 111–12, 129
responds to partisan attacks, 267
and role of CIA, 121, 205
and rule of law, 2–3, 5–6, 8, 19, 63, 131–32,
185
and search for bin Laden, 43–44
and Shahzad's capture, 190
and "signature strikes," 39–43, 117–18, 256
and signing statements, 231, 270
and "state secrets" doctrine, 45–46, 58–59,
117
and strike against bin Laden, 234–36,
241–44, 245–48
Tea Party opposes, 5
and Warsame trial, 259–60
Obama, Michelle, 82, 171, 258
Obama's Wars (Woodward), 21
Odierno, Ray, 48
Ogden, David, 141
and closure of Guantánamo, 90, 156
tries to undercut Holder, 85, 86–87
Ohlson, Kevin, 85, 88, 161, 196
and Mohammed trial, 227–28
and possible torture investigation, 68–69
Olsen, Matthew: and civilian trials of
detainees, 155
and Guantánamo Review Task Force,
55–57, 93, 98
and Mohammed trial, 147, 149
and resettlement of imprisoned Uighurs,
98–100, 105–8, 111–12
Operation Eagle Claw (1980), 204, 235, 242
Operation Neptune Spear. *See* bin Laden,
Osama: strike against
Otisville, New York: as venue for
Mohammed trial, 226–29

Padilla, José, 175, 179
Pakistan, 57–58, 261–62
CIA missile strikes in, 39–40
duplicity in war on terror, 21
protects bin Laden, 234–35, 242
Taliban in, 121, 189–90
US diplomatic relations with, 42

Palmer Raids, 143
Panetta, Leon: as CIA Director, 32, 66, 121
    and CIA's covert drone program, 120–21
    and closure of Guantánamo, 54
    and possible torture investigation, 66,
        74
    and release of "torture memos," 61–62
    and resettlement of Guantánamo
        detainees, 102
    and strike against bin Laden, 234–35, 244,
        245–47
Parhat, Huzaifa, 108–9, 115
Pelosi, Nancy, 130–31
Petraeus, David: and closure of
    Guantánamo, 159
Pfeiffer, Dan, 38, 104, 166, 175
Plouffe, David, 266
Project Juno: and Mohammed trial, 226–29
Putin, Vladimir: "assassination campaign"
    by, 134

Qaddafi, Muammar al-: Libyan insurgency
    against, 254–55
Qaeda, al-. See al-Qaeda

Raging Bull, 184–85
Rahman, Gul: killed by CIA torture, 67
Rapallo, Dave: and closure of Guantánamo,
    159
Raskin, David: and civilian trials of
    detainees, 146–49
    and Mohammed trial, 147, 148–49, 159
Rasul v. Bush (2004), 28
Reid, Harry: denounces resettlement of
    Guantánamo detainees, 109
Reid, Richard: convicted in civilian court,
    150
    sentencing of, 9–11, 184
Reno, Janet: Emanuel's attitude toward, 78
Republican Party: attacks health care
    reform, 229
    gains in midterm elections (2010),
        228–29
    threatens American constitutional values,
        191–92
Rhodes, Ben: on Cheney, 180
    and Obama's "framing speech," 129–31,
        136
Rich, Marc, 78–79
Richardson, Bill, 25

Riedel, Bruce: and search for bin Laden, 43
    and war on terror, 57–58
Rizzo, John, 206
    and CIA's covert drone program, 32
Robow, Mukhtar: considered as US target,
    221–23
Romero, Anthony: friction with Obama,
        134–35, 137, 233
    on photos of prisoner abuse, 129
    on "state secrets" doctrine, 46
    urges torture investigations, 135–36
Romney, Mitt, 142, 234
Roth, Kenneth: and long-term detention
    policy, 134
Rouse, Pete: and closure of Guantánamo,
    157
Rove, Karl, 87
Rumsfeld, Donald, 19, 49

Sabour, Abdul, 96
Saleh, Ali Abdullah, 93–94, 253, 255
Salt Pit (CIA prison), 67
Saudi Arabia: and Guantánamo detainees,
    94–95
Sautter, Chris, 84, 86
Savage, Charles, 231
Schiliro, Phil, 107, 112, 166
    and Mohammed trial, 8
Schumer, Chuck: and Mohammed trial, 183
SEAL Team Six, 19, 204, 238–39, 241–42,
    246–47, 262
Semet, Abdul, 96, 108–9, 115
Shabab, 34, 122, 203, 212–13, 218–20, 237,
        250–52, 254, 258, 261
    attacks Uganda, 220
    Johnson declares off-limits, 213, 218, 221
    joins with al-Qaeda, 220–21, 249
    proposed strike against, 49–51
Shahzad, Faisal, 119
    Bharara and, 190
    failed terrorist attack by, 189–90
    Holder and, 190
    Obama and, 190
"signature strikes," 49–50, 252–56
    Hayden defends, 40–42
    Kappes on, 41
    Obama and, 39–43, 117–18, 256
signing statements, 231, 270
Slavery by Another Name (Blackmon), 71
Smith, Jeffrey H., 29

Somalia, 122
  and Black Hawk Down debacle (1993),
    125–26
  Ethiopia occupies, 220
  proposed strike against, 49–51
  war on terror in, 201, 203, 205, 209, 213,
    218, 220–21, 237, 251, 252, 254
Soufan, Ali: on Abdulmutallab, 177
Standish Maximum Correctional facility
  (Michigan): and closure of
  Guantánamo, 157–58, 166
"state secrets" doctrine: Bush and, 45, 117
  Obama and, 45–46, 58–59, 117
Strautmanis, Michael: and resettlement of
  Guantánamo detainees, 113
Straw, Jack: supports civilian trials of
  detainees, 163
Stupak, Bart: and closure of Guantánamo,
  157
Summers, Larry, 89
Supreme Court: rules military commissions
  illegal, 150
Sutphen, Mona, 112

Taliban, 18, 21
  in Pakistan, 121, 189–90
Tannenbaum, Andrew: interviews
  Guantánamo detainees, 100–101
Tea Party movement, 158
  opposes Obama, 5
Tenet, George, 22
Thomson Correctional Center (Illinois):
  and closure of Guantánamo, 166
torture: CIA use of, 14, 20, 23, 26, 28–31,
    45–46, 62–63, 66–69, 74, 145, 147–48
  Obama bans use of, 37–38, 131
  political hypocrisy regarding, 31–32
  possible investigation of, 69–71, 73,
    79–80, 88, 135–36
  produces inadmissible evidence, 147
  Yoo supports, 59, 207
"torture memos," 46, 65, 73, 207
  CIA fears release of, 60–61
Tribe, Laurence: Emanuel attacks, 189
  Obama consults with, 188–89
Trump, Donald, 244–45

Uganda: Shabab attacks, 220
Uighurs: in Bermuda, 113–16, 155
  resettlement of, 98–116, 127, 156

  resistance to Chinese government, 95–96
  wrongly imprisoned at Guantánamo,
    97–98
United Nations: reaction to CIA's covert
  drone program, 118–19
United States: diplomatic relations with
  Pakistan, 42
US Congress: denies funding for civilian
    trials of detainees, 153, 161–64, 169,
    170–71, 183–84, 186–87, 226–27, 230,
    237
  encroaches on executive power, 186,
    230–31
  exploits fear of terrorism, 156, 157, 248,
    269
  Keep Terrorists Out of America Act,
    156
  prevents resettlement of detainees, 129
  rejects closure of Guantánamo, 89–90,
    129, 230
  restricts transfer of detainees to US for
    trial, 89, 129, 186, 230–31, 237, 250,
    260, 267, 269
USS *Cole*: al-Qaeda attack on, 44, 93–94
  Obama meets with families of, 44–45

Varney, Christine, 88–89
Verrilli, Donald, 47
Vilsack, Tom, 80

war, laws of, 125, 128, 146, 203, 208, 211–12,
    217–19
war on terror: Beers and, 17
  Brennan and, 22–23, 51–52
  Brown and, 5
  Bush's policies in, 2, 4, 13, 16–17
  Cartwright and, 51–52, 254
  Clarke and, 13–17
  in "denied areas," 200–201
  Emanuel and, 4–5
  Graham and, 151–52
  and Guantánamo detainees, 128–29, 131,
    138, 140, 147, 148–49
  Giuliani and, 19–20
  Holder and, 77, 150
  human rights in, 108, 118, 211
  legal position redefined, 59–60
  limits on executive power in, 133
  McCain, 19–20
  McConnell and, 21–23

war on terror (*cont.*)
    Obama's overall policy in, 130–37,
        205–6, 252
    Pakistani duplicity in, 21
    reform of, 2, 4, 14–19, 25, 30, 32–33, 41–43,
        46, 48–49, 53, 58–59, 76, 95, 98
    Republicans and, 5
    Riedel and, 57–58
    role of lawyers in, 205–8, 213–14
    in Somalia, 49–51, 201, 203, 205, 209, 213,
        218, 220–21, 237, 251, 252, 254
    Supreme Court rules illegal, 150
    in Yemen, 199–201, 203, 205, 209, 219, 237,
        252–54
Warsame, Ahmed Abdulkadir
    capture and detention of, 237–39, 241,
        249, 256–57, 260–61, 262–63
    interrogation of, 250–52, 260, 263
    as policy problem, 249–52, 256–59
    trial of, 259
waterboarding. *See* torture
Weich, Ronald, 90
West Wing, 176–77
White House staff: Craig leaves, 112–13
Emanuel leaves, 243, 266
    Holder's friction with, 2, 8–9
    methodological disputes among, 3–4
Whitehouse, Sheldon: and CIA use of
        torture, 65–68

Willett, Sabin: and resettlement of
        imprisoned Uighurs, 103–4, 108,
        113–15
Wilner, Thomas: and closure of
        Guantánamo, 232–33
    and detainee rights, 27–28
Wolf, Frank: denounces resettlement of
        Guantánamo detainees, 105–6,
        109
Woodward, Bob: *Obama's Wars*, 21
Wright, Jeremiah, 82

Yemen: al-Qaeda affiliate in, 174, 177, 178,
        193, 199, 215, 221, 237, 249, 251–52,
        258, 261, 262
    Guantánamo detainees from, 93–95
    proposed JSOC "signature strike" in,
        252–56
    war on terror in, 199–201, 203, 205, 209,
        219, 237, 252–54
Yoo, John: supports torture, 59, 207
Young, William: and sentencing of Reid,
        9–11, 184

Zawahiri, Ayman al-, 18
    as US target, 261
Zazi, Najibullah, 119
    background, 159–60
Zubaydah, Abu: CIA torture of, 67, 73–74